Ah Les Femmes!

Tribulations, Struggles and Triumphs.

DR. LOUIS B. ANTOINE, M.D.

From the same author:

Lone Survivor: Judge Jury and Executioner.
Published by Vantage Press, New York February 1999

Naked Souls/Ames A Nu.
Published by Les Editions du CIDIHCA, Montreal 2001

Mahogany Island: The Lost Pearl
Published by Moon Shard Media, TX 2024

Haunted Soul: The Curse of the Black Skull
Published by Moon Shard Media, TX 2024

TABLE OF CONTENTS

Dedication

This book is dedicated to the memory of my mother, who went to her grave silently. Had she wanted to tell her story, it would have been impossible because she could neither read nor write. This book is for all mothers who have countless stories of courage and selflessness to tell. The story of their world is waiting to be told.

Preface

The Unborn Child Prodigy...

Once upon a time in the 90's...

An expecting father, on the night after he returned with his wife from an exciting trip to the obstetrician, had the most unusual dream:

"Dad," said the unborn child, as he floated around in a sac of warm water that felt more like a Jacuzzi, "you seemed overjoyed today. What was that all about?"

"You are right about that, Son. It was quite a thrill to learn from the good doctor that you are going to be a boy."

"So, what is the big deal? From my vantage point, I do not see any difference. Boy or girl? Don't I still have to swim around attached to this cord?"

"Are you kidding, Son? When you are born as a boy, you own the world. You get better jobs than girls do. When you speak, everyone listens. You can act as If you know everything. The world is at your feet. This is power."

"Are you sure, Dad? I've heard Mom's conversations with her women friends and she seems to think that she makes all the decisions at home. Isn't that where the power really counts?"

"Never mind what you might have heard, Son! No one will believe the women. We have the political power. We control the public opinion. We

basically own the media. We control the jobs. We make all the rules. We enforce them. Hey! What else could you ask for?"

"Dad, are people really happy out there? A world without equality must be very unsettling. If Mom and the other women don't have a voice, isn't the world getting only part of the story?"

"Hush up, little man... keep your mouth shut! You have been hanging around women too much. They have already co-opted you. Wait until I start taking you to hang out with the boys."

The unborn child prodigy was not amused. He made a promise to himself that he would keep his antennas out for a more equitable solution. There had to be a better way.

Introduction

I feel I should start this essay with an apology. In the course of my research, I have reviewed many writings about women and the picture is disheartening. It seems that there has been a pervasive misrepresentation of women throughout history, beginning with the ancient philosophers, through the Holy Bible and the Koran, and continuing with the psychological and medical literature. Women are depicted as inferior and unimportant. Rarely are they given the opportunity to express their own views. In the Bible, one can hardly find a woman speaking for herself or expressing her own feelings.

This warped view of women that has been presented to the world throughout history is grossly incomplete and therefore inaccurate. It reveals a systematic censorship by omission similar to the dearth of information on Blacks and other minorities' contributions to history. Consequently, I feel I have been robbed of the tools necessary to fully understand women and, in turn, the world around me.

If we agree that both men and women are living in gender societies where inter-dependency is a fact and that these societies have been defective, both men and women are victims. To those who will look with suspicion at the endeavor of a Black male psychiatrist who has become interested in women's issues, I pose these questions: Why should racism be the discourse of one race? Why should feminism be the discourse of one sex? Don't racism and sexism have the same color? It seems to me that they both have the color of oppression. Don't they both generate in me the same feeling of anguish? They both leave on my back the same painful tracks of the master's whip. Tania Modleski believes that there is room for "male criticism supportive of the feminist project." She makes an argument for men not needing equal space in a male/female debate. (Feminism Without Women: Culture and Criticism in a Postfeminist Age, Tania Modleski, Iris 1992) Did she mean to overlook Black men who cannot claim to be part of the White male power structure? However, as a Black psychiatrist who has been granted the training and the opportunity to practice in the White male designed world, I must come to grip with and accept responsibility for the fact that I am a "collaborator." Protagoras long ago recognized that the truth is relative. Every day I collaborate and acquiesce to the truth as it is currently defined. I argue that the so-called truth is the mere opinion expressed by a group that has the political and economical power to spread it and impose it on the amorphous masses. In the order based on that truth, normal is defined as any behavior that stands in support of the powerful order. As Szasz put it, "If a person disagrees and disobeys authority, when that authority is religious, then he is the devil or is possessed by the devil. Likewise... when that authority is scientific, then he is insane or mad. In the last analysis, this is matter of definition..."(Tomas S. Szasz, In the Manufacture of Madness, Harper and Row, 1970). The least that I can do is to continuously ponder and question the reality around me in search of alternative viewpoints that might have made it, as truths were the tables of power turned. What if the dicta from the great philosophers of ancient Greece did not receive the canonical backing of the church fathers? What If the matrilineal cultures of pre-Colonial Africa or the pre-Columbian cultures of the Americas were allowed to develop without the intrusion of the invading Europeans? The factoids that make up history as we know it have been collected over millennia. We could go back and marvel at the complexity of the world that preceded us. No matter what our political leaning might be, we cannot escape the fact that we have been left to examine only crumbs and remnants of civilizations dominated by "racism, sexism and other affronts to human rights." The whole world would be known differently as different truths would abound. Therefore, I should not remain silent lest I am held back by the discomforting fear of transcending my peer-defined male and ethnic characteristics. As a Black male, could I ever live up to the machismo image that the patriarchal system expects of me? Would it be in my best interest, the interest of my family and my community that I do so? Isn't this the pressure to keep up with this image that is at the roots of the race to consumerism, our endless and fruitless attempts at keeping up with the Jones, our lack of appreciation for others, stress and even domestic violence? Do I foster instead less patriarchy-valued attributes like intuitiveness, emotionality, better communication skills, and attunement with my environment? If I cannot live up to this expectation of machismo, if I cannot demonstrate enough athletic talent to play professional sports, am I condemned to being discarded as a misfit? In the early nineties, as I was coming back from a conference in Pittsburgh on immune response to stress, I got into a taxicab with a much older Jewish colleague, a university professor. The taxi driver, bewildered by the strange fare and lamenting over the poor performance of his local football team, the Steelers, told me in a squeaky voice, "Gee! Maybe you should go to the Steelers trial camp, they sure could use your help." Racist stereotypes are as caustic as sexist ones. Therefore, I feel that I cannot be excluded from the discourse about sexism lest I fear to offend my mentors and pastors who taught me a lot, but did not teach me the whole story because they did not have the whole story. I fear that if the debate about feminism is not allowed to continue, the victories so hardly fought for are in danger of being reversed, just as some elements of the conservative wing are trying to do to Blacks. They could not have because as those who in the words of Mao Tse Tung "hold up half the sky" women have been excluded, misrepresented and lied about, as have Blacks and other minorities.

It sounds like an oxymoron to say that a man could be without a voice. Well, in the late seventies, as a newcomer in this country going through post-graduate medical training in the culturally exclusive American hospitals, I was a man without a voice. As I sat through the abstract discussions about medical and psychoanalytical literature, I remained silent. I would have given anything to be able to tap into the vast amount of knowledge that I had acquired through reading that I started at age 10 in French-speaking Haiti. All my arguments lay dormant in a language that none of my fellow trainees from India, the Philippines, Ethiopia, nor my American professors could understand. Like an ignoramus I sat there thinking how I could have dismantled the point in discussion if only I was not a man without a voice. Silent no more! The explosion of information of the early 90's with the popularization of the Internet has allowed me to get re-acquainted with Greek philosophers and all the other classic authors who for years were the nourishment of my hungry brain. For the sake of better attunement with those who come to me for help, I have since shed many layers of male biases and prejudices and I am constantly seeking to unmask the more dangerous ones, the veiled ones. I realize that one can only see that many trees out of the forest. Using both the traditional method of literature review and a more voice-centered relational approach of psychological research, as suggested by Carol Gilligan, I have been examining many issues. One of the first utterances that I could exclaim, "Ahhh, les femmes!" as I remain awestruck by the degree of oppression that women have been enduring throughout history. It is our hope that every woman will be able to retrace, with the help of this essay, the story of her own tribulations, struggles, and undoubtedly her triumphs, however small. It is an attempt to bridge that huge gap in knowledge that has been allowed to persist for too long.

However, an apology without an attempt at repairing the damage is reminiscent of the feeble apologies of White America for slavery while apartheid and discrimination continue to plague our communities. Not only must we admit that injustice has been done, we must also stir up the debate and formulate practical suggestions to help solve the problem. This proposal may seem like an impossible task. However, let me suggest that the only impossible task is the one that is left untried. For someone who is not suffering from it, there can be comfort in keeping the status quo. Our survival will depend on the ability of all people, especially that large majority of oppressed people, to recognize that the real enemies are racism and sexism while acknowledging the diversity of our cultures. Let me suggest that a world without racism and sexism should be a better world for everyone. Therefore, we must make an attempt at solving the problem -- no doubt that the road to change is arduous and difficult. What choice do we have lest we want to sit around and wait for the next big bang to begin the world anew?

In the first part of this book, I will take a trip back in history as far back as the Greek philosophers, the early theologians, and the Church Fathers, the ones who have laid down the foundations, the canons of Western civilization. We will listen to the voices of politicians and writers in their portrayal of women. We will see how events based on this philosophy have contributed to the making of a very oppressive world.

In the second part of this book we will see that women have not remained silent. We will retrace the steps of the Women's Rights movements starting with the "Declaration of Sentiments." Women have not remained silent; in fact they have screamed at the top of their lungs. The oppressive world around them seems to have remained impassive. We will show the tremendous contributions of the ones who have always been kept at the bottom of the totem pole, Black women. We will tell about their efforts to articulate their own priorities in the well-defined movement "womanism," which promotes the redemption of all members of our society, especially Black men who seem to be on their way to extinction. We will end the second part with a review of a new psychology of women that would be based on the voices of women.

In the third part of this book, we will listen to the voices of different women who will tell us real stories about their daily tribulations with a system that has changed some but still has a long way to go. We will hear from an abused woman who has shown courage under fire. A Black woman psychologist will recount her struggle with a male dominated academia. We will hear a modern-day madam denounce the hypocrisy of a system that drives man to a life of stress, enjoy the services of hired women, and then see them officially as bearers of sin. We will listen to two lesbians who will give us their perspective about women's plight today. We will be reminded of the tragedy of Indian women who still bear the consequences of a male dominated culture. A well-educated woman will retrace the steps of her psychological journey as her life takes a new meaning after she became a voodoo priestess.

In conclusion, we will advocate a new approach to human relationship, one based on "eco-feminism." Men and women together will chose to reinstate the attributes of both sexes as equally valuable. Autonomy, independence, and rationality will be invoked whenever necessary. The power of emotionality, inter-dependence, and intuitiveness will regain their

former places of honor. We will strive for a world where everyone can hope to find internal peace and harmony. In such a world there cannot be any room for mistreating the environment. The sanctity of life, every life, will once again be proclaimed. As we approach the new millennium, the recent explosion of technological advances made in communication will serve to unite us rather than divide us.

PART 1

THE MAKING OF THE OPPRESIVE WORLD

Judge One-thousand-years A.K.A Better-must-Come, presiding...
"Hush up! Columbus? Combossus? It don't matter. (sic) He did come
trick us.

It was you who went to the Americas and Africa with your
doctrine of civilizing the savages...

You taught Black people to pray with their eyes closed. When
they opened them, you had their land, they had the Bible. With the
Bible and gun, you robed, raped, murdered their foreparents in the name
of Jesus...

You are also charged for misinterpretation. You have twisted the
Bible to suit White supremacy... You have painted women as originators
of sin. You have made women look inferior in all your religious books.
You have been preaching a sexist doctrine to our people. From Eve to
now, you have blamed women for the downfall of the world. You
blamed Delilah for Samson's stupidity"...

People's Court II, Mutabaruka, Shanachie Entertainment Corp. 1996

Chapter One

Idyllic World of Ancient Times: Myth or

Reality?

There exists among men, because they are men, a solidarity through which each shares responsibility for every injustice and every wrong committed in the world, and especially for crimes that are committed in his presence or of which he cannot be ignorant...

(Karl Jaspers, La culpabilite allemande, Jeanne Hersch's French translation, pp. 60-61)

In January 1997, a group of enthusiastic archeologists excavating In Athens, Greece made what they believed was an extraordinary historical discovery. What they found under that Athenian parking lot seemed to be the ancient lyceum of Athens, the teaching place of the renowned philosopher, Aristotle. Naturally, word of the discovery spread like wildfire throughout the globe, for the cradle of western thinking had been found! It was as if the intellectuals of the Western world had found their roots. It was at that peripatetic school that a mature Aristotle, after having separated from his master, Plato's, idealist view, advocated a return to nature. Maybe those who still held the view that Aristotle was an usurper who had nothing to do with the hundreds of writings of which authorship he claimed, were nourishing a faint hope that the real story would be unearthed. The importance of this find cannot be over-emphasized. A table of citation indexes published by Michael Mahoney (1991) placed Aristotle as the most quoted philosopher in the history of psychology (107.64). Descartes, the renowned French philosopher and the father of rationalism, came a distant second with an index of 53.36.

Philosophers influential in the History of Psychology

Name	*Citation Index*[1]
Aristotle	107.64
Descartes	53.36
Plato	45.76
Locke	37.44
Hume	34.08
Kant	32.16
Augustine	30.24
Leibniz	27.37
Berkeley	25.76
Herbart	23.69
Aquinas	22.86
Brentano	20.64
Spinoza	20.52

The citation index reflects the simple product of the number of texts in which an individual was discussed and the average percentage of pages in that text on which they or their work was discussed.

Before the beginning of the Western world there was ancient Mesopotamia, there was the Sumerian Civilization and there was Egypt. It had all the makings of a perfect world[2]. It was promising to be a near-perfect world built on mathematical and scientific principles waiting to be discovered. Such principles were to be verified and re-applied for the betterment of mankind. Satellite communication and electronic technology was not yet discovered but who could doubt that progress was being made. We still marvel at the seven wonders of the ancient world. The largest of the great pyramids of Egypt, Khufu covers thirteen acres and contains 2.3 million blocks of stone, the stones themselves averaging 2½ tons and some weighing 30 tons. Remember the Seven Wonders of the Ancient world like The Temple of Artemis built in honor of goddess Diana3. These works are not only a testimony to the physical strength of these African men but to the intelligence of the engineers behind them. Such exploits have not been attempted or duplicated. Mechanized tools were not used, or were they? There was harmony in the universe. Philosophers and scientists of the time were determined to discover its mystery. Astrology, magic, divination, healing, or studies of natural phenomena were all geared toward that quest. The complexity of the task did not go unnoticed. In the ancient civilizations labor was divided not according to gender but according to skills. No one was excluded. The value of women's relatedness, emotionality, and

---

[1] See Mahoney, M. J. Reference No. 42
[2] See Ancient ... Reference No.2
[3] See Reference No. 73, under References.

intuitiveness was recognized. Their unique ability to stay in tune with the different facets of nature was counted upon to resolve some of the difficulties facing this society. Although there was a gradual subordination of women, they continued to enjoy important roles in those societies as goddesses and priestesses. The priestesses were to carry the offerings and the prayers of the afflicted to the goddesses. Such goddesses were seen as all-powerful and capable of tremendous metaphysical exploits. Under different names, mother goddess was venerated because she symbolized cosmic unity between humans and nature. The women/goddesses had the characteristics and the duties of humans. They could feel love and hate. They could show mercy, as they could be vengeful. Like mother earth they could be fertile and procreate to maintain life. Such ability was celebrated through very elaborate rituals and festivities. Before Aristotle there was ancient Egypt and many centuries of religion, philosophy and sciences.

Then suddenly came Alexander the Great. Egypt fell to the king's invincible army. Not only were the territories annexed, the culture also fell under tutelage. Flanked by his former tutor Aristotle, the victorious monarch could claim ownership to the vast body of knowledge accumulated over several millennia. Winner takes all. The city-sized library of Alexandria and its invaluable contents had fallen into the hands of the triumphant king. Aristotle, a man whose earlier years were basically unknown, is suddenly catapulted into fame. Aware or not of the importance of the war booty, Aristotle wasted no time putting together a group whose only duty was to catalog that huge amount of information[4]. Like it or not, Aristotle had become the de facto author of the famous writings and a dictum from him would carry a heavy weight for generations to come. As if this were not enough, Aristotle and the philosophers of his time would find themselves suddenly elevated to the status of prophets who had received revelation from the gods and would guide their brethren to salvation. Men were to shed the fetters of their humanity and elevate their souls to eternal life. Anything that would stand in the way of their fulfilling that divine destiny would be considered sinful, including money, women... furthermore from that point forward science would be based on empiricism and practical observation. He was now ready to rule the intellectual and ideological world. Just like the other philosophers of his time, his own fellow Athenians persecuted him. However, he managed to become the leading authority on many topics. Surprisingly, a man who for twenty years was said to have been the pupil of Plato, a philosopher, had suddenly become the author of countless number of science treatises. The Greek imaginary world was suddenly enriched with an unprecedented number of rituals, religious beliefs, and practices. Mysteriously, however, the Egyptian goddesses were

____

[4] See James, George G. M., Reference No.30

removed. Banned was the popular cult of Osiris. Isis, the woman/goddess with ten thousand names, the mother of heaven, the lady of love, the female Ra was no longer worshipped. The gods were virtually subjected to a process of character assassination. They would be demonized and their cult suddenly referred to as idolatrous. The gods would be evicted from their pantheon. It was not quite Niestche's cry, "God is dead," but for centuries to come, an all-out campaign would be put into motion to eradicate all of these gods from the minds of the brethren in the name of salvation. Gone would be the vision of a world where men and women live in harmony with mother earth under the watchful guard of a pantheon of goddesses as numerous as the needs of the people. Humans could no longer be gods. Gone was the matrilineal society where inheritance descended through the female, from mother to daughter, where Merneith, Hatshepsut, Nofretari, Nefertiti Tiy, and Cleopatra VII ruled as queens and kings.[5] The society where women could be priestesses, magicians, scribes, and head of the temples was disappearing very quickly. Isis had all the attributes of a well-balanced androgynous being who was in touch with both the masculine and the feminine side of her personality. She could display self-confidence, authority and yet show love and compassion. She was goddess herself, but remained loyal to the memory of her dismembered husband soirees. She used her

---

[5] See Knapp, B. Reference No. 34

magical power to bring him back together and make him immortal. In January 1997, a group of enthusiastic archeologists excavating in Athens, Greece made what they believed was an extraordinary historical discovery. What they found under that Athenian parking lot seemed to be the ancient lyceum of Athens, the teaching place of the renowned philosopher, Aristotle[6]. Naturally, word of the discovery spread like wildfire throughout the globe, for the cradle of western thinking had been found! It was as if the intellectuals of the Western world had found their roots. It was at that peripatetic school that a mature Aristotle, after having separated from the idealistic view of his master, Plato, advocated a return to nature. Maybe those who still held the view that Aristotle was an usurper who had nothing to do with the hundreds of writings of which authorship he claimed, were nourishing a faint hope that the real story would be unearthed. Like it or not, Aristotle had become the de facto author of the famous writings and a dictum from him would carry a heavy weight for generations to come. Furthermore, from that point forward science would be based on empiricism and practical observation.

It was Aristotle who was credited with the invention of the branches of Science as we know them today. He supposedly wrote lengthy and detailed treatises on topics as complex as the phenomenon of dreaming and the

---

[6] See Kyriakidou, D. Reference No.35

thinking process. He invented logic, rhetoric, and the art of public speaking - basically, he invented the language of scientific arguments. One needs only to observe an attorney at work to witness the imprint and influence of a philosopher who lived between 384 and 322 BC. Aristotle is often referred to as the man who laid the foundations for the science of psychology. In fact, there are very few modern concepts used in Western culture that cannot be traced back to Aristotle.

Chapter Two

The World As Seen By Aristotle:

Retrospectively, one could say that some of his views were erroneous and should not have survived the test of simple inspection. For example, how could a man of such position maintain the belief that women were of inferior intelligence because, "...they had a lesser number of teeth than men..."[7] Unfortunately, modern day society still bears the influence of this "great" philosopher. How else can one explain the aristocracy's oppression of the masses throughout history? Truly, any time the members of a specific class use their social status to claim entitlement to economic privileges, they are following an Aristotelian-based model of society - a society viewed essentially as static.

Aristotle believed that one's position in society is determined at birth. If one happened to be of the wrong sex, the wrong color, or the wrong nationality, that person was doomed to live a life of oppression. Looking ahead into the Judeo-Christian era, it seems that these very principles were in full swing. How else could certain groups of people have been subjugated for so long by other groups of people? How could slavery have lasted for so many centuries? How could members of one sex have dominated, so overwhelmingly, the members of the other sex? How else could people of a certain race or gender have been kept away from polling stations? How recently have we witnessed such occurrences? Look at South Africa, where members of a small group excluded the majority of the population of a whole nation from the avenues of politics.

---

[7] See Aristotle. Reference No1

Aristotle held the view that the family is "...the association established by nature for the supply of men's everyday wants...the household consists of master and slaves, husband and wife, father and children...not father, mother and children." In Aristotle's society, the children belong to the father and the woman is a mere Instrument of procreation," the slave is not only the slave of his master, but wholly belongs to him. He who by nature is not his own but another man's, is by nature a slave, a possession. To the question "Is there anyone thus intended by nature to be a slave?" Aristotle answered, "From the time of their birth, some are marked out for subjection, others for rule... that for inferior men [the ones with inferior souls] slavery is both expedient and right." He makes a distinction between the rule of a father over his children and the rule of a husband over his wife. The former is seen as a royal rule and the latter as a constitutional rule. He believed that the male is, by nature, more fit to command than is the female and that the inequality between male and female is permanent. He saw men as having the virtue of the rational, and women as having the virtue of the irrational. He concedes that the soul is present in freemen, slaves, and women, but in different degrees. To Aristotle, the courage of a man is displayed in commanding, whereas the courage of a woman is displayed in obeying. Silence is woman's glory.

In Aristotle's society, one's position in life is predetermined by nature and is not expected to change. Borrowing the following quote from Socrates, Aristotle reasons, "For the gold God mingles in the souls of men is not at one time given to one, at another time given to another. It is always given to the same. God mingles gold in some and silver in others, from their very birth, but brass and iron in those who are meant to be artisans and husbandmen." The aristocrats, the dictators, the supremacists of the world, and all those who claim to be members of the noble class must love Aristotle! For in his writings, they can find more than ample proof for maintaining the status quo. However, for those poor souls who were born to follow and serve, there is still hope, according to Aristotle. The slave can find virtue in being a good slave by applying himself in doing the work of his master. Such elitist views are echoed by conservative Edmund Burke (1729-1797) and related by Auerbach (1968), "Social order is part of the natural order that God has created and it exists prior to the individuals who are born in it. Inequality is inescapable in society. But social leadership is most properly founded on the natural sense of dependence, subordination, and affection, which respond to ability, virtue, age, and graciousness. These qualities of leadership are best institutionalized in a hereditary aristocracy." The woman can display virtue by keeping silent and submitting to the rule of her husband/master. The child can show courage by obeying the royal rule of his father. As for formal education in Aristotle's society, its only purpose would be to help the lesser beings to perform better in their predetermined roles. Parts of the very elaborate Egyptian mystery system were incorporated into a whole new religious philosophy. In the emerging post Egypt invasion era, philosophers and poets had finally found a more practical role. By default, they found themselves with the prestigious and unique task of making the unimaginable imaginable. Whenever the connection between this world and the great beyond could not be demonstrated through some mathematical theory or through some esoteric philosophical construct it was simply created or fantasized about.

TIMELINE OF AN OPPRESSIVE WORLD

800-400 BC: THE BIBLE

Several versions of the Bible are written.

469-399: Socrates

Search for truth ("know thyself")

427-347 BC: Plato: Father of Idealism.

384-322 BC: Aristotle: Theories of Ethics, politics and physics

336-323 BC: Alexander The Great reigns

THE BIRTH OF MONOTHEISM

THE NEW ERA: The advent of Jesus Christ, the Messiah

The Apostles give us a written account of the Messiah's life, the Gospel.

182: Origen: Christian doctrine is established

The assault on women continues

249-313: Persecution of Christians

306: Constantine makes Christianity the official religion of the Empire.

354-430: St. Augustine

The Confessions: He links Plato and Aristotle to theology.

570: The birth of Mohammed

TIMELINE OF AN OPPRESSIVE WORLD (Continued)

1095-1204: The Crusading Era

Popes and Kings go on wars to deliver the Holy Land from Islam.

1202: The Last Crusade starts

1204: The Fall of Constantinople

1225-1274: From Philosophy to Theology

Thomas Aquinas establishes Plato and Aristotle's philosophical principles into the canons of Theology.

The doctrinaires of the Church declare women the cause of all the ills of the world.

THE INQUISITION: The Dominicans (Order of Preachers) create a war machine to combat heresy

1492: Christopher Columbus "discovered" the New World

1500-1800: The slave trade becomes a multimillion-dollar business.

Black Holocaust: Millions of Blacks perish in Slavery

1594: Descartes: Rationalism

TIMELINE OF AN OPPRESSIVE WORLD (CONTINUED)

1650: Church & State: The Alliance Continues

Gospel to the world

Salvation and Colonization

Civilization, Exploitation, and Slavery

Blacks and women are subjugated.

1694: Voltaire denounces French nobility

1712-1778: Jean-Jacques Rousseau

Father of French Revolution.

Emile: A blueprint for the rearing of the "ideal man"

Church and State partners in the crime of Slavery (Black Holocaust)

1789: The French Revolution

Assault on the Monarchy: Marie Antoinette guillotined

Nothing changes: Third Estate disappointed

1809: Charles Darwin

1856: Origin of the Species.

1863:   The Emancipation proclamation

TIMELINE OF AN OPPRESSIVE WORLD (Continued)

1861-1864: The American Civil War

Brothers go to war over the great evil of Slavery

1884- 1914: The Jim Crow's era

1914-1918: First World War

1929: The Great Depression

1889-1945) Hitler goes to war to create an Aryan nation.

The Holocaust

6,000,000 Jews are sent to the gas chambers.

1856-1939: Sigmund Freud

Drive Theory

Psychosexual stages of Personality Development

Freud's Triad to characterize women:

Passivity, Masochism and Narcissism

Hysteria, Penis Envy

TIMELINE OF AN OPPRESSIVE WORLD (Continued)

1925-1965: Malcolm X

By all means necessary

Assassinated

1948: Boer ideology: Apartheid established in South Africa

1939-1968: Martin Luther King Jr.

I Have A Dream

Assassinated.

1949: Simone de Beauvoir

Le Deuxieme Sexe (English version in 1953)

1957: Fidel Castro

The Cuban Revolution

1965: The Vietnam War

Civil unrest: The cities are burning

Black men die in White men war in South Asia

Black women and their families are forced into welfare.

TIMELINE OF AN OPPRESSIVE WORLD (Continued)

1969: Sit-ins in the universities around the world

> Catholic priests from Holy Spirit order expelled from Haiti

> Catholic Church authorities tacitly approve.

1970: For a theology of liberation

> Assault on progressive wing of the church

> Bishops, nuns, and priests assassinated in Latin America

1978: the Islamic revolution triumphs in Iran

1980-1992: The Reagan-Bush years

> Death squads clean up leftist opposition In Latin America:

> Archbishop Oscar Romero assassinated

> The Sandinistas Revolution triumphs in Nicaragua

> The Contra war

> The Death Of Communism: Cold War Ends

1990: Anita Hill V. Clarence Thomas

TIMELINE OF AN OPPRESSIVE WORLD (CONTINUED)

1991: VIOLENT COUP IN HAITI: DEATH TOLL ESTIMATED AT 10,0000

> THE GULF WAR: MEN WITH BIG GUNS DRAW LINE IN THE SAND

1994: Rodney King: Can we all get along?

> California Proposition 213: Affirmative Action Reversal

Genocide in Rwanda, Africa

800,000 Hutus and Tutsis slaughtered.

> Leaders of the New World order watch passively

1992-1995: The Balkans Conflict: Ethnic cleansing

Genocide by Bosnian Serbs on non-Serbs

1995: Louis Farrakhan's "One million-man March"

1996: Bill Clinton reelected.

He promises a race relations dialogue

Chapter Three
The Church Fathers Espouse Aristotle Worldview
The Birth of Monotheism

Meanwhile, around the same time that Aristotle came to the scene, other events of tremendous importance were occurring in the religious world. Judaism, Christianity, and Islam were born. The church authorities did warn against subscribing to Aristotelian philosophy without prior review by "capable Catholic scholars." Such review was left to one of the best scholars from the Dominican ranks, Thomas of Aquinas. Aquinas was such an avid Aristotelian that it seemed difficult to the modern reader to dissociate Aristotelians to Thomas. His essays on various topics are strikingly similar to that of Aristotle. In Aquinas' discourse on fornication, he sees any emission of semen for purposes other than procreation as sins against nature. He sees the human female as "clearly insufficient of herself for the rearing of three offspring..." Woman by herself is not capable of raising a child. He finds the inordinate emission of semen repugnant and sinful, a sin second only to the sin of murder. He holds the view that a son, as long as he is without the use of reason, does not differ from an irrational animal, just as an ox or a horse belongs to some owner, the son belongs to his father[8]...he did not see philosophy and theology as contradictory. He sees all things as created by God. Reason demonstrates it. Faith holds it. A group of elderly men had committed to writing revelations they supposedly had received from God. The logistics of these happenings remain puzzling to scholars and lay people alike. Thomas Aquinas is credited for recognizing the right of an oppressed person to rise against his tyrant, but he did not seem to extend these same rights to women. However, no critique has been able to take anything away from the book, which is seen by some as a religious instrument and by others as a historical reference text. Possibly the most discussed and the most controversial part is the book of Genesis. No matter which side of the argument one stands on, one could safely say that chaos is described in some of the books of that text. It would seem as if it was the rendition of an epic fight between two civilizations, one dominated by old pagan beliefs and customs under attack by an inspired and exalted belief system operating under a new convenient sealed by powerful symbols. This book is like the first artistic draft of an emerging god who is allowed to be temperamental, hesitating, angry, whimsical, and definitely partisan, almost like an unsettled artist who is still uncertain as he stands in front of his canvas[9]. In the mind of the writer, this god has made very hard, and one might even say controversial, choices. How could an all-loving, all-knowing, and immanent god select one person over the other? Were the church fathers setting up the premises for inequality in the world? If one people are presented as the chosen one, others had to be un-chosen and are ipso facto inferior. How could the creator of all people chose one people over the others? He could create man in his image, yet find it sinful for man to attempt to conquer the ultimate knowledge by eating the forbidden fruit. Shouldn't man aspire to be like his creator? The all-knowing god is depicted as going into a fit and taking the extremely serious step of bringing about the Apocalypse. God soon realized these humans, his very own creatures, are up

---

[8] See Bourke, V. Reference No. 3
[9] See Moyers, B. Reference No.47

to no good. Let's start the world over except for Noah and his entourage, the chosen elite.

Just imagine...

Imagine a society that would build its code of conduct solely and exclusively upon the unabridged, unedited story of Genesis. Let us leave out for a moment the religious connection. Let us look at the book of Genesis without the leaven of faith and spiritual guidance. What kind of society do we see unfold in front of our eyes? A society filled with chaos and inequity. Woman would start out with an insurmountable burden on her shoulders. She would be told right from the start that her sole purpose in life is at the side of her man as his servant, sex object, and the bearer and raiser of his children, yet she could claim no rights to these children. Imagine a society where women who represent more than half of the population would have no voice. They would not be allowed to express their feelings about anything. They would always sheepishly and silently align themselves behind their husbands' position even when such position goes against their very essence as women and their best interest. The children belong to the father. When something goes wrong, the woman would take the blame. She would become known as the one who "violated Jesus in the past, robbed her children of heaven, [the one without whom] ... There would be no hell, no grief..." A mere instrument of sexual pleasure and procreation, she would remain a tool to be used and traded in the name of a greater cause. She would be on display when it was profitable to do so and would be kept in a back room whenever necessary. Such a creature would be deprived of a voice and would be left with little or no opportunities to express her opinion, let alone her feelings. For women, life would be toil. The moral expectations would be different for men and women. For women, infidelity to her spouse would be a crime punishable by flocking or death. For men, as long as they could claim some raison d'etat, their libidinal excesses would be welcome. After all, men have been given the divine task of creating and safeguarding a nation. The end justifies the means. Gratitude and loyalty would have no place in such a society. An infertile, married woman could use her servant as a surrogate mother by giving her to the insatiable sexual appetite of her husband. After the child is born, the wife could turn the table on the poor woman in fear that the child might inherit the family estate. Would such women have been on welfare today? It was all in the name of a god who is omnipresent and omniscient. A god who operates more like a *Deus ex machina*, intervening whenever and however he pleases in the pursuit of a plan that only he knows. After going through all this trouble, the patriarch, maybe because he did not have to go through labor pains or maybe because he had the faith of a giant, could in a flash get ready to offer him in sacrifice to his god. One would believe that such a decision would have warranted a serious discussion around the campfire. Not in that society! It was the patriarch's decision and his alone. The human feelings with which we are all too familiar in today's world would be magnified. In that society, the feelings of jealousy would be so raw and competition would be so fierce between brothers that simple sibling rivalry would be allowed to degenerate into murder. What is the fuss all about? Am I my brother's keeper?[10] Would the murderer respond to the voice of conscience? Whatever happened to justice? Innocent Abel would get no justice, as Cain the murderer was marked for protection by a capricious and mysterious God. Was that the signal for future fatidic wars to come whenever one could invoke a noble cause, a more global justification, such as the building of a nation or the protection of the status quo? Where was these children's

---

[10] See New Living. Reference No. 50

mother? Could she have intervened to teach the feuding brothers how to get along? Did the children fall victim of parental neglect? When it comes to getting the patriarch's blessing and the material wealth that came with it, intrigues, deception, and subterfuge are all allowed. Jacob had to get ahead and a little trickery was played on Eusace. This time, the mother is given the role of the conning, morally shaky woman who did not hesitate to lie to get her way. Jacob was destined to carry out God's plan...discrimination and segregation was not only expected but also encouraged. "Swear by the Lord, the God of heaven and earth, that you will not let my son marry one of these local Canaanite women."[11] What was wrong with the Canaanite women? Did a different god create them? In that society people did not always keep their word. Jacob was tricked into sleeping with and marrying Leah after she was promised Rachel. Heh! What is a daughter between friends? Jacob could have both Leah and Rachel. Were Leah and Rachel asked what they wanted to do? In that society the only way women could shore up their power was by the number of children they could have from the coveted husband. Leah and Rachel were allowed to play out their animosity toward each other by competing for Jacob's bed using their women servants, Bilhah and Zilpah, as surrogate mothers. In the grand finale, as his death was near, Jacob gathers his twelve sons, the twelve tribes of Israel, and predicted what was going to happen to them. Absent from the story line were any references to these men's wives or daughters. When God was ready to answer men's prayers, he gave them more sons, no daughters. Where did all of their mates come from? Was it a mere omission or were the women simply not important? One could always come up with some justification to deviate from the set rules as long as you are of the right sex. The more land, cattle, oxen, and slaves you could accumulate, the closer you were to

---

[11] ibid

fulfilling the prophecy. Imagine a very materialistic world where it is quite acceptable to manipulate, lie, and scarify other people's lives in order to wrestle wealth out of the competitor's hands. The weak and the unprotected would be run over by the powerful. The leader would manipulate his way into wealth, even if it means selling his own family member, especially his wife. The law of hospitality would take precedent over all the other rules. In order not to violate such sacred rules, the head of the household could, without hesitation, offer his virgin daughters, his wife, and his concubine to attackers to protect the stranger. The guest in the man's home must be protected at all cost.

Over a thousand years later came Muhammad, the orphan, who reported that he has been visited by archangel Gabriel and given the mission to preach the message of God, the compassionate, the merciful. It is believed that he received revelations over a period of twenty years (612 to 632 AD). Again, the central message is monotheistic. Severe punishment awaits those who are guilty of "joining other gods with himself." The inequity between men and women is again reflected in the Koran. Men are superior to women because of the qualities with which God hath gifted the one above the other...Virtuous women are obedient, careful during the husband's absence, because God hath of them been careful. The moral code seems to be full of double standards. It was okay for men to do certain things and forbidden for women to do the same. If any women be guilty of whoredom, bring witnesses, and if they bear witness to the fact, shut them up within their house till death. If two men commit the same crime, punish them both, but if they turn and amend, then let them be[12]. Women are alluded to over and over as impure. They will also question you as to the courses of women, say they are pollution. Separate yourself therefore from women and approach them not, until they are cleansed. Women are equated to objects, "Your wives are your field: go in, therefore, to your field, as ye will...[13]"

With Islam making progress in Persia and Christianity, along with all the forms of Greek culture, spreading in the ancient world from the Atlantic to India, all of the elements were in place for the making of a very powerful and authoritative system. The establishment of the doctrinal foundations of the church continued to receive contributions from theologians who basically saw themselves as chosen for the mission of saving the world. They were designated as the church fathers. Origen, a prominent ascetic, went to the extent of emasculating himself in order to be certain that he would not yield to sensual pleasure. Amongst the fathers was Augustine, whose writings describe clearly the lower position of women considered as "unstable animals" under Christianity. "We are men, you are women, we are the head, you are the members, we are the masters, you are the slaves." Sex, Augustine believes, is merely tolerated because it is necessary for procreation, one of God's mandates. Parenthood is seen as inferior to celibacy. From the fourth century priests had to take a vow of celibacy as it was believed that marriage would contaminate their souls[14]. St. Thomas Aquinas was no different. Women, he believed, were frustrated males. The female fetus received the soul much later than the male, causing women to be less rational. Timothy, in his first letter, wrote that women should learn in silence and humility, "I do not allow them to teach or to have authority over men, they must keep quiet. For Adam was created first and then Eve. And it was not Adam who was deceived; it was the woman who was deceived and broke God's law." Tertullian, another important figure of the early church

---

[12] See Rodwell J.M. Reference No. 58
[13] ibid
[14] See St Augustine. Reference No. 66

writes: "Women, you ought to dress yourselves in mourning and rags, representing yourself as a penitent bathed in tears, redeeming thus the fault of having ruined the human race. You are the door of hell: you corrupt him whom the devil dares not approach; you finally are the cause why Jesus Christ had to die."

Misogynism persisted long after the dark ages. The church fathers continued to set the tone on how women should be treated. It gets much worse when St. John Chrysostom declares, "Among all savage beasts, none is found as harmful as women." Balthasar Gracian saw women as a perpetual temptation, a threat, and "neither the youth, nor the adult, nor the old man, nor the wise, nor the brave, nor even the saint is ever safe from woman." Francisco de Mello insisted on seclusion of women stating that, "Woman should leave her house on three occasions only: baptisms, marriage, and burial." Any difference from the old feudal teaching from Confucius? He wrote, "A woman is bound to three obediences: that of being subject to her father prior to marriage, to her husband after marriage, and finally to her son if she became widowed."

Had the God followers been left with the choice of discounting the teachings of the church fathers as pure diatribe from frustrated males who have had very poor childhood experiences or no experience at all with women, the above words would have felt less caustic. On the contrary, the Church fathers quickly erected themselves as the sole interpreters of God's words. The authorities of the church created a magisterium from which every word spoken was to be accepted without question, on a pure act of faith, just because "magister dixit." The Pope is infallible. The domination would be incomplete without the church authorities establishing individual codes of conduct that would make the handling of personal matters a state matter.

> Once torture has begun the game is won. The witch must confess, the witch must die. And whether she confesses or not, it amounts to the same thing, for once a woman has been brought into the prison, she is guilty, whether she has been brought there rightly or wrongly.

> Friedrich Spee (1591-1635)

Sexuality was sinful and would go counter to the goal of salvation. The heathen was to mortify the flesh in order to save his soul. Any infraction of the rules set by the church fathers were to be confessed to the authorities of the church and the sinner was to seek forgiveness through even more sacrifices. Women and sexual gratification could only lead to eternal damnation. Sexuality had just moved away from the bedroom to become a discourse by individuals whose ascetic life often excluded sex. Marriage, a sacrament sanctioned by the church, was no longer acceptable to its own elite. Attempts at giving moral direction to an emerging Christian society would be welcome were it not for the biased view of the authorities that were too willing to accept and defend the status quo. Never mind that such status quo excluded women and Blacks. All spontaneity was removed from sexuality. Sexuality had moved away from "Ars erotica" to become "sciencia sexualis," to borrow the words of French philosopher Paul-Michel Foucault[15]. Anything that did not support the dominant, authoritative view of the patriarchy would be deemed pervert and abnormal. A whole set of

---

[15] See Foucault M. Reference No. 19

psychopathologies would derive from this notion. Enter the medical scientists whose mission was to find the etiology of any deviant behaviors.

If an ideological basis was ever needed at a time when it was customary to use one's military might to subjugate all territories and appropriate all their resources, the church was going to provide it. In the name of God, in the name of salvation, pope and kings would become allies. Popes became kings and kings became popes. They would go on crusades at times to protect themselves from the influence of paganism, with the expressed purpose of expanding God's flock, while filling their coffers with gold and precious stones earned through the sweat of slaves condemned to forced labor[16]. The first salvo of colonialism and imperialism was shot from the pulpit and the world would never be the same again.

---

[16] See Roberts, J.M. Reference No.59

Chapter Four

In The Name Of Salvation and Civilization, Colonialism and Slavery Start an Era of Exploitation and Genocide

In the Americas, a civilization lay dormant for maybe as much as 40,000 years. Burial sites, artifacts and majestic ruins in Honduras, Peru, Guatemala, Hispaniola, and Mexico remain the irrefutable proof that the native people of the "new world" were not all that new because they have always been there. Christopher Columbus did not discover them as the official version of world history often reports. Without immune defense against European diseases and with their weapons still from the Stone Age, the indigenous population stood no chance against invaders driven by greed. No one knows for sure how many Indians lived on the island of Hispaniola, but fifty years after their "discovery," their numbers were reduced to a mere 500[17]. On the island lived many queens. One name that comes to mind is that of Anacaona, who offered fierce resistance before the Spaniards captured her. The Indians were subjected to forced labor; their way of life was destroyed, causing them irreparable psychological stress. Women were abused and children were captured. Christopher Columbus landed with the cross in one hand and a rifle in the other hand. His royal mission: To save the Indians from false gods and bring them civilization, all in the name of

---

[17] See World History. Reference No. 76

Father God. The Indians were described as "savages", "devilish heathens", and "primitives" when all the evidence points to the very organized and quite advanced society for the epoch. Who were the real savages, the Indians or the Europeans who showed no mercy and did not hesitate to use their superior firepower to subdue and kill unprepared Indians? It took another century before the Europeans took interest in the land of North America. The Europeans' appetite for easy wealth could not resist reports from famous Spanish explorers like Cabeza de Vaca and Francisco Coronado about North American lands plentiful and rich just waiting to be taken[18]. Absent from the fantastic stories was the fact that these lands were inhabited by millions of Indians who had established a way of life in accordance with the rule of nature. They saw Mother Earth as a source of life and therefore sought to protect it. They venerated the sun and stood in admiration of waterfalls and other natural wonders. Some authors would have you believe that the idea of a peaceful savage or primitive harmony is a myth and that the evil nature of human beings is a universal phenomenon that preceded the arrival of the Europeans in America. As evidence, they report about immense burial sites where people of different ages seem to have fallen victims of massacre. No one can be certain about the exact date these events allegedly took place. One should be free to speculate about other possible causes of death. The fact of the matter is that greed caused one group to exterminate another using the false pretext of the need of this people for salvation. The above argument does not justify the hypocritical and antidemocratic act of colonization. The focus of the argument must remain on the central question of whether or not the pre-Colombian cultures were primitive at all and on whether or not the silence and the omission of women in those cultures was justified. Women like the capullanas led entire communities in

---

[18] See Purcell, E. Reference No.59

the pre-Colombian era. Myths still persist about an Amazonian society where six-foot tall women ruled with courage. Men-gods representing storms, mountains, and other natural forces stood side by side in the pre-Colombian pantheon with women-goddesses representing fecundity and fertility of the earth. Lured by the exoticism in all of us, the Westerner is often attracted to far, remote places. Rarely, however, does he give any serious consideration to understanding, accepting, or integrating the historical and cultural context of the coveted subject. Why should he bother since he often presents with an air of arrogance and superiority visible only to the native? A free and egalitarian exchange between the "dominant" culture and the "primitive, savage, and inferior" culture is never allowed. No true marriage is ever possible between the two cultures. This phenomenon is well described In Julian Viau's novel, "The Marriage of Loti," (1880) between a Polynesian native and a Westerner. The Western character will go as far as expressing doubts as to whether or not the two lovers were created by the same God. It is the same bug of exoticism that once again struck Disney when the story about Native American, Pocahontas, was made into an animated movie. The world reacted with nostalgia to Disney's folkloric and romanticized rendition of Pocahontas' story. Maybe such movies are necessary as they have the virtue to exorcise America's psyche from the ghosts of a hideous and shameful past. However, such artistic licenses do little justice to the surviving native Americans whose cultures, which were established over several millennia, have suffered violent and irreparable assaults and are fast disappearing from the planet. For every Pocahontas who befriended her captors, accepted their culture, and ended up falling in love and marrying John Rolf the Englishman, thousands of women were abused, raped, and exterminated. Amongst the pre-Columbian cultures, it is believed the Mayans were the most advanced. They contributed greatly to the field of astronomy and mathematics. Recently reported findings in the Amazonian rainforest of ancient painted caves seem to support a more communal-type society. Everyone, including men, women, and children, participated in activities such as hunting and food gathering, rather than a society where men dominated because of their ability to use their muscular strength to go hunting. More discoveries by Czech archeologists at Dolni Vestonice and the neighboring site of Pavlov revealed that the contributions of women were overlooked. They were engaged in net hunting and were far from the image of the passive little cave-mates[19].

---

[19] See Pringle Heather. Reference No.59

Chapter Five

Racism and Sexism, A Deadly Mix...

Long after the colonial era was over, the assault on indigenous culture persisted. In the middle of the twentieth century, almost one hundred and fifty years after Haiti became independent, the Catholic Church joined forces with the state and attempted to eradicate all traces of African religions from the Haitian culture. Soon after the departure of the American marines that occupied Haiti from 1915 to 1934, the church, in alliance with the bourgeoisie, started to attack voodoo openly. In September 1935, the Haitian government promulgated a decree condemning superstitious beliefs and forbidding associated practices[20]. The marines were gone, but the venom of racism and discrimination against anything indigenous was well ingrained in the Haitian society. The assault against the African beliefs and communal rural society persisted. The literature of the era is replete with satire of the behavior of members of the bourgeoisie who were suddenly stricken with a desire to be Anglo, to sing the blues, and to speak American. In 1942, Elie Lescot, a mulatto president, ordered a second anti-superstition campaign. Haitian Voodoo temples were destroyed and priests were persecuted. Peasants were discouraged from serving their gods or participating in voodoo rituals. Tens of thousands of sacred objects were destroyed. This movement was known in Haiti under the name "rejection."[21] The Haitian people were to reject their indigenous culture to adopt the

---

[20] See Cosentino Donald J. Reference No.12
[21] ibid

European religion. What the church leaders did not acknowledge was that harm was being done not just to the cultural heritage of the nation, but to the very social structures of the Haitian families. At no time was it acknowledged that voodoo represented more than a religious cult although it was also a social system that provided a support network to members of the peasantry. The "mambos"[22] were female leaders of the community. They were healers and advisors. Voodoo practices kept community cohesiveness. By destroying the voodoo temples, the invaders were actually breaking the back of whatever power structures existed in the country and were preempting any embryo of resistance. No longer were women to continue to assert their leadership roles. The voodoo pantheon full of goddesses and feminine symbols were to be depleted. No effort was made to understand the cultural value of these practices. The European priests did not mince their criticism for the voodoo practices seen as barbaric and superstitious. These views reflected the prevailing racist doctrine of the epoch. Whatever happened to the teachings of brotherly love advocated in the gospel?

---

[22] A "mambo" is a voodoo priestess. She is the female equivalent of the "hougan" or Voodoo priest.

Chapter Six

Women Around the World ... Brainwashed Into Submission...

There is a tendency to view women and minorities as a large amorphous and homogenous block, where the members lack personal characteristics and are incapable of holding individual point of view. Most policies about Black women are based on preconceived ideas, born out of stereotypes, which rarely if ever represent the view of the majority of the groups. They are often based on the assumption that Black women do not want to work and would rather receive handouts from the government, that most Black women are single mothers and the heads of the household, and that they came from disintegrated families. Women who do not fit the above categories are not newsworthy and are unlikely to be featured in national newsmagazines. Black girls are raised with the belief that successful Black women do not exist and that it would be utopia to aspire to be anything but a "welfare queen." Left with very few role models, the Black girl is brainwashed into believing that to be beautiful is to be White or to at least be as White as possible. The literature and the media are replete with such examples where "norms of femininity and beauty are mercilessly dictated" by the dominant culture. Our culture has become addicted to media clips and sound bites. When watching the evening news, we hardly realize that the story being forced into the format of the show is constructed reality. Elements of the story that would allow the viewer to formulate his own opinion are often left out. And since White males dominate the network, the views that are forced upon us are bound to be theirs and theirs alone. Excluded are the women's views. Excluded are the Blacks and other minority views. A 1979 survey by the National Organization for Women published in 1980 in NOW National Times revealed that for every 700 pages about men in U. S. history texts, only 14 pages are about women.[23] What the report did not say is how many of those pages were about Black women. The voice of the Black woman has been silenced in many ways. She is silenced not only as a Black person in a society that is yet to accept that racism does exist, but also as a woman in a patriarchal culture. Women who allow themselves to be frivolous or spontaneous in African literature are quickly turned into monsters that need to be destroyed at once. Dumping all women in the same cesspool can only beget confusion and alienation. This characterization further dehumanizes women. It is a known fact that different individuals subjected to the same stresses will use personal attributes and degree of resiliency to offer different responses. The stresses are perceived, processed, and experienced differently. Minorities and women must be allowed to display the same diversity and heterogeneity as the members of the majority group. White women need to acknowledge that minority women are confronting a much broader form of oppression that encompasses both racism and sexism and that these evils are generated by the same oppressive machine. African women have not been allowed to exorcise themselves from their traumatic past. The literature about African women still reflects that struggle. Female writer Mukabi Kabira, in "Gender and Politics of Control," gave a rather mythical explanation on how women have lost their dominance in African society and how men have become the rulers. She attributed the loss of power to women's excessive

---

[23] See Van Howe. Reference No. 89.

demandingness and to ruse from men who encumbered them with pregnancies and the care of children. Male authors describe the situation in terms of rationality, power, dominance, and nationalism, while female authors are more interested in the emotional experience. The problem is further complicated by the fact that members of the minority group do not always remain loyal to their original characteristics. They are often enticed into adopting the value system of the dominant culture, thus loosing their own cultural identity.

The psychological impact of such indoctrination through continuous bombardment with subliminal messages from the media cannot be minimized[24]. The conditioning affect is not just of women, but the response of men. The minorities often see it as a sign of progress when they received the stamp of approval of members of the dominant class. They feel that they have moved up the social ladder and often quickly distance themselves from their own group. This approval, however, is often very superficial and hypocritical and is almost always based on economical reasons. The newly "accepted" member is not judged on who he is but on what he has. It is never based on bi-directional cultural exchanges. The minority has to espouse the values of the dominant culture. Women and minorities often succumb to the brainwashing process which has them believe that they are inferior, causing them to seek affiliation with the "superior" group as a means of improving their lot.

In Africa, the murdering and the plundering of a whole race was of an epic magnitude. Not brave enough to venture inland, the Europeans used African mercenaries to capture other Africans and bring them to the coast to awaiting ships. Women came often to the painful conclusion that it was better to kill their own offspring than to let them face a life of endless suffering through slavery.[25]   Men and women were stripped of their humanity. They were stripped of their names, their family affiliation, and their identity. To the slave owner, the women were nothing more than slave making machines whose best asset was her ability to procreate. Women often doubled as concubines. The master could engage freely in sexual experimentation with them that could not take place within the Victorian constraint of the marriage. The women's sexual abilities were tried out at the slave market before the trade was concluded. The African women who made it to the master's bed did not lose any opportunity to advance the cause of freedom. They often were able to extract valuable tips that would prove very useful when rebellions were being fomented. Children were taken away from their mother and submitted to castration. The more children they could have, the better. What a reversal from the current belief that having too many minority children would be a burden to the economy! To justify such a large-scale genocide, the truth had to be recreated. Stories about Africans hanging from trees in the jungles were widespread. Africans were described as ignorant and superstitious. Africans made their contribution to the technological advance of the world. Men and women worked well together as they tried to pierce the mysteries of the inclement environment. Priests[26] and priestesses sought alliance from the gods to learn about nature. Africans from the Ethiopian area developed a very sophisticated civilization. The Africans were respected trade partners with China and other empires of the time. Capitalism would not have taken off without the slave trade. Whether pre-colonial Africa was matrilineal, as the idealized anthropological version reports, twin-linear, or African-style

---

[24] See Welsing, F. Reference No. 80
[25] See Anderson S. E. Reference No. 3
26 ibid

patriarchal, one thing remains certain: Class oppression was not gender-free. Division of labor in the family structure was in accordance with the patriarchal frame of reference. Women's labor remained unpaid. Other contributions in the form of healing, participation in religious services, and their role as spirit mediums, although essential to the life of the community, were either unrecognized or undermined by the authorities of the church and the state. The pre-colonial societies were able to "create" human beings that lived according to the just principles of harmony, truth, balance, and right order. During the past decades, the Black Diaspora has mounted a serious effort to return to these traditions. Dr. Maulana Karenga, Professor at California State University, started the Kawanzaa celebration in 1966. He recognized seven principles that should be the guideposts of the life of Black people living in America. The principles are unity, self-determination, collective work and responsibility, cooperative economics, purpose, creativity, and faith. The facts seem to indicate that Africa is the real cradle of civilization, not Europe. When the freedom bell rang, women were in the forefront, playing the roles of spies, information gatherers, and warriors. For centuries, millions of Africans were uprooted from their hometowns and newborns were separated from their mothers. Like sardines, confined to spaces less than the size of a coffin, they were sent to the perilous journey across the Atlantic. A very small percentage of them made it alive. When it was no longer fashionable to trade slaves, the Europeans, lured by a land full of splendor and natural resources, descended on the African continent like prey birds. A new form of exploitation was invented, neo-colonialism. Often times they allied themselves with the local leaders to subjugate the masses. The Europeans did not go to Africa as students of ancient history and civilizations as they often pretended, but as gold diggers, ivory collectors, and con-artists. More often than not they were ignoramuses, outlaws, misfits, and rejects who were not accepted even in their own countries. They came with a proverbial complex of superiority and a head full of racist theories and prejudices. They portrayed themselves as demi-gods that would save the Africans from barbarism and cannibalism. A whole section of the history of humanity was pushed aside. Never mind that Homo erectus started his long journey from the depths of Africa or that the ancient civilizations of TA Seito (Sudan) and Hemet (Egypt) were the cradles of modern civilization, Africa was christened the "Dark Continent."[27] If the roots of racism could be traced back to the ignorance of the first European colonies, it is the silence from the more enlightened members of the "civilized" world that has allowed it to persist into the third millennium of the Christian era. When the Europeans set foot on the African continent, they violated the soul of a people. In that society, the Egyptian queen Hatshepsut, the first female pharaoh, was held in high esteem. In that world, women stood side by side, equal to men. In the word of an Ugandan president, Africa stood "like a sitting duck" ready to be shot and plucked, and plucked she was. Back in Europe, large fortunes made of gold, diamonds, and other precious gems were accumulated. More than the natural resources of a continent, it was a whole approach to life, a whole philosophy that was eradicated. How could people who were rejects of their own society or their own religious order be so arrogant?

The prevailing Manichean theory[28] of a world divided between good and evil and the need for salvation offered a golden justification to the Spaniards, fresh out of the Inquisition era, to go around the world with relentless missionary zeal to save the world while taking away their temporal fortunes. They, the Spaniards, were god's people; they were good. The Indians did not

---

[27] See Roth M. H. Reference No. 69
[28] Mani religion based on a strict dualism opposing principles of good and evil.

know God; they were bad. They could either submit or perish. The alliance between religious doctrines of the church and the military might of the state was going to find a perfect application in the New World. Church and state were operating under very ill-defined boundaries. Was it still under the inspiration of God or was it greed and the prospect of immense fortune to be collected? In the name of salvation, popes and kings would go at war. The darkness of paganism and false gods were to be pushed as far as possible.

The Swahili society of the nineteenth century offers researchers and scholars a unique opportunity to study the influence of colonialism on the status of women.[29] Situated on the East Coast of Africa on the shore of the Indian Ocean, it was a hybrid society where many cultures met. Unlike the African on the Western coast who was taken across the Atlantic Ocean into the New World, the Swahili were exposed to Islam. This allowed some comparison between the fate of Christian influenced society and the parallel dominant role of monotheistic Islam. It also speaks to the survival ability of the indigenous cultures and gives us an excellent example of an idealized situation where, within the local religious practice, all societal barriers seem to fall and men and women seem to enjoy an equal footing. Elite women (Ungwana) of the stone towns had much higher status than the women of the rural area did (Ushenzi). Even so, they were still subjected to many discriminatory practices of their society. The practice of seclusion (purdah), the exclusion from most aspects of Islamic life, and the acquisition of concubines through trade for the sexual gratification of the men were still prevalent. The elite women remained aware of their perceived importance in perpetuating the elite lineage. They displayed no solidarity and did not identify with the struggle of the slave women. The Swahili women are also interesting in that they prove the fact that when the choice is between gender status and class status, the economic factors tend to prevail and women, like men, tend to associate with members of their social class. This phenomenon is important. Maybe this can explain why the social gain of the White feminist movement did not always translate into gain for women of minorities group. Thus, Bell Hooks echoes the cry of a great African-American named Sojourner Truth: "Ain't I a woman?" The exploitation of women did not disappear with the end of colonialism. In a view that will be later echoed in "The Bell Curve,[30]" the colonizers have established a hierarchy of civilization with Europeans on top, Indians second, Arabs third, and Africans last. Swahili women, unlike other African women, were able to enjoy secular education and were exposed to ideas about equality between men and women, marriage, and women identity. Like any other Black women groups, the Swahili women were also victims of the double-headed snake of racism and sexism. Long after modern African nations had become independent, the archaic system under which women could not enjoy the same rights as their male fellow citizens persisted. In fact, it seems that it was well ingrained in the mind of the now well-established patriarchal society. At times, the liberated colonies would remain silent about women's contributions in the identity-building task of keeping the oral traditions alive and at other times would simply modify these traditions to place male heroes in the leading roles. Women in many West African nations have managed to keep the oral traditions alive through songs and dances. These women were called the griottes.[31] Such practices were also in effect as a literary movement in the nation of Haiti In the middle of this century. Yet, in recounting the stories, modern historians have persistently substituted the

---

[29] See Gower and al. Reference No. 24

[30]

[31] See Ogede, O. Reference No .56. See also Reference No. 28.

women heroines for men in the middle of these epics. The stories were often distorted to reflect the views of the contemporary male dominated society. Needless to say, once again women were blamed for everything that could possibly go wrong. Lost was the original essence of the production. The poems or songs were used by men to voice their discontent about marital life and the depravation of the women who have espoused the view of the city people and are no longer under the control of the husband.

This degrading attitude towards women is very much alive in countries like Haiti where the rallying cry for the first slave revolt against the White master took place in 1791 and where the role of women was essential. Modern time popular folk artist Coupe-Cloue sees women as parasites that are obsessed about marriage. Even though the woman does not have any education or assets, Coupe-Cloue comments, she cannot wait to get married to continue her libertine ways. Coupe-Cloue goes on to describe women as dishonest, calculating, and cold blooded. He persistently portrays men as the victims of women who can use the power of seduction and the apparent dependence of men on women for sex. The artist typically will use appropriate tempo of the music to converse with his audience and tell the fans in a very joking way what his experience has been. It is almost always about women cheating on their husbands, getting caught, and blaming their insatiable sexual appetite and the irresistible lust of a sexual organ for falling to temptation. This view is remindful of a prevailing myth in the seventeenth century according to which an enormous devil's penis would compete with the husband to satisfy women's voracious sexual appetite.[32] Women are often compared to appetizing and delectable fruits to be savored to the very end. The burden of family planning and contraception remains exclusively women's responsibility.

Back home, violence is cultural. In the adopted country, violence is criminal

Women, no matter how long they have been living in America, are constantly reminded of the low status in which they are held. Back home, it is customary for women to earn the good graces of the boss by being totally submissive and servile. Men are, by definition, the masters and if they happen to control the purse strings because they have the power to hire and fire, they wield a lot of power. The boss, at times, will expect total control over the women and will even extract sexual favors. Women are not expected to protest even when the injustice seems to be the most flagrant. Immigrant women will sometimes suffer years of domestic violence without protesting, feeling that their world would collapse if the powerful man would withhold his bittersweet love. Many reasons have been advanced as to why women stay in abusive relationships. Dependency on the man's financial support is definitively very high on the list. Other reasons might include the fear of upsetting the equilibrium of the family. A child who has been sexually abused, for example, tends to grow up to become an abuser later on, perpetuating the cycle of violence.

When they moved to more industrialized countries, these women had a hard time understanding or taking advantage of the protection afforded to them by the law. They sometimes live in enclaves, completely sheltered from any exposure to the law. Immigrant women often do not know that sexual harassment is illegal nor do they know that there are recourses against domestic violence.

In fact, immigrant women are at particular risk for abuse. For some women it is the first time that they are confronted with very different and

---

[32] See Rowbotham S. Reference No.79

conflicting roles in their home. They feel obligated and their husbands expect them to continue to fulfill all of their duties as housewives and caretakers for the children while, for the first time, they have to seek employment outside the home. Stuck in low paying jobs, they can hardly meet their monthly expenses and must remain dependent on the husband who enjoys an inordinate amount of leverage on how decisions are made in the home. If the women ever made it to a more professional position a whole new set of problems were created. The spouse might become excessively envious, insecure, and jealous and find all kind of excuses to mistreat the woman. He feels that he needs to re-assert his authority and resorts to verbal abuse and physical violence. Often times, this situation becomes the precipitating factor that serves to reopen old wounds. Dramatic situations unfold with, at times, the most regrettable consequences both for the woman and her children, who remain forever scarred after witnessing their mother being assaulted and bruised. I could quote the example of a patient of mine who describes how she feels torn between two masters. On the one hand, she needed to be firm and protect herself from injuries by enforcing a restraining order against her violent, alcohol and drug abusing husband. On the other hand, she faced the wrath of her children who do not want her to send their father to jail. The abused mother was reliving her own story of being abandoned by her mother who placed her on a bus and shipped her away with her siblings to a cousin hundreds of miles away. The memories were so vivid that the abused women could describe the little red dress that she was wearing, even the smells that were part of her experience, and the very words that the cousin used to express her displeasure at being dumped on. My patient felt like she was being disposed of like a puppy that was not wanted. For years she remained in the abusive relationship. She kept on getting pregnant, hoping with each new child that the family she never had would magically be created and that her abusive husband would turn around and become a caring father, ready to give up his addiction for the sake of the children. For months the abused woman lived on the verge of disaster and never gave up hope.

Chapter Seven

Transposing An Oppressive Heritage Into Psychology of Everyday Life.

The psychological world, as seen through the eyes of Freud and his followers, is male defined and phallocentric. The male's development and psychic structure dominated early theoretical formulations. Females were seen as a variant of the male. Having a priori decided what the feminine and the masculine characteristics would be, the derived definition of normality was bound to be inaccurate. For example, should a male behave in a submissive and dependent way, the behavior might be define as abnormal, while it might be seen as normal for a female.

Sexuality: While the Victorian society was outwardly displaying a world of Puritanism, sexual activities were running rampant inside the bedrooms *des gens de bien*.[33] And should we believe Freud and his colleagues, these sexual acts were being forcibly imposed on young girls with lasting and damaging consequences. The psychological foundations laid by Freud were a logical follow-up to the patriarchal, monotheistic thinking discussed earlier. It is a variation on the same theme: Man is an animal enslaved by his sexual and aggressive drives (Eros and Thanathos). Only societal rules are keeping him from unleashing the beast within him. As an immature being, he is guided by the pleasure principle, but soon is confronted with the reality of an imperfect world and finds himself having to negotiate with his

---

[33] refers to people of the aristocracy.

environment. Society has its rules and he must abide by them. Hopefully, he will move from a narcissistic, totally dependent individual to a more self-sufficient being that can reconcile his own personal needs and the restrictions imposed by society's needs. This adaptive process is not without pain and discomfort. The individual causing symptoms of neurosis will put forth various defenses. The drives can be so powerful that unrestrained fulfillment would cause a state of turmoil for the individual. Therefore, the individual is constantly repressing his innate desire to fulfill his needs. At first Freud supported the view that all man's emotional problems stemmed from the fact that men have been repressing the knowledge of actual traumatic experiences. He later modified this view to suggest that such traumas did not need to have happened, but could have been fantasized. In fact, the world as seen through the eyes of Sigmund Freud is replete with abusive parents who sexually traumatize their children, leading to serious psychopathology. In economical terms, such pent up energy seeking to free itself by all means possible and finds its expression in maladaptive behaviors. When left to float freely, this energy causes pathology specific to women. The word hysteria was invented. In his paper, "The Etiology of Hysteria," Freud uses various words to depict the traumas that he calls "infantile sexual scenes," but he also implied some participation from the girl who changes from the role of the seduced to that of the seducer. This theory, described as a fairy tale[34] by his contemporary, Count Richard Kraft-Ebing, Chairman of the Department of Psychiatry of the University of Vienna, would have very serious implications for generations to come. Not only did his descriptions place the blame for emotional disturbances on the parents, it also placed a heavy burden of guilt and fear on little girls who, in Freud's world, are not innocent little victims.

---

[34]See Masson J.M. Reference No. 46

Facing isolation and ostracism from his colleagues, Freud would retreat from the strongly stated views at the expense of his nemesis, women. At the Salpetriere, with his friend and mentor Charcot, he would find a forum to further build his theory about hysteria. The reported infantile sexual scenes, he would later write, were nothing more than "fantasies of hysterical women who invented stories and told lies."[35] These fantasies would later be characterized as genital hallucinations. Girl victims were often suspected of accusing their fathers of imaginary assaults in order to gain their freedom and give themselves over to debauchery. The persisting practice of blaming the victims that still prevails today must find its roots in these early writings which are the foundations of our understandings about the topic of sexual abuse. The consequences of the controversy created by Freud and his followers have not ceased. Later on, other psychiatrists like Lazarre and Klerman would further define the concept and have described the hysterical personality with the characteristic traits of demandingness, dependence, egocentricity, exhibitionism, fear of sexuality, lability of affect, sexually provocative behavior, and suggestibility. A link with depression in women was suggested. Psychiatrists are often accused of planting false memories in the mind of abused children. The question is, does the prevalence of sexual abuse in the late nineteenth and early twentieth century establish causality between trauma and mental illness in female victims? Psychological theoreticians of the time seemed to be obsessed with sex. Fliess, a Freud's associate, saw a causal connection between the nose and the sexual organ. Emma Eckstein, Freud's first psychoanalytical patient (poor soul!), was even subjected to a complicated surgical intervention on her nose to cure her masturbatory tendencies. Even when the poor woman suffered life-threatening, post-surgical hemorrhage, the diagnosis of hysterical bleeding

---

[35] ibid

was still under consideration. Later, treatment with cocaine to the nose would be suggested.

Sigmund Freud's and Helen Deutsch's Feminine Triad:

Passivity: The female as a masculine being who goes into "castration shock" when she realizes that she is not like the boy. Not only does she not have a penis, but also whatever she has, her clitoris, seems to be truncated. Since in Freud's male-dominated word the phallus is so valued, the woman is seen as inferior. In his view the woman develops a continuous state of low self-esteem, longing to own a penis. And since the woman is irreversibly penis-less, the only thing left for her to do is to have a child to make up for that valued penis. In fact, the concept of penis envy is so pervasive in Freud's theory that there is "scarcely any character trait in women which is not assumed to have an essential root in penis-envy." There seems to be no doubt that the whole theory is based on cultural prejudices. The connection to the prevailing theological and philosophical views of women and the origin of sin in the world seems obvious. The woman sees her mother as devalued and wants to be like her father.

Masochism: Women are not supposed to display aggressiveness; therefore, women seem to be predisposed to develop masochistic impulses. In Freud's world, masochism is a feminine characteristic. Women are supposed to have an emotional dependence on others. Masochism is defined as a condition in which sexual gratification depends on suffering, physical pain, and humiliation, women are seen as engaging in behaviors seeking this kind of gratification as a result of some innate predisposition.

Narcissism: A narcissistic is a person who is in love with himself. He is both the observer and the object of love. This individual has a morbid need to self-aggrandize to compensate for feelings of low self-esteem. Chased by inner feelings of inadequacy, the narcissistic seeks refuge in a world of fantasy. The problem with this concept in Freud's world is that Freud seems to imply that it is a trait that is more likely to be encountered in women who are anatomically inferior. Such a view is echoed in the literature when Rousseau states in Emile, "Even the tiniest little girl loves finery: they are not content to be pretty, they must be admired." (Page 393)

It is true that the other psychologists and psychiatrists of the era did not always agree with Freud's outlandish views. His own disciple, Karen Horney, MD, had her doubts about Freud's psychological concepts, especially as far as his views on feminine psychology were concerned.[36] In spite of her admiration for Freud, whom she called a genius, she was one of the first to realize that Freud's views were mere reflections of an era characterized by prejudice and exclusionary practices. Although the era was depicted as one of tolerance and liberal thinking, it was still dominated by male bias and exclusion of minority construct. We cannot run away from the fact that the end of the nineteenth and the beginning of the twentieth century were still dominated by racism. Freud could not step out of his time. At the outset, Horney disagreed with the view that narcissistic, masochistic, and perfectionist trends were derivatives of instinctual forces. Rather, she saw them as attempts by individuals seeking "their paths through a wilderness full of unknown dangers." The tenet of psychoanalysis lies in the ability of the analyst to be attentive to the thoughts and feelings of the patient and to offer interpretations. These interpretations have been criticized as arbitrary and subjective, therefore prejudicial and biased. Much has been made by the fact that Freud's views were biologically based. However, one must admit that the biology in Freud's era was still in its

---

[36] See Horney K. Reference No. 29

infancy. Cherry[37] will characterize this biological basis as "metaphysical rather than scientific." When one thinks today about Freud's insistence that Eckstein's post-surgical bleeding was due to hysteria rather than a blood dyscrasia, one will have a clear idea of the state of the art in that period. In fact, Freud seemed to have been stuck in his own early commitment to an instinctual theory based on poorly defined physiological concepts. "Anatomy is destiny," Freud wrote, pointing toward the definitive and permanent nature of woman's attributes. One cannot change what is determined by biology. Freud himself made numerous references to the fact that he felt abandoned by his colleagues, but it was his writings and influence that would mark the world for generations to come. It is his conceptualization of the psychic world that would dictate how people's emotional problems were handled, not to mention the plethora of writings that sprung up around the same period.

---

[37] See Cherry, A. Reference No. 6

Chapter Eight

When Literary Arts Start To Copy Reality.

Revisiting Jean-Jacques Rousseau, Gustave Flaubert, Honore de Balzac, and Other Classic Authors: The Dark Side.

As I re-read the work of Jean-Jacques Rousseau, I have a confession to make. Having come to this world through a difficult childbirth myself, I was given little chance to live by the midwife who had to travel through mountains and valleys to come and bring the process of delivery to a fortunate outcome. In reading the story of Rousseau's birth and the death of his mother, I quickly took a liking to this man. Like me, he had no athletic abilities and became a bookworm. I was ready to devour and accept everything that he wrote and every statement that he made. Maybe I was drawn to the clarity and beauty of his literary style. I fell for the rendition of the story of his childhood. I made every hesitation, insecurity, and trepidation about his burgeoning sensuality my own. I shared his indignation when he discovered injustice for the very first time. Having been punished for a petty mischief that he did not commit, he let it all out. I placed myself in the shoes of that cousin of his and with him I repeated a hundred of times: Carnifex! Carnifex! Carnifex! Executioner, tormentor!

Maybe in my own naiveté, I was fantasizing that this veneered author would stand for justice and protect me and my peers from all the affronts to justice that were going on around me in the terror years of the Duvalier dictatorship. I wanted a hero and became blind to the fact that further in the readings of the same confessions, the once jolly fellow had grown into a disappointed, grouchy old man who was barely surviving the rebuff of his first love. This man had resorted to theft, lies, roguery, and other subterfuges to quench his frustration. As he put it himself, he had fallen from "the sublimity of a hero to the baseness of a villain." I guess my schoolmates and I did not have much of a choice but to admire this character that was touted as the greatest writer of his time. Besides, what could possibly be wrong with a statement like, "Men are naturally good, it is society that corrupts them"? Was this statement the words of a narcissistic man who felt endowed with unrecognized talents and who was forced to act more like a commoner? Was it the reflection of a man with good insight into society around him? After all, this man was branded the "father of the French revolution" and was seen by many historians as the precursor of our own slave revolt in the colony of Hispaniola. Little did I know that this man's writings would be at the center of a political debate that would cause him to flee his native Geneva after a warrant was issued for his arrest. Rousseau, a troublemaker? Great! In the prime of our adolescence with heads full of ideals, like my schoolmates I was ready to save the world and Rousseau's ideal was going to help us. What we did not know was that we were being shielded from a much bigger picture, the darker side of Jean-Jacques Rousseau. Rousseau, the heretic, the skeptic! He exclaims, "I love truth, I seek her, and cannot find her...!" He was the man with many questions. He only lasted a few weeks in the seminary and in his "Profession De Foi Du Vicaire De Savoyard" (the creed of a Savoyard priest), he questioned the very basis of organized religion, especially the notion of a blind trust in the church authorities' interpretation of the message of God. Were the Catholic priests, our teachers and members of the same church under attack from all azimuths, going to poison our young minds with the philosophical thinking of this man? At least from a rhetorical standpoint, Rousseau and his friend and colleague, Diderot, raised the right questions and were on target when they talked of Europeans having constructed a system of law and government for the sole purpose of conservation of property, inequality, and slavery. They fell short, however, of condemning it. "What is," he declared, "is good, and no general law can be bad." The real question is what was Rousseau's reality. To perceive is to know. It is now clear that Rousseau and his contemporary knew very little about biology and almost nothing about the cultures and the history of the world around them. The man who advocated that his Emile learn by experience had a head full of quotes from Plutocrat, Socrates, and the Greek classics, but little experience about the world he was living in. Many times, chased by his own demons, he sought refuge in the imaginary world of writing. There he had complete control. Only his own emotional instability, his mood swings, and his delusions of persecution limited him. He was admired by many, but did not always believe it. Often, he secluded himself and hardly mixed with people. Feeling like an unsung hero, he probably had some manic episodes, like after he found himself all soaked in his own sweat upon learning that his "Discours Sur Les Sciences Et Les Arts" was awarded first prize by the Academie de Dijon. The world that Rousseau would create is a man's world. Women's roles are predetermined by nature and they should not deviate from it. Women who leave their home and devote themselves "gaily to the pleasures of the town" are doing it at their own risk. The survival of the race depends on women not forsaking their duty to breastfeed their children. It cannot be a matter of choice. In the cheerful home, the woman has sweet duties imposed by nature and the man has pleasant recreation. The real teacher of the child, according to Rousseau, has to be the father. In his education system there would be no provision made for the physically challenged or for that matter, for any woman. In his world, their mothers will educate women at home. In his world there is no place for a woman soldier, "If the young men of Paris find a soldier's life too hard for them, how would a woman put up with it?" (Page 390) There is a feeling of uneasiness that grabs everyone who is bearing the weight of oppression, as he seems to constantly remind his reader of the futility of any fight to change what has been determined by nature, the stern law of necessity. Stagnation is the order of the day. "Oh, man! Live your own life and you will no longer be wretched. Keep your appointed place in the order of nature and nothing can tear you from it." The nature versus nurture debate rages on. Little did I know that Rousseau's whole philosophy had been in defense of the status quo. How could I, as a Black individual, have been made to adore someone so reactionary? This is the whole point. This is the subtle inner working of a Eurocentric, patriarchal system. I argue that this system was meant to be oppressive and that censorship by omission and exclusion is an integral part of it. In his kingdom, Rousseau would have had only women and cripples working in the garment industry. A woman is to be seen as a "helpmeet" to be consulted in bodily and sensual matters, while men are to be consulted in moral and intellectual matters. He sees no role for women as writers or book critic. (p.366) The role of the woman is to please the man, as she is a creature made for man's delight. In the intercourse between men and women, women are like a city-besieged, ready to be run over. Should there be any violence in that encounter, the woman is to blame, for nature has endowed women with the power to stimulate men's passion in excess of men's power of satisfying those passions. Weak is the woman and she is proud of it. He seems to indicate that if a woman is forced into a sexual act, she should remain silent and in support of his view he quoted a law of Deuteronomy, stating that women should not let themselves be surprised in lonely places. In Rousseau's world there is no personal right to movement for women, they belong between the four walls of their home. Inequality, he claims, is not mere man-made prejudice, it is the result of reason. Women should not complain. Women should not engage in family planning as they have the duty to procreate and perpetuate the race. Rousseau will readily admit that men are imperfect, vicious, and even faulty. It is the responsibility of women to learn to submit to injustice and to suffer the wrongs inflicted on her by her husband without complaint. How could the teenager that I was possibly know that the famous statement meant that one is born with some endowed qualities and that they were better left alone? And if a racist/sexist and therefore oppressive world had decided that a group was endowed with inferior qualities, such a group was condemned to a life of servitude and inferiority. How could a man who had so eloquently lamented about the injustice that he had felt as an apprentice turn into a defender of the status quo? How could he have let die the fire of indignation that he had felt burning within him when the father inquisitor bluntly asked him during the rituals that preceded his conversion to Catholicism, "Is your mother damned?" The same man who had experienced first hand what prejudice was like while traveling as a Catholic in a Protestant country and had to change his name temporarily to Vaussore. What was the hidden lesson that my Europe-trained or European educators wanted me to get by shielding me from the darker side of this man?

The story of my first encounter with the work of Rousseau bears witness to the very thesis of this book in several ways. First, it demonstrates that it is almost impossible to develop an accurate and independent understanding of a philosopher's thinking without access to both the whole work of the person and its historical and cultural context. If not, the view that one develops is bound to be erroneous. The facts can easily be manipulated by the selection itself of what the reporter chooses to present. It is like censorship by exclusion. Emphasis can be placed on aesthetic rather than content, as was the case with my literature teacher who presented Rousseau's work for its literary value rather than its content and historical significance. As consumers of information, we are susceptible to being drawn to whomever the establishment presents through the powerful media. As human beings we have an inclination for heroes. Maybe heroes are there to fulfill the narcissistic needs in all of us. We usually choose models that are valued by our culture. When Jesse Jackson got on that podium in the democratic convention in 1984 and delivered his famous speech, didn't we all wish that we had his oratory talent? When Barry Sanders does his foot dance and takes the football to the end zone, don't we all wish we were on that field in his stead? When Florence Kersee-Joysner makes her dash to the finish line leaving her competitor to eat dust, once again we feel the tension in her every muscle and we cross the finish line with her. For every one of these exceptionally talented individuals offered to us as heroes, there are countless stories of courage and achievement that have not or will not get a chance to be told.

Madame Bovary: Gustave Flaubert describes the women of the epoch.

Three-quarters of a century later, Gustave Flaubert (1857) will give us a whole different flavor of how women were viewed in the classic literature.

In his famed novel, "Madame Bovary," Flaubert created a character unmistakably marked with the stamp of the romantic era. In his wordy characteristic style, he depicts a heroine whose insatiable taste for life is pursued relentlessly but never achieved, almost like an anorgasmic woman. His heroine is both fascinating and painful to watch as she constantly struggles and hesitates between her phantasms and the reality that surrounds her. She always seems to be willing to take one more try at capturing elusive and fleeting moments of happiness. She describes her temperament as more sentimental than artistic, seeking emotion rather than landscape. She is, however, full of insight and declares her disappointment at man's inability to bring her happiness. She expected "man to initiate her in the turbulence of passion, but this man taught nothing, knew nothing, wanted nothing." The author seems to be at ease with the traditional gender roles, describing Madame Bovary's father-in-law as unconcerned with domestic matters yet hoping to raise his boy child in a Spartan-like manner, while the wife is consumed with house chores, withdrawn and resentful. Mr. Bovary states that clearly, "a man would always get ahead in life if he has enough nerve." A man is free to explore exotic feelings and his passions. A woman is "constantly thwarted. Inert and pliable, she is restricted by her physical weakness and her legal subjection." Some convention is always there to hold her back. A woman is also viewed as a love object, a coveted prize that is suddenly placed on a pedestal and loses her bodily attributes. At times there seems to be nothing conventional about this heroine. In spite of her sarcastic statement to Leon that "a good wife and mother does not worry about how she looks," Madame Bovary challenges the puritan view en vogue in the earlier epoch. She became increasingly annoyed with her husband's apparent lack of ambition. When her heart fills up with chagrin over the departure for Paris of her unconsummated love, Leon, she does what many modern women do, she goes on a shopping spree. Although Flaubert seems to struggle all throughout his masterpiece between his desire for a purely literary novel and the need to have it grounded in reality, he could not escape the religious and philosophical discussions of his time. He does not hide his admiration for the Greek philosophers and embraces a faith based on reason without the mediation of religion. "My God," he exclaims, "is the God of Socrates, of Franklin, of Voltaire, of Beranger! I stand for the religious credo set forth in Rousseau's Emile." Madame Bovary was troubled and she did what most church-going Catholics would do, she approached the parish priest, Father Bournisien, with her moral dilemma and internal turmoil. The man of God seemed more interested in temporal matters and in his parishioner's social status as a doctor's wife than he was in helping the heroine find spiritual comfort. Still tormented and longing for the fulfillment of her impossible dreams of love, she fell for calculating Rodolphe's stratagem when the latter appeals to their common duty to feel what's great and cherish what's beautiful. The fate of their nascent love affair was sealed. Rodolphe was going to rescue her from herself. It seemed that they were heading for a life away from the small town, when suddenly a bolt of light suddenly strikes Rodolphe as he is going through his collection of mementos from all the women in his life. The implied thought here is that Emma Bovary was not capable of reason and Rodolphe, the all-powerful male character, had to instill it in her. The situation would take a turn for the worse as after being jilted by her secret lover, Emma went into a long period of poorly described illness that sounded just like the hysterical episodes which would be made famous by Charcot and Freud in the next century. Weakened and broken-hearted by the monstrosity and the oppressive nature of the small town where the power structure consists of an all-male cast, from the notary to the pharmacist to the dry food dealer, the loan shark, and the court, all of a sudden Emma seems to have no friends in this town. She is financially ruined and has nowhere to run. Desperate, she rekindles her old love for Leon and consummates the relationship, hoping that maybe her quickly fading karma would be re-energized. Not a chance! When opportunities present themselves one needs to seize the moment at once. Carpe diem! When they are lost, may seem to be gone forever. The second time around, it is never quite the same. Facing the execution of an order to seize from the court, Emma swallows her pride and finds her way to la "huchette" where lives her former lover, Rodolphe. There she faces a rude awakening. Reality has finally caught up with her. She utters the famous words that have been like a curse even in today's relationships, "You are no better than the rest." Vanquished, she confronts death with courage after looking at herself one last time in the mirror. She takes a large dose of arsenic and commits suicide. Before his own death, the husband, Charles Bovary is made to appear very magnanimous. He forgives Rodolphe. All is well that ends well. The all-male dominated society lives on. The pharmacist has been awarded his Legion of Honor. For Mademoiselle Bovary, the heroine's daughter, the cycle of poverty and subjugation continues. She will be working in a cotton mill to earn a living.

Another Voice From The Past Seals Women's Fate In The Literary World: Honore de Balzac.

Many authors have depicted the situation of women in their works and could have easily been quoted here. However, no one has excelled like Honore de Balzac in the art of describing the physiognomy of his characters. Honore de Balzac (1799-1850) was a very prolific writer. His works included many descriptions of women as he saw them. He has left us with many psychological profiles in the novel genre. His very first notable work was "La Physiologie du Marriage," where he wrote about the wife, "Pay no attention to her murmurs, her cries, her pains, nature has made her for our use and for bearing everything: children, sorrows, blows, and pain inflicted by men." Balzac was a serious writer who set out not only to write the social history of France, but also to diagnose the ills of society and to propose remedies. It is in his novels, however, that he freely let out his hatred for women. He sees them as essentially inferior. In his acclaimed novel, "La Duchesse de Langeais," he seems to degrade women almost to nothing. After going through rather gruesome details about how to dispose of the heroine's body, the perpetrator exclaims, "C'etait une femme, maintenant ce n'est rien" (It was a woman, now it's nothing). He clearly believes in the primacy of man in society. "Les peuples comme les femmes," he wrote, "aiment la force en quiconque les gouvernent..." (People, like women, want to see strength in their rulers....). He also talks about women who want to be beaten at will. Was Honore de Balzac just a narrator or was he expressing his own philosophy of life? One thing is sure, his work reflected the views of the era. His influence was tremendous and many of the great authors that followed, like Emile Zola and Marcel Proust, are "unmistakably indebted to him."

PART II

THE WAR IS ON...

THE FEMINIST RESPONSE

"Tremble not before the free man, but before the slave who has chains to break."

Margaret Fuller

"It is time to effect a revolution in female manners--time to restore to them their lost dignity-and make them, as a part of the human species, labour by reforming themselves to reform the world."

Mary Wollstonecraft, *A Vindication of the Rights of Woman, 1792*

First Wave.

Chapter Nine

Contributions of the Strategists

In face of the hostile and oppressive environment described in the first part of this book, it was only a matter of time before women would rise up to at least offer an appropriate response. The yearning for freedom and justice seems to be an instinct present in all humans. Once a human being becomes conscious that there is such a thing as freedom, the fate of the chains are sealed. There is no battle too hard to fight, no blood too precious to shed. The war will be waged, no matter the cost. The former slaves of Hispaniola did not hesitate to take on Leclerc's army. The Americans started with the Boston harbor tea protest and went on to earn their independence from the British Army. The third estate in France, under the leadership of some luminaries, stood up to the arrogant but powerful French monarchy of the eighteenth century and took over la Bastille. Many heads rolled under the guillotine. The Bolsheviks kicked the Czar of Russia out of his luxurious and glittery palace into the somber and cold halls of the dungeon. The Shaw of Iran went from port to port, unwanted by his former allies, while the Ayatollah was making his triumphant entry Into Teheran. All of those wars were waged in the name of freedom and justice. To the idealist or the poet, these words carry with them a very abstract meaning, but to the materialist these words can only be defined in economical terms. Justice can mean equal pay for equal work or it can be defined as equal treatment under the law. In the early capitalistic society, many factors contributed to make the situation unbearable for women. Women were no longer allowed to be Brewsters or spinsters, as these trades were quite lucrative and were taken over by men. The healing arts, like midwifery and surgery, were gradually transformed into men's professions. Women were devalued and their worth was directly related to their ability to work or procreate, thereby multiplying the number of hands available for labor. The laws gave full protection to men's property, which also included women. Vagrancy and poverty became a crime. The first real attack on patriarchy came from an explosion of prophecy and spirit possession. One thing is certain, if under the influence of the spirit, women could not be held responsible for their deeds. The Puritan revolution of the mid-seventeenth century did not fully benefit women and children. Women, and especially children, were considered naturally sinful and needing to be beaten into holiness.

People became conscious of the existence of an exploitative situation. From then on, the fate of the shackles was sealed. When pushed into a corner, anyone is capable of heroic acts. In the response put forth by the women's liberation movement, many heroes and heroines rose to the occasion. The heroines took diffcrent approaches. Some acted more like army generals who mapped out the strategy for the long battle ahead, using their literary talents and their eloquence. Others were more like activists who departed from their aristocratic background to engage in the fight in the name of moral decency. They shifted their methods in accordance with the sociopolitical currents of the time. However, all these women had at least one characteristic in common, they were determined to see women benefit from the transformation of the country from a colony into a more industrialized, young, democratic nation. They had their work cut out for them. They soon realized that piety, purity, submissiveness, and domesticity, the essential qualities of "true womanhood," would no longer be enough. They needed new skills that only education could provide and that women were being denied.

Mary Wollstonecraft:

Mary Wollstonecraft's book, "Vindication Of The Rights of Women," is by far the most influential book of the women's right movement. It was a direct rebuttal of Edmund Burke's, "Reflections On The Revolution In France," which came in support of the status quo. She does not hesitate to ask the hard questions. She refutes the notion that "gentleness, docility, and a spaniel-like affection" should be the cardinal virtues of the sex. Have women so little ambition as to be satisfied with such a condition? She suggests that women should fortify both their bodies and their minds through education. Mary Wollstonecraft jumped into the Puritan radical fight to make the case for the inclusion of women. Women, too, should have the right to decide on their own fate. That was quite a bold position since all the Puritan talk about freedom and participation in government was only to include the head of the household, the property owner. Women should have access to education and in "Thoughts on the Education of Daughters" she argued forcefully that a girl's intellect should be developed. She made her contribution to the nature/nurture debate, recognizing the influence of the environment on human nature. If girls are passive, it is not because of some natural defect, but because of lack of exposure. Rousseau was no friend of women. He declared that "a woman should never, for a moment, feel herself independent, that she should be governed by fear to exercise her natural cunning and made a coquettish slave... a sweeter companion to man." Mary Wollstonecraft would not leave such an assertion unchallenged. Using her pen like a sword in the hands of a skillful fencer, she exclaimed, "What nonsense! When will a great man arise with sufficient strength of mind to puff away the fumes which pride and sensuality have thus spread over the subject!" She predicted that with education, women would embrace all kinds of professions now reserved to men like Medicine, Politics, and Business and that midwives would be replaced with *accoucheurs* (italicized to mean male obstetricians). She stated, "I will venture to affirm that a girl, whose spirits have not been damped by inactivity, or innocence tainted by false shame, will always be a romp, and the doll will never excite attention unless confinement allows her no alternative."[38]

Girls, she argues, are what child rearing practices are making them. Were they raised like boys, they would behave like boys. Mary Wollstonecraft did not live to see her ideas in action. Her stingy and direct writing style earned her the title of "hyena in petticoats." After attempting suicide, she became depressed and would die a couple of years later. Mary Wollstonecraft was a woman ahead of her time when she wrote that there are no innate racial, sexual, or social class differences among men and women and that all differences are rooted In the social environment and can be eradicated by changes in that environment.

Frances Wright:

Frances Wright was probably one of the first women lobbyists in America. Born in Dundee, Scotland, she devoted her life to the cause of democracy. She got close to the great men of her time, befriending French General Lafayette and receiving invitation from President Monroe to visit the United States. She witnessed first hand the inhumane treatment received by the slaves, seeing them in chains being led to the slave market, and set out to do something about this cancer which was a "threat to the young democratic nation." She envisioned a colony, "Nashoba," where ex-slaves would live freely after earning their freedom through surplus labor. In

---

[38] See Wollstonecraft M. Reference No.81. See also Reference No. 67

this integrated society, Blacks and Whites would intermarry and live in harmony.[39] These revolutionary ideas were counter to the ongoing religious revival movement of the time. Middle class America reacted negatively to the project and Wright retreated. She switched gears and became one of the most popular lecturers of her time. She campaigned against slavery, the religious revival movement, and the poverty and ignorance of the urban American scene. Her personal problems did not keep her from devoting all of her energy to the translation of her political ideas into social action. Her ideas about political reform are true to this day. There cannot be any freedom without economic empowerment. To illustrate the veracity of this concept, one only need look at the plight of third world countries which, decades after gaining their independence, are still languishing in economic stagnation.

Harriet Martineau:

Like Frances Wright, Harriet Martineau was another transplant from England. She managed to describe the early American societies in such detail that scholars and social scientists invariably turn to her "Society in America" to get an original view of the era. She discussed topics like mercenary marriages where parents would break up relationships between their young girls and their boyfriends to marry them to rich old men.[40] She was branded as a writer of the liberal left, a title that was certain to raise some eyebrows in conservative American society. She stunned everyone when she quickly embraced Garisson's abolitionist views. She quickly denounced the treatment of women. The men were full of gallantry, but could not stand women becoming successful in areas that really mattered. "She has the liberty to get her brain turned by religious excitements, that her

---

[39] See Rossi, Alice. Reference No. 67
[40] ibid

attention may be delivered from morals, politics and philosophy...In short, indulgence is given as a substitute for justice." Education is restricted, thus "nothing is thus left for women but marriage." She was one of the first to denounce the lack of solidarity between the women (White slaves of the north) and the suffering race. She did not spare the hypocrisy of professional Christians who would act as if there was a separate gospel for women.

Margaret Fuller:

Raised by a very stern and demanding father, who graduated from Harvard College, Margaret Fuller had the privilege of a very erudite education. However, she soon found herself with the responsibility of running the affairs of the family after her father suddenly died of cholera. Her contributions to the cause of women are multiple. She showed a lot of courage by discussing the differences in pleasure-seeking activities between men and women. She also approached the subject of homosexuality. "It is true," she wrote, "that a woman might be in love with a woman." But she fell short of seeing this relationship as necessarily a physical one, "It is undoubtedly the same love that we shall feel when we are angels..."

In "The Great Lawsuit," she made a case for an end to slavery, "Extended freedom such as has been achieved by the nation, should be also for every member of it," and said the fight against racism and the fight against sexism are all in one, "If the Negro be a soul, if the woman be a soul, appareled in flesh, to one master only are they accountable."

They were ready to fight for it with every breath and fiber of their body. In a way, the religious revival movement following the second great awakening at the turn of the century (1795-1810) aided this moral high ground approach. Salvation would not come as a gift from heaven while the brethren passively waits, it would depend on individual efforts on concerted social action. A wave of antislavery sentiments was sweeping across Europe and the echoes could be heard all the way in America across the rural farms of New England. The British are coming... The British are coming... This time it came in the form of antislavery literature and political tracks. The first American antislavery society was born in 1834. The discourse had taken a more religious tone. Slavery was not just a cancer, it was a sin.

Chapter Nine

Contributions of the Activists

The Grimke Sisters:

It was within this context that Sarah and Angelina Grimke, the Grimke sisters, made their appearance on the battle scene. With the proliferation of the local antislavery societies, the battle was going to take a political turn. The U. S. legislators could no longer sit by the sideline. Women were succeeding in making Christian and democratic America feel very uncomfortable about the monstrous tentacles of slavery. In 1843, the antislavery debate had finally reached the National Congress and would remain there for quite some time, until it came to fruition some twenty years later.

The Grimke sisters did not hesitate to break away from their familiar and comfortable environment to embark on a lifelong fight against slavery and later against sexism. Their South Carolina family was slave owners and instead of sheepishly following the laws and traditions of their time, they broke away. There is some poetic description about how they taught their slave girl how to read and spell around the flickering light of the fireplace. Sarah was not permitted to study Latin and law, a domain reserved for males. She acquired her vast knowledge on legal issues from her father and brothers. The sisters became fervent abolitionists and inspired many of the lieutenants of the women's movement. Raised as devout Episcopalians, they joined the Quakers. They saw slavery as morally wrong and did not mince their words to denounce it. Angelina Grimke ruffled quite a few feathers of the southern slave owners when she directly addressed the women in an appeal to the Christian women of the South. The response from the church authorities was swift. The power of woman, she was reminded, is her dependence, flowing from her consciousness of the weakness that God has given her for her protection. The pastoral letter went on and on, reiterating centuries of biases and prejudices in one breath. The polemic continued, as Sarah responded to every single assertion in the pastoral letter. She did not lose the opportunity to once again make the link between the right of women and the right of slaves. She laments about the condition of female slaves, comparing it to the situation in Athens, Greece, "In Athens, the female slave could seek the protection of the temple and demand a change of owner. In Christian America, the female slave has no refuge from unbridled cruelty and lust."[41]

Sarah combated the biblical justification for slavery with her publication, "Epistle to the Clergy of the Southern States." The Grimke sisters are believed to have greatly influenced Theodore Weld's work on slavery, "American Slavery As It Is: Testimony of a Thousand Witnesses (1839)." This book is a precursor to Harriet Beecher Stone's masterpiece, "Uncle Tom's Cabin." These books created a real breach in the granite walls of slavery. No American would ever look at slavery the same way again.

A Man Joins The Fight

John Stuart Mill's main contribution, "The Subjection of Women," was published only four years before his death. It quickly became the reference book documenting the position of women in the society of the time. It brought instant prestige to the suffragist movement. He became closely associated with Harriet Taylor and many believe that he could not have

---

[41] ibid

written such an essay without her help. He promoted the idea of the complementarity of the sexes. From very early, women were made to believe that their ideal character is the very opposite to that of men, not self-will and government by self-control, but submission, to make complete abnegation of themselves, to have no life but in their affections. How can one claim to know the nature of women when the only time women have been observed was as subject, under the control of men?

The turn of the 19th century saw the birth of two women who would turn out to be the best political team in history: Susan B. Anthony and Elizabeth Cady Stanton. They met fortuitously in 1851 and became inseparable. Never had a cause brought together such a dynamic and energetic duo. They combined their talents to literally shake the world around them. Neither one spoke without the other's blessing. When one wrote, the other one critiqued. They both had the fighting spirit and vision that was necessary at the time to advance the women's movement. They offered each other the moral support they both needed to manage their housekeeping and child-rearing responsibilities (Elizabeth bore seven children) together with a hectic lectures schedule that took the pair all over the country, traveling by the means of transportation of the era. Elizabeth was a woman full of emotions and she did not hesitate to express her feelings whenever she felt that she was about to break. "I am at a boiling point!" she once wrote to Susan, "If I do not find some day the use of my tongue on this question I shall die of an intellectual repression, a woman's right convulsion." (Stanton and Blatch 1922: II, 41) Her own father did not recognize Elizabeth's genius. Neither her father nor her husband were supportive of her social activism, feeling maybe that all that agitation was not becoming of a woman. Her father went as far as disinheriting her, although he changed his mind before his death. These two women did not just start the women's suffragist movement, they laid the blueprint for women's struggle towards the right to vote granted in 1920, almost two decades after the pair had died. Elizabeth was also consumed with other women's issues. In her numerous letters to her sister in arms, Susan, she debated the question of marriage and divorce. She denounced the complicity of religion, laws, and customs in degrading women. She experienced genuine moments of exhilaration as women responded to her speech on divorce, "Oh, how the women flock to me with their sorrows. Such experiences as I listen to, plantation never equaled." (Stanton and Blatch 1922: II, 127)

It Was Their Fight, Too.

In recent times, in the name of multi-culturalism, there has been some effort to bring to light the contributions of non-White males to the apparent strength and prosperity of this nation. These contributions were not always voluntary. Nuclear testing happened unbeknownst to the inhabitants of small towns of Middle America. African-Americans were used to test the natural course of syphilis in Tuskegee, Alabama. The buffalo soldiers were finally recognized. How many more historical facts are still waiting to be brought out in the open? Should all these facts about women, Native Americans, Blacks, and Black women be discovered and should the country decide to do a complete about face and start educate its citizens completely and accurately about history, what then? How many generations will it take to undo the pain and suffering caused by centuries of exposure to half-truths, if not right out lies? Can the White women, the Black women, and the Black men ever get over the psychological scars they have endured from lack of identity, low self-esteem, and feelings of alienation in a country that has excluded them?

Freedom, equality, and justice are not synonymous, but they seem to be irreversibly linked. One without the other seems useless. Angelina and Sarah Grimke, Suzan B. Anthony, and Elizabeth Cady Canton, among others, were very much aware of that fact. They understood that their struggle for a just society would have been hypocritical if some women, the colored ones, did not have any rights at all. Slavery was an abomination and they fought to eradicate it from their country. They were not Blacks, but as women they personally suffered from inequality. Once abolition was won. What next?

Chapter Eleven

Enough Is Enough: Simone de Beauvoir's Pointed View. A Review of The Second Sex.

A powerful woman's voice from the French literary elite set the record straight: Madame De Beauvoir writes "Le Deuxieme Sexe"

One hundred years after the publication of Madame Bovary and one hundred years after the death of Honore de Balzac, came Madame Simone de Beauvoir with "Le Deuxieme Sexe," published in 1949.

In an unprecedented display of phallic might, the allied armed forces had just warded off the threat of world servitude or annihilation by vanquishing Hitler's Third Reich army and dashing this crazed man dream of an eugenic world. Then came Madame de Beauvoir and "The Second Sex." This woman, the long time companion of existentialist philosopher Jean-Paul Sartre, was one of the many authors who have lived and suffered directly or indirectly the atrocities of the war. It seems as if they all were waiting to unleash their verve. Using her pen like a scalpel in the hands of a skillful surgeon, no area of accumulated knowledge seems to be safe from her tedious, detailed, and careful dissection. De Beauvoir's goal is stated right in the introduction. "One is not born, but rather becomes a woman," she declares. She does not hide her annoyance with the feminist movement which in spite of "the voluminous nonsense uttered over the past century seems to have done little to illuminate the problem."[42] The methodology she employs is not new. She reviewed the fields of biology, philosophy, theology, literature, and politics to create a long dossier of the exploitation of women. This is the way it is. This is the way it has been. Women, she argues, have not demonstrated the ability to give any kind of organized response about the inequality. "What is a woman anyway?" she asks. Can she be defined by her own accord? Or is she to be defined as a negation of man, a non-man? No one ever questioned the essence of man. Men define the world. Strongly influenced by the existentialist philosophy en vogue at the time, she seems to be tormented by the question and asks it in many different forms. She laments the difficulty that she encounters in trying to come up with an acceptable definition, "A man is in the right in being a man; it is the woman who is in the wrong." They are defined by their physical attributes. "Women are in danger," she heralds. Can women save themselves from a feeling of alienation? For a woman who reportedly was quite comfortable in the elite intellectual circle, she seems to be almost full of disgust when she describes the powerlessness of the other sex, a stranger in a world of which she could claim half. She asks rhetorical questions and seems to a priori know the answers. By asking why, the sovereignty of males is not being contested. She opens the door for more difficult questions without directly accusing her fellow women of ineptitude. At times, she seems to exaggerate the obvious to make her point. A statement like, "Women have no past, no history, no religion of their own," might sound inaccurate at first, but when you take it with you and start turning it in your head, you cannot help it, you have to marvel at her ability to force you to think. How many Joan of Arcs or Madam Curies do you know? In the above-mentioned citation index, how many women philosophers were represented? Who is the female equivalent of

---

[42] See De Beauvoir. Reference No.14.

Shakespeare? Is the world of philosophy only made up of Socrates, Aristotle, Aquinas, and Nietshche? Not that they do not exist, but no one bothered to write about them. History as we know it is the history of men. She could not escape the still prevailing dualistic, binary theory of the era. She borrows heavily from Levi-Strauss to make her point. She seems to know the psychological make-up of members of the oppressive group very well and describes their apparent complex of superiority. She does not hesitate one moment in using the sometimes-raw language of some authors when they put down women.

In book one she starts with a very expansive expose of biological data that, in the words of some literary reviewers, belongs more to a medical textbook than to a philosophical essay. All of that in order to establish that woman is who she is by destiny. Woman's anatomy and her physiology define her.   Woman is imprisoned in her biological characteristics. Womanhood is destiny.   Woman is endowed with certain attributes indispensable to her predetermined duty, procreation. She presents the facts dispassionately. The reader is taken through the labyrinths of comparative embryology. She questions the validity of any theory that would present one sex as superior to the other. The only aim of the sexes is the survival of the species. She quotes Hegel's notion of necessity. She subscribes to the view that the two gametes, after they unite, lose their individuality. She shows remarkable ability to switch back and forth between the biological and the philosophical arguments. The ovule is likened to immanence, the sperm to transcendence. The ovule is passive; the male gamete is rational. Sperm the very data she so carefully presents. One is not always sure where De Beauvoir stands on an issue. Sometimes, she tends to become over-inclusive until she suddenly and unequivocally lets it out, "They [the biological data] are one of the keys to the understanding of woman, but I deny that they establish for her a fixed and inevitable destiny."[43]

Discarding Freud's psychoanalytical views was very easy for de Beauvoir, because, as she pointed out, Freud never demonstrated any understanding nor did he show any concern for the destiny of women. In fact, his own contemporaries and admirers have leveled the same criticism at Freud. She made light of Freud's penis envy theory, rejecting it as overgeneralization of Freud's experience with women or lack thereof. The psychoanalytic system has been complemented, however, by Alder's inferiority complex theory, which causes woman to want to reject her femininity. If there is one essential weakness that De Beauvoir sees in the psychoanalytical theory, it is the rejection of the notion of choice. The whole theory is based on psychic determinism, meaning that there is no such a thing as accident. De Beauvoir seems to strongly disagree with the reductionistic notion that every human activity evolves around sexuality, as the psychoanalysts would have you believe. If woman wants to have a penis, it is because she has come to realize that in a male defined and dominated world, being a male is positively valued. It might mean access to a world from which penis-less women have been excluded.

As Madame de Beauvoir continues, we seem to be defined by history. Humanity is a historical reality. Invention of tools, for example, was developed to extend the ability of the hand. According to Engel, the distribution of labor started on an egalitarian basis between the two sexes, but things fell apart when men started to enslave his fellow men. Safeguarding the private property line became the first priority and families were rearranged, shifting the chain of authority and inheritance to a matrilineal model.

---

[43] ibid

One becomes much clearer on de Beauvoir's purpose as we go along. Men and women find themselves linked by a common destiny and each aspires to dominate the other. So far, it seems that man has had the upper hand. Claims have been made about man's dominance being due to superior musculature, although history reveals that it might not have always been that way. Woman was definitely at a disadvantage since she had the added duty of bearing children to ensure the survival of the species. That duty was not received with joy though, it was seen more as a matter of fate. Communal life rested for the most part on the work of women. Women were doomed to a sedentary existence. Madame de Beauvoir bluntly rejected as myth the notion of a golden age of woman when matriarchy existed, although she presents no strong argument to that effect. She uses more recent history to show that when women made it to a position of leadership, it did not necessarily bring any improvement in the lot of the other women. She argues that societies that have remained matrilineal have also remained primitive. Even the belittling of women by the church fathers has not escaped her scrutiny. The authorities of the church often saw the institution of marriage in a negative light. Maybe that is why it was soon forbidden for the cadre of the Catholic Church to get married. Ironically, with chastity and puritanical family life put into effect, prostitution became a necessary corollary of the institution of marriage. Women who became too interested in intellectual matters were ridiculed. "Femmes Savantes" and "Precieuses Ridicules" were published and had a huge success. One would think that with the French revolution there would be some improvement in the conditions of women. A repressive apparatus was quickly put into motion to reverse the gains made by the French Revolution. Women were the first to fall victims. In "Beyond Good and Evil," Friedrich Nietzsche assesses the situation as follows: "Since the French Revolution, woman's influence in

Europe has decreased proportionately as her rights and claims have increased...There is stupidity in this movement." It would take French women another one hundred and fifty-eight years before they could enjoy full political rights. Besides, great numbers of them were guillotined in the aftermath of the French revolution.

De Beauvoir also reviewed the literature and presented a different point of view on how women are represented by different authors. Montherlant blames his mother for his being a person with physical limitations. He sees his physicality as an impediment that makes him less than God. Women are presented as incomplete beings doomed to slavery. Lawrence believes that the powerful phallus will bring the sexes together. Claudel reflects the views of his church and sees salvation and redemption for women in dedication to church and family. She presents Breton as the poet and Stendhal as a genuine friend of women.

Book II is a study of the human life cycle starting with the formative years that include childhood, adolescence, and the entry in the adult world with sexual initiation. Childhood is viewed as a period of sexual undifferentiation where the world is represented by "immanent sensations." He is suddenly turned loose and has to face the world seen by him as the other. He has to fight abandonment either by rushing back into the arms of his mother or by seeking others' approval. Later on, boys are abandoned again when they find out that society does not expect them to cling at their mother's skirt. He is made to believe that he is superior because he has a penis, while the girl is encouraged to be pretty, homely, and passive. Messages of man's superiority are all around her. Her essence can only be accomplished through the advent of a prince charming. De Beauvoir also gave her views on lesbianism. She was much ahead of her time when she tried to differentiate physical appearance and sexual orientation. She sees the lesbian as a woman who was able to make a choice and has refused to play the part of the "true woman" that society has tried to impose on all woman, i.e., a life of submissiveness, passivity, and inferiority. She goes as far as saying that every woman is a bit ... homosexual.

What de Beauvoir did not say? What de Beauvoir could not have said?

De Beauvoir does well when she lays down the facts, the bare facts, although she tends to get lost in intricate details. Nowhere else can a researcher find any other single source where so many aspects of the question of woman has been so thoroughly treated. She came very close to threading a complete quilt of women, were it not for the obvious absences. Missing from her fresco are accounts from live, contemporary women themselves. Maybe she could have gotten away with it if she did not set out to depict such a huge portrait. Her statement, "All that women have done is to symbolically agitate," sounds very stereotypical and is at least inaccurate on several accounts. Whatever happened to the feminist movement? (It will be reviewed in the second part of this book.) Whatever happened to the heroic efforts of Harriet Tubman who risked her own freedom to shuttle scores of Blacks through the Underground Railroad track out of slavery? Whatever happened to the resistance of queen Anacaona who refused to be led away in chains by her Spanish captors? De Beauvoir seems to accept too quickly the idea that the status quo cannot change. Mentioning in passing that the "Negroes of Haiti" were successful in freeing themselves from the chain of slavery is not enough. One would have liked to see her expand a little bit more on the historical facts of this struggle. She lost a golden opportunity to expose the fact that this triumph was only possible when men and women of Haiti were able to unite and work together towards the common goal of freedom. She would have also exposed the fact (alas!) that the triumph was very short-lived as the superpower has conspired to "keep the emancipated Negroes in their place." The analogy to the fate of the Third Estate in France after the French revolution would have been obvious. When the euphoria of the takeover of La Bastille was over, the French society went back to its old conservative ways and the fate of women did not change much.

Maybe asking so much from de Beauvoir in the historical context of her work is unreasonable. One cannot help but to feel that de Beauvoir's torment is purely intellectual, somewhat of an intellectual masturbation. She seems to stand away from the crowd, watching. Many questions seem to be in order. Is it her role as a writer to get into the fray, jump into the trenches, and get her hands dirty? Is it the role of a writer to stir up the debate while enjoying the coziness of her recliner by the fireplace? It is a matter of choice, of course. And Madame De Beauvoir made her choice. De Beauvoir did not write a revolutionary manifesto. Her work is far from being a call to arms. Fifty years later, in spite of the huge success of The Second Sex (witness the hundreds of reviews in the literature), the fate of women has not changed much. The best way to describe her work is to use her own words, "The truth is that these notions are hardly more than vagaries of the mind."

Chapter Twelve

The Second Wave and Beyond: Feminism Africana Style.

Black women did step into the trench and contributed immensely to the struggle. It is quite appropriate to start the long list of Black contributors with Harriet Tubman, who made the trip north all the way to St. Catharine, Canada. She was so thrilled by her newly found freedom that she decided to go back behind enemy lines, at the risk of getting captured or killed, to ferry other Negroes into freedom. She became known as the conductor of the Underground Railroad. Neither her own physical limitations nor fear could stop her. She was a woman on a mission. She stood a mere five feet tall and suffered from seizures secondary to a severe head injury, yet did not hesitate to threaten escapees who were having cold feet. "No coming back" was her rule. After liberating more than three hundred slaves, she was not satisfied. She became a spy and worked for the Union army as a spy. She earned her title of General, the first U. S. Army woman general. Not too bad for an ex-slave! A freedom fighter, a spy, a general, and a nurse, Harriet Tubman was a woman of many talents.

Then there was a legend of a lady named Sojourner Truth. When the movement needed a trusted soldier, she was there. She relentlessly campaigned around the country as the leading female abolitionist of the nineteenth century. She deservedly has been branded one of the "founding mothers" of modern America. Her inner strength and her unique ability to overcome adversities and pursue her goals was attributed to her faith in God and her belief that she was invested with the power of the Holy Ghost to advocate for changes in the condition of her fellow Blacks. She remained illiterate until the very end. She was a staunch supporter of the Union Army during the Civil War. Guided by her faith as a Pentecostal, she faced some of the social problems confronted by women head on. She even joined the Magdalene society, a group dedicated to the reformation of prostitutes. She was probably one of the first Black leaders who supported the workforce and was critical of Blacks living off handouts from the government well before welfare came into existence. Sojourner Truth, along with Harriet Tubman, brought needed credibility into the movement since they could talk from a very vivid perspective what kind of suffering the oppressive patriarchy had created. She did not coin the term "Womanism," but she could have. Her statements at that time take a prophetic tone. She insisted on the connection between slavery and sexism. " If colored men get their rights and not colored women," she stated, "colored men will be masters over the women and it will be just as bad as before." Over a century later another African leader will state the fulfillment of this prophecy. Nelson Mandela will declare, "I have known White masters, I have known Black masters." Sojourner Truth has suffered in her flesh the damaging effects of slavery, as she put it so eloquently in a speech before women's rights a convention in Akron, Ohio in May 1851:

> "I have plowed, and planted, and gathered into barns, and
> no man could head me! And ain't I a woman? I could
> work as much and eat as much as a man-when I could get
> it-and bear the lash as well! And ain't I a woman? I have
> borne thirteen children, and seen 'em mos'all sold off to

slavery, and when I cried out with my mother's grief,

none but Jesus heard me! And ain't I a woman!"

Are there any muscle men out there who want to take this woman on? The above statement epitomizes the statuesque nature of this woman who has also been called "The Black Joan of Arc." It is no surprise that she became a mythic figure, a legend even before her death.

Many other Black women followed in the path of the two pillars of American history just mentioned. They brought their own perspectives to the fight. Mary McLeod Bethune, for example, did not have the fiery speech of a Sojourner, but with the cool-headedness of an academician and a scholar, she broke many grounds. She insisted on African-American girls receiving an adequate education. She also took the position that changes could come from infiltrating the enemy lines.

She represented Blacks at high levels of Government and made her case in a very methodical way. She founded the Daytona Normal and Industrial Institute that would later merge with the Cookman Institute to become the Bethune-Cookman College. Her most famous statement remains "What the Negro wants"- a prelude to the avalanche to come with the civil rights movement of the sixties.

On that momentous evening of December 1955, Rosa Parks boarded that bus in Montgomery, Alabama like she had done many times before. Little did she know that she would mark the world's history forever. She became an agent of change, a catalyst, and a voice for a movement that had been festering underground for quite some time. She sounded the cry for resistance against an oppressive system that, years after Blacks had obtained their legal freedom, was still treating them as second class citizens or no citizens at all. Enough was enough. She was too tired, as she recounted, "to give in to White people," and Rosa Parks was going to hold on to that seat no matter the consequences. The whole world, and especially African-Americans, is grateful that she did. Seven thousand Americans responded to a call to a peaceful march. The march to freedom was on.

There is no doubt that the White feminists presented above contributed enormously to the cause of the Blacks who, in addition to sexism, had to confront racism. However the contribution of Black women to their own liberation cannot be minimized. For centuries, they were kept invisible. Never could they succeed in silencing them. Their White counterparts pushed them aside when it was time to march on Washington because the White strategists could not afford to offend the Southerners by letting the Black ex-slaves adopt such a public posture. Several amendments were made to the original Voting Rights Bill. They excluded Black women in order to increase its chance of passage by Congress. The Black women fought on. Like chameleons, they mastered the art of dissimulation. Black women could not take their enemies head-on. Therefore, they went underground and created one of the most sophisticated networks of freedom fighters using Black Churches as their haven. There they fought without fanfare, but very vigorously, a system that discounted them as inferior beings incapable of success. No issues about African-Americans were off limits to this extremely dynamic group of women. They proposed hard work, sobriety, integrity, and self-help over dependency on others. Today they stand on the sideline of the main stream of the feminist movement, feeling that the time has come to formulate their own agenda. They see their interest as not necessarily the same as that of White middle-class women. They might be taking the same position on some issues for completely different reasons. If Black women are against abortion, as some recent polls seem to indicate, it is not necessarily for religious reasons, but because they feel that birth control and abortion have been pushed down their throat by policy makers. The motive might even seem suspect by ethnic minorities who often wonder if they are not being targeted because they are depicted as poor, uneducated, and a financial burden to the community. Besides, they do not necessarily see abortion as a civil right issue, but as a personal issue to be examined in terms of its emotional implications.

What womanism means is that Black women will no longer be satisfied to have other women lead them. They want to set up their own priorities. Womanism wants to build on the Black women's tradition of emotionality, spirituality, intuitiveness, and cooperation with their men to raise their children like in the old traditional African village. Womanism will liberate Black men from the entrails of the patriarchal system that has kept them enslaved to violence, drugs, poverty, and diseases. The patriarchal system has failed both Black men and Black women and freedom for both groups will only come if they remain supportive of each other. Womanism calls for a total transformation of men and women. This transformation will bring all of us closer to nature. Under the womanist philosophy there cannot be room for domestic violence, drug use, or continuous assaults on the environment. Womanism calls for the elimination of the binary thinking that seeks to oppose masculine and feminine, mind and body, nature and nurture, and rational and spiritual. As Alice Walker explains, "Womanism is not a movement against Feminism, it is a special nuance of feminism" that seeks to restore Black women to their rightful place. It is a movement that will finally acknowledge the invaluable contribution of Black women in their immanent role in nurturing everyone. Black women have nursed children of White families during the day and tended to the needs of their own children in the wee hours of the night. They have cared for the children of their neighbors as teachers and educators. They have dressed the wounds of everyone in the hospitals. They have striven to keep the peace at home.

Who ever said that this role was any less important than building highways or operating a Hercules crane at a construction site? Who ever said that the art of negotiating the best compromise between warring factions, an art that has remained the purview of women, was any less important than operating a forklift? In spite of Black women's tremendous contributions, they have had no recognition whatsoever. They have displayed extraordinary resiliency. They have come out swinging, resisting and combating the negative characterization. Building on their talents, many Black women have changed forever the landscape of the entertainment world. Their influence seems to be everywhere. No one has mastered the art of daytime chatting like talk show queen Oprah Winfrey. No issues are beyond her reach. No one can tell a story and bring tears to the eyes of her riveted audience like she can. Whoopi Goldberg is in a league all by herself. Can anyone challenge the singing ability of a Whitney Houston or a Tina Turner? As an opera singer, Leontyne Price has forever broken the color and the sound barrier in bringing about the most memorable rendition of "Aida." These women are very few and one might say that they are just tokens of success in a world dominated by White males and females. However, they signify that there are no longer any mountaintops too high for Black women to climb. Black women must not just continue to sing and entertain, they must not be afraid to speak up about the issues confronting our communities. Who can be better voices for these problems? Many Black women have either witnessed them or experienced them first hand. The struggle is tiring and the road is tortuous and tricky, but it must go on. The process of healing and establishing a self-concept must continue for both Black women and men. To have its full impact and be truly liberating, however, Womanism has to bring Black men into the fold. Black males are still invisible. They are in danger of extinction. Successful Black men whether in sports, politics, or professional careers like medicine or law are just like artifacts on the radar screen of a busy metropolitan airport. They carry an inordinate amount of weight on their shoulders. They are like sitting ducks to be used as target practice by overly critical and scrutinizing agencies. The Willie Horton syndrome still haunts us and seems to be replayed ad nauseam every night on the evening news. Black men are lagging behind Black women in terms of education, income, and other indices. I do not see Black men standing any chance of redemption or survival without the help of the sisters. The destinies of Black men and women are forever linked together. It would indeed be very foolish for Black men to see Black women's affirmation as a threat. Instead, this movement should be seen as the last ticket out of stagnation. When Black women bail Black men out of jail, the trip should not end there. The journey should continue into the nearest College registrar office. They must resist the temptation of going after the Black males just because they look like hunks. Black women are not just crowding the welfare lines; they are also outnumbering Black males on the college's campuses. Black women have a historical role to help Black men realize that there is no salvation in the relentless pursuit of the White man's macho image of Rambo and the Terminator. We have blindly espoused the view that expressing our feelings is not a manly thing to do. We have neglected the most balanced part of our psyche, the part that makes us into a caring and nurturing being. Children are walking around in part of the community "packed" with a gun because they fear they might have to respond in kind. The more fragile the ego, the bigger the pistol. We have allowed violence to steal the innocence and the spontaneity of our children. Whatever happened to conflict resolution through communication? Black men must voluntarily find their way to the psychotherapist or the psychiatrist office to resolve marital conflicts and prevent domestic violence well before they are mandated to do so by the judicial system. No, It is not a sissy thing to do. To talk about issues that are gnawing us inside and cause us to lose control, smack women that we love, or become abusive to our children is the right thing to do. Women talk things out all the time. Men, on the contrary, feel that they have to compete and emulate their peers. This race to consumerism's only purpose is to keep everyone in check. We have become enslaved to our materialistic needs. Consumption of goods has become the symbol of our newly achieved status. This process has alienated us. We multiply our jobs to keep up with our bills while our children are being "educated" (brainwashed) by messages from the television set. We have lost our sense of family, our connection to nature. We have lost our ancestral African soul. Womanism seeks to recapture that soul and spread its healing and repairing virtues. This movement aims for an egalitarian society where women's inherent qualities are valued. No longer should the focus be on emulating males attributes that, whether displayed by men or women, have lead to disaster of gargantuan proportions. In the early weeks of 1998, a sequel of the Gulf War seemed inevitable. Many Americans were lounging in front of their television sets, rooting for the home team. The mighty American Navy fleet was awaiting orders to launch satellite-guided missiles at their targets in Bagdad. Came in Kofi Annan, the man from Africa. Diplomacy triumphed. Everyone wins. He used qualities usually associated with women. Why can't they be used more? The struggle should be for those inherent women's attributes to become positively valued and put to use to bring about real changes. One might argue that this is a utopic dream and that the obstacles to its realization are insurmountable. I beg to differ. One only needs to look around to see the progress that has been made as we approach the third millennium. The only task that anyone is certain not to ever complete is the one that never gets started. Did you ever wonder what America would be like if the African-Americans did not force the Whites to live up to the ideal of the American Constitution? Because of the struggle of the civil rights leaders, America is a much better place today. Therefore, isn't it fair to say that the debt of the country to African-Americans is priceless? The Womanist movement can now claim the leadership of the feminist movement and bring about irreversible changes on this nation's way of thinking.

Timeline of the Women's Liberation Movement

The First Wave

"To Restore Women to their lost dignity"

Strategists	Activists

1786: Mary Wollstonecraft:

Thoughts on education of daughters

1790: Judith Sargent Murray:

On the equality of the sexes

1816   The Blackwell Clan starts:

Celebration of spinster-hood

1820   Harriet Tubman (1820-1913)

General Tubman, the conductor, the nurse, and the spy

1834   First American anti-slavery Society

1836   Angelina Grimke:

Appeal to the Christian women

Of the South

Sarah Grimke:

Letters on the equality of the sexes

Epistle to the Clergy of the Southern states

TIMELINE OF THE WOMEN'S LIBERATION MOVEMENT

STRATEGISTS   ACTIVISTS

1839 Theodore Weld: AMERICAN SLAVERY: AS IT IS

1843   Margaret Fuller THE GREAT LAWSUIT

1848 The Seneca Falls, NY meeting: Declaration of sentiments

1851 Sojourner Truth: *AIN'T I A WOMAN?*

1860   Elizabeth & Emily Blackwell: American Women: Medicine, a profession for

1863 The Emancipation Proclamation Legal freedom achieved

TIMELINE OF THE WOMEN'S LIBERATION MOVEMENT

STRATEGISTS   ACTIVISTS

1861-1864   The American civil war:

Abolitionists v. Anti-abolitionists

To keep the union at all cost

1869 John Stuart Mill:

The subjection of woman

1875   Antoinette Brown Blackwell:

The sexes throughout nature

1881   Elizabeth Cady Canton & Susan B. Anthony

History of women's suffrage

1892   Frederick Douglas denounces lynch law

1884   Jim Crow's Era

1895   Elizabeth Cady Stanton:

The woman's bible

1856-1915   Booker T. Washington

Accommodationist:

Self-help, Self-reliance, Education

TIMELINE OF THE WOMEN'S LIBERATION MOVEMENT

Strategists   Activists

1891   The Tuskegee institute

"Cast your bucket where you are"

1909   NAACP founded

1910   Urban League founded

Interracial   Cooperation   &

Education

1915   W.E. Dubois:

The immediate program of the American

Negro

A matter of survival: social,

1920   Voting rights for Women

1944   Mary McLeod Bethune:

What the Negro wants

1949   Simone de Beauvoir:

Le deuxieme sexe

The Second Sex (1953)

Kinsey: Report on Sexual Behavior in Human Female

1955   Rosa Parks:

The bus incident: "I

am   tired   of

giving   in   to   White

people"

TIMELINE OF THE WOMEN'S LIBERATION MOVEMENT

The Second Wave

Equality for All women Equal Partnership of the sexes

1963   Betty Friedan

The Feminine Mystique:

Women not totally fulfilled

In marriage and motherhood

Martin Luther King Jr.:

"I have a dream" speech

1964   Civil rights act of 1964: Title VII Prohibits

DISCRIMINATION ON THE BASIS OF SEX

1966   NOW (National Organization for Women) founded

1968   Pope's Humanae Vitae:

Against artificial methods of birth control

and voluntary sterilization

1969   Stonewall Inn incident:

Modern Gays and Lesbians Rights movement starts.

1970	ERA passes us House of Representatives
1972:	Shirley Chisholm : Black Congresswoman

Challenges "Healthy good-looking White male "

Seeks the presidential nomination of a major

party.

TIMELINE OF THE WOMEN'S LIBERATION MOVEMENT

1973   Roe v. Wade

ABORTION   LEGALIZED   ROE   V

WADE

1978   100,000 people march on Washington DC

In Support of ERA

The Third Wave   Generation X

Cindy Lauper

Girls just wanna have fun

Madonna

Papa Don't Preach!

The Spice Girls

If you wanna be my lover

The   Jerry   Springer's

groupies

1982:   Carol Gillian: In a different Voice

Psychological   Theory   and   women's
Development

1991   Anita Hill v. Clarence Thomas

1992:   750,00 Abortion rights supporters

March on Washington DC

1994 Federal Law to stop violence against women

TIMELINE OF THE WOMEN'S LIBERATION MOVEMENT

THE OTHER WAVE 1981-

WOMANISM: RECLAIMING   BLACK   FEMINISM

CONSCIOUSNESS

BELL HOOKS

AIN'T I A WOMAN?

KILLING RAGE ENDING RACISM

SISTERS OF THE YAMS: BLACK WOMAN AND SELF-RECOVERY

CORNEL WEST

RACE MATTERS

LISA JONES

BULLETPROOF DIVA

PART III

THE TRUE NATURE OF WOMEN:

A NEW PSYCHOLOGY.

Chapter Thirteen

Identity and Self-image

In the first part of this book, we have established how Western philosophy and psychology have derived from a male supremacy model of thinking. We have traced the roots of this system back to the Greek philosophers and have witnessed how a whole theology of oppression has been put into action. Popes and Kings have started a series of Crusades to defend or impose their points of view. We propose to review existing psychological theories and their historical impact on women and other minorities.

Our experience is the sum total of what we perceive. As social beings, we crave feedback from our environment to validate our very essence. We depend on our environment to set the outer limits beyond which we simply cease to exist. The process of perception through which we let environmental stimuli sieve is highly selective and culturally determined. We see as important and valuable what the society we live in tells us is important and valuable. Racism and sexism have contaminated that process. For women and Blacks the environment has been extremely hostile and prejudiced. The pursuit of self-affirmation and autonomy has been, for these groups, a dream both elusive and difficult to attain. Individuals often feel helpless in their dealing with the outside world. The locus of control in the dyad self/non-self or being/non-being has been situated for too long out of the individuals' reach.

For too long, women and Blacks have been deprived of their humanness and "relegated to the status of things among things."[44] How can a woman define her self-ideal independently of the constraints imposed upon her by centuries of silencing and exclusion? How does a woman gather the necessary qualities to reach her full potentialities, to self-actualize? How does she meet her fundamental need, in the words of Maslow, to be loved, respected, and accepted by herself and others? Women cannot escape their uniqueness as human beings and the exhilarating power associated with that discovery. This process, however, has been thwarted by years of interference from oppression and subjugation. Individuals should feel free of pressure and should not be forced to effectuate changes that do not fit their pursuit of love and happiness. Such changes, when contemplated, should represent no threat to the individual's sense of continuity and self-consistency. Oppressed individuals live continuously under the threat of annihilation. Slavery did not only deny Black people their individuality, but deprived them of an opportunity for self-consistency. There have been discontinuities in the victims' experiences of self, both collectively and individually. Racism and sexism have left women and Blacks groping in the dark for an explanation for their psychic experiences. Their collective memory is like a disjointed mosaic of tribulations, struggles, and small triumphs. However, this experience is awaiting validation. The absence of such validation has constituted a major hindrance to the ability of women and Blacks to act as their own pathfinders. Often they have found themselves following the tracks of Judas goats.[45] Untested psychological

---

[44] See Gale R.F. Reference No.24

[45] A Judas' goat is a goat that has been conditioned to lead the pack of goats down the chute at the slaughterhouse. The Judas's goat knows to jump at the last minute as the followers are getting their heads chopped off.

theories have been advanced and put into practice, causing catastrophic damages.

Challenging these erroneous views of White male supremacy has been difficult for various reasons. The voices of dissenting theories about women have been kept quiet by the power of the main system that dominates the publications, the media, and expressive art in all its forms. Challenging the prevailing all-male generated views has been made difficult by many problems such as the non-inclusion of women in research samples and the absence of a language designed to convey the woman's perspective, causing the premature generalization of theories not tested on women. Fearing that women's menstrual cycles and lability might complicate the interpretation of their data, psychological researchers have avoided women as subjects. For decades the racist and sexist views have remained unchallenged. People have come to believe that some qualities are inherent to White men because of some predetermined and permanent biological attributes. The longer these views have remained unchallenged, the more accepted these views have become. In fact, these views were fast becoming the canons of the science until some very powerful women's voices started to resonate. After the work of Carol Gilligan was first published in 1982, women would no longer be looked upon through the mold created by Sigmund Freud and his disciples. This powerful voice has made every researcher in the field of psychology very uncomfortable and hesitant to accept the definition of women as non-men. Throughout her writing, Carol Gilligan has established the defining characteristics of women. Men are not the norm, and women should not be "fashioned out of the masculine cloth." In her letter to readers of the 1993 edition of "A Different Voice," Carol Gilligan denounces two lies. "The first lie is in the psychological theories which have taken men as representing all humans and the second lie is women's psychological development in which girls and women can alter their voices to fit themselves into images of relationship and goodness carried by false feminine voices." She conducted a series of studies where Lawrence Kohlberg's six-stage hierarchical model of moral development was revisited. Gilligan's goal was not to debunk the work of her mentor and friend, but to point out the fact that the model might be full of male biases. In her college student study, her "subjects" are faced with a morally ambiguous situation, Kohlberg's original Heinz's dilemma: A man's wife is dying. He cannot afford the drug at the price proposed by his pharmacist. Should he steal the drug or should he let his wife die? There is a whole hierarchy of conflicts attached to this situation. Should the man violate the rule of personal property and do as he pleases without regards for the pharmacist's rights? Such choice is sure to draw some sanction from society if he is caught or some feeling of guilt if the man has bought into the Manichean system of right and wrong. Should the man betray his responsibility towards his wife and let her die? He is then sure to face internal guilt from himself and opprobrium from society. Can he live with the sin of theft or the sacrifice of the sanctity of life? Should he take a "justice approach" or a "care approach"? Both choices seem as justifiable as they are difficult. The boys take a mathematical, logical approach in solving this real life dilemma, while the girls take a more relational approach to the same problem.[46] The boys' approaches were scored as conventional on a mixture of stage three and four, while the girls were scored at a mixture of stage two and three. On what basis can one say that a mathematical approach is superior to a relationship approach? First of all, Kohlberg's stages of development were based on the study of 84 boys, no girls. Second, the higher value placed on logic over emotionality seems arbitrary. This is

---

[46] See Gilligan C. Reference No. 25.

the crux of the matter. The whole system, created from a patriarchal male dominated perspective, has arbitrarily and positively valued one set of characteristic over the other. Autonomy, rationality, logic, and self-reliance, attributes traditionally characteristics of men, are deemed superior to emotionality, inter-connectedness, communication, and intuitiveness, qualities found in women. In fact, in examining the above dilemma, Gilligan believed that Jake and Amy, the eleven-year-old boy and girl in her study might have been looking at a completely different question. Amy took her time and pondered the possibilities. She lamented over the relationship implications of her choice. She seemed "evasive and unsure." The eleven-year-old girl is looking at the situation from a care perspective. There is a relationship at stake here and, in Amy's view, it cannot be put into a mathematical formula. Having a different approach does not mean having an inferior approach. Janet Surrey supports the concept of "self-in-relation," a notion that "for women the primary experience of self is relational, that is, the self is organized and developed in the context of important relationship." What we are proposing to do here is to review the alternative views. We hope to demonstrate that the concepts put forth by the tenets of modern psychology are inaccurate because they were based on false premises in the first place. Ask the wrong question and you will be bound to get the wrong answer. We will review the work of authors like Joan Borysenko and Carol Gilligan and seek a more accurate portrayal of the psychology of women. We have tested concepts like gender identity, gender differences, gender behavior, choices, and expectations. We wanted to hear women's voices. We wanted to create an environment where women could talk from the heart without fear of criticism, away from the scrutinizing eyes and ears of people who could make our core group uncomfortable. We started out with our friends. The first meeting received rave reviews. And then something very interesting happened. The women who participated in the first debate started to spread the news and to invite their own friends. They had also made it clear that they wanted these discussions to continue and that men would not be invited. At least not yet! The series of focus groups was baptized the "What if...? Series." It has been going on for almost a year now. It has brought together scores of women from different socioeconomic and educational background. Women with a large variety of life experiences have painstakingly shared with us their point of view about different issues. We have been able to discover some common threads in the discussion. We do not pretend that these debates will solve all the mysteries that surround the psychology of women. At the very least, however, we hope to make some progress in our attempts to understand the true nature of women.

What would the world be like if women could rewrite the book of Genesis?

It was a mere coincidence that a question about the first book of the Bible was chosen for our very first meeting. For hours their voices resonated against the four walls of the small conference room of my office. The initial hesitations about the fact that the question might have a religious connotation were quickly addressed. The discussants were to focus on the impact of women representations in that book, on their self-identity and position in society. The book was seen as a story with a lot of holes. If the purpose of this book was to serve as guidelines for women to carve out their own humanity, many participants saw it as a rather scary proposition. The holes left too much to chance. It has been left too much to different groups' interpretations. It was a story told by men. As such, men have used it to advance men's agenda in a purely male-dominated society. It is not a book without a very strong cultural flavor. It is a book full of symbolism. It is a very powerful book. In spite of the consensus of opinion that the world would be incomplete without women, the relationship between the sexes has been one of total domination and subjugation of women. The participants were unanimous in pointing fingers at the Bible for setting the tone. The women expressed the view that they have been made to feel guilty for the so-called original sin, when all that Eve wanted was to share God's infinite wisdom and divinity. Some found the book to be exclusive of people with a minority view or sexual orientation. What if Adam had wanted a Steve instead of an Eve, or Eve an Yvette instead of an Adam? Could it be that the very essence of women was mutilated right from the start when her role was limited to procreation? How about eroticism and sexual pleasure? Maybe, the participants conceded, the transcribers of God's grand plan, being the products of their time, did not see women's issues as important and totally excluded them. The Bible has been used as a whipping stick to oppress women. Why then didn't the fathers of the monotheistic religions, who claim the Book as their blueprint, offer a more inclusive interpretation? Some of the participants did accept some responsibility for allowing themselves as women to slip into a state of passive acceptance. Without women's acquiescence there would be no oppressive system. Others made it clear in a very loud way: Not a chance. If women have accepted the status quo, it is only because they were forced to do so. There was no choice. They do not make the rules. We, as women, have been powerless. If women were to rewrite the book of Genesis, there was no way they would create Eve as a servant to Adam. Woman would be a creature in her own right. Her name would not be a derivative of man. She would take the initiative in choosing her own name. Throughout the book of Genesis the power of naming has been illustrated over and over. The participants did fully identify the many symbols established in the Genesis and could not help but notice that women have been carrying the burden on their shoulders since the beginning of time.[47] They take off their shoulders the burden of the original sin, that curse that has haunted them forever. They would have Adam take responsibility for his own decision in sharing the forbidden fruit. The participants even fantasized a scenario where Eve would look God straight in the eyes in a charming and sassy way and ask, "Oh God, what can be so wrong in wanting to share in your knowledge? Wasn't it your intention for your creatures to be like you?" Why were men so lucky as to be the only ones to be confided the words of God? Why haven't we heard of some wise women entrusted with such spiritual gift? If they were to rewrite the book of Genesis, Isaac would not be taken to that mountain without some kind of family discussion. After all, Isaac had a mother. Women would definitely have a voice that everyone could hear loud and clear all around the planet. Not everyone was comfortable about the idea of re-writing the first book of the Bible. A small minority contended that women just had to accept what was and not second-guess God's plan for humanity. The participants did recognize that inertia could become very comfortable. There is comfort in accepting and rationalizing a system that you feel powerless to change, it is called coping. Society tends to reward those who are deemed as having "good coping skills." Wasn't it God's intention to place men and women in a situation full of ambiguity in order to define better the purpose of Creation? Others were very puzzled, if not outright suspicious. How could there be freedom without a choice? How could Eve and Adam be blamed for something they were destined to do? If we were just toys in the hands of an Almighty and all-knowing God, how can Eve be blamed for a transgression that was all part of the plan?

---

[47] See Moyers, B. Reference No 55.

Chapter Fourteen

Gender Definition and Stereotypes

The women's debate probably went on in their heads well after they left my office. A couple of weeks later they came back in force. This time, the echoes of their voices resonated against the wall of a ballroom at the Wyndham/Fort Lauderdale Airport Hotel. They were challenged with more questions about gender and stereotypes.

What would the world be like if gender roles were reversed?

This question elicited a lot of emotions from the audience. The majority of the group did not agree with the arbitrary nature of gender assignment. It is true that over the past decades women have done a better job demanding that men participate and take more responsibilities for sharing the chores around the home. Men are being dragged kicking and screaming to do chores traditionally assigned to women. However, this in no way should be seen as a redefinition of gender role. For the most part, certain duties are widely viewed as women's duties. In a way, they are being dragged kicking and screaming into the 21st century. The women offered some flexibility. They did not need to engage in a tit for tat struggle with their partners. In dividing the labor, one's personal attributes, tastes, and affinities should be taken into consideration. Why not allow men to excel in the outdoor chores around the yard, if it is where his forte is? If the woman is a better cook, why not let her take care of the kitchen or vice versa? The Black women participants did not buy the idea that Black women could be housewives. Black women, they offered, always had to go out and work hard. They did the housekeeping and other service jobs in most of the hotels and offices. They served as maids and nannies in upscale middle class neighborhoods. More importantly, women are the ones left with the task of educating and raising children, the lawyers, educators, physicians, executives, and political leaders of tomorrow. Women are the primary socializing agents. Why was the job of educating and rearing children, a job traditionally assigned to women, seen as any less important than that of designing an airplane or trading stocks? Behind the façade of autonomy and strength, men are depending more than ever on their wives for support and relief from the grueling effects of the work environment. Women are teaching their girls that their future endeavors should not be limited to what society wants to impose as their place. How are women doing it? They are discovering new bargaining chips and they are using them to shape men into compliance. Women are realizing that relationships can be advantageous or disadvantageous for both men and women. Once women have learned about the virtues of self-sufficiency and financial independence, they no longer feel compelled to stay in a non-fulfilling relationship. The participants reported a very positive change about men. Men-in-relation, some participants believe, are learning that they, too, could be nurturing, patient, and caring. Men-in-relation[48] are not afraid to bond with their children. No longer do they seem afraid to show their more tender, gentler, and kinder side. Women are standing up and demanding self-respect and the right to control their own lives. The role of women as sexual objects in a relationship is no longer as widely accepted and is being challenged more and more. The participants did see these gains as direct results from the sexual revolution that followed the women's rights movement even though they, too, were guilty of bashing the movement often described as too radical. They also recognized that the technological revolution and the advances of the

---

[48] See Borysenko, Joan. Reference No. 10.

communication age were also responsible. Women can compete at the work place without the muscle mass of their male counterparts. The group was very conscious of the fact that educators often reinforce boys and girls differently. Boys tend to get all the praises, while the girls get the harsher punishments. Much needs to be done. In some enclaves of this modern metropolitan city, women are still abused and treated as if the women liberation movement never happened. It is not all about education, one participant commented, it is about men's own sense of insecurity. It is like a vicious cycle. The more they mistreat their women, the more afraid these men are that the women might be taken away. It is like a caged bird that cannot wait to fly away. It is paradoxical. The same men that want to control the kind of outfits their women wear on the street will be the same one lusting over a provocatively dressed women at a club or in a store. And then some women take the opposite extreme. They take pleasure in portraying themselves as rough and boyish, from the no-frills jeans to the unkempt hairstyle. They live in protest of their own femininity. Many participants saw this period as very confusing for most people, but they proposed that this transitional period was even more confusing for men, who by definition have to have order and need to find logical explanations and specific solutions to every situation. The expression "survival of the fittest" could take a whole new meaning. The one who will survive may be whoever is more comfortable with the chaos, whoever is able to deal with the emotional turmoil. Who can doubt that women are better prepared for this challenge? If we were to take a count of the casualties today, men would outnumber women by a mile. It behooves women as parents to better prepare boys and girls to meet these challenges.

At no point did we observe any animosity towards men. A true spirit of camaraderie dominated the debate. Many of the participants were familiar with the work of John Gray, Ph.D., "Men are from Mars, Women are from Venus." Men, they noted, cannot stand being close to anyone for too long. They tend to experience the adult equivalent of what Melanie Klein describes in the early stages of human development as "fear of being engulfed." Because of this fear, men can only tolerate intimacy and closeness for short periods of time. They tend to internalize pain and discomfort instead of letting it flow. Women, on the other hand, will not hesitate to express those feelings, sometimes in very colorful and dramatic ways. These behaviors have become so characteristic that they have been accepted as a societal code of conduct. Any deviation is looked at with suspicion. An outwardly emotional man is described as effeminate. A very independent and firm woman who displays little emotion is described as manly. Women do not allow themselves to totally disconnect from a problem. When a couple is presented with a problem, the man will perform his quick appraisal, contemplate a few options, make his choice, and move on. There is very little or no emotional investment into the debate. Women, on the other hand, will stay with the debate for a very long time, sometimes days after the initial question was raised. They are likely to seek advice from their peers. A whole array of emotional expressions can easily be observed. This moodiness will often be a mystery to the man who has long forgotten about the original question. The job of coming up with an acceptable solution is taken very seriously.

Some women brought into the room a defeatist attitude, seeing little point to all this agitation. Even if gender roles were reversed, nothing would really change for women as long as men continue to hold the power, to make all the rules and all the corporate decision. Others have been very forceful in realizing that no matter how much progress women seem to have made, the fight to break the glass ceiling is yet to be fought. Maybe, one of the participants suggested, the answer is not about becoming like men. Why would we want to do that anyway? They have failed miserably. The next millennium will find many major issues around the globe unresolved. Hunger, high infant mortality, and families living in poverty are still major threats. Maybe, she continued, it is about time that society started paying attention to our voices, our way of handling conflicts. We have a different way of knowing.

Chapter Fifteen

Leadership Roles and Social Engineering.

What would the world be like, if most world leaders were women?

The words that come to mind to describe leaders are strength, power, patience, wisdom, and charisma. Unfortunately, the participants concede these words are not readily associated with women. Should a woman start showing any of these qualities, she is viewed in a very negative light. Such women are likely to be described with the B word. They are likely to be said to be experiencing PMS. The truth of the matter is that we have all been brainwashed into believing that women are not capable of being leaders, although for the longest time, they have led the basic unit of our society, the family. Women are said to be too quick in displaying their emotions. Evita, the famous Argentine first lady, the force behind Presidente Peron, cried in public. Imagine if she was a man. For a long time, men have been conditioned into believing that shedding tears is wimpy. Some might argue that there has been a softening of the macho image. The fact that Ed Muskie would lose the Democratic primary after he cried seems almost unbelievable. When tears started to roll off the cheek of President Clinton while sitting in the front row of a Baptist church during his first inauguration there were no comments from the major networks. Men are only very timidly starting to do what women have done all along. Women weep four times as often as men do. Not only have men been taught not to cry, there also seems to be some neurological reasons for the differences. There are fewer fibers in that large structure that connects the emotional brain (the right brain) to the logical brain (the left brain) in men than there are in women. We are living in a society where expression of emotions is not acceptable. Our grief over the death of a loved one is left up to a professional mortician. Every aspect of the quickly put together ceremony is planned and allowed to unfold in a very smooth and emotion-free environment. Mothers and educators, who know the virtue of being in tune with one's emotion, face a serious dilemma. Are we entering an era where people in touch with their feelings run the risk of being run over by a very violent and unforgiving society? How do parents handle less socially acceptable human emotions like anger, frustration, jealousy, and greed? How do mothers channel these feelings into more mature defense mechanisms? Leaders need to perfect the art of negotiation. Are mothers and educators equipped to deal with the task of educating the children? Do they prepare children who are fit for the part in a barbaric world? If so, aren't we preparing the children to assimilate into a society that we understand is wrong? Many participants quickly stated that if most world leaders were women, not much would change. Quite a few of those who made it as leaders did not rule any differently than men. They cited the example of the ex-Prime Minister of England who ruled with such a firm hand that she earned the nickname of the Iron Lady. The truth of the matter is that this chief of state was just implementing a patriarchal agenda. In that same country another woman, Princess Diana, a lady full of panache with a heart full of nurturing qualities, was given the status of an icon only after she was dead, when she was no longer a threat to the status quo. Hilary Rodham Clinton's social agenda and plan for universal health care for all Americans were shot down as liberal and counter to the male conservative agenda. The point is that the advent of a woman to the reins of power, although rich in symbolism, does not necessarily guarantee a non-sexist and free society. Geraldine Ferraro came very close when she was chosen to be number 2 on the democratic ticket in 1984. The other candidate won by a landslide.

Chapter Sixteen

Relationships: The Making of Mr. Right.

What if women could plant, grow, or clone their mates?

It did not take long for the participants to lay it all out in response to this most unusual question. Loyalty, honesty, ambition, and faithfulness are important qualities, but above all, they want their men to be attentive and available. Is there any room for compromise? Maybe. If he is a workaholic and is willing to share in the responsibilities of raising the kids or do some house chores, he does not have to have a very high hunk factor. In other words, he does not have to be like Brad Pitt, Denzel Washington, or Leonardo DiCaprio. The participants were very eager to describe their ideal man, but somewhere in the mist of the debate, common sense and the voice of reason prevailed. No one wanted to take responsibility for portraying the group as outer beauty without substance. Perhaps, it was the presence of the more mature women in the audience who extolled the values of a well-rounded, mature, educated, and nurturing man. No, they reminded the younger crowd, you cannot get everything in one package. You need to get your priorities right. Successful relationships take a lot of work. It takes some degree of personal stability and self-confidence. Women who do not love themselves cannot expect to be loved. Love is not as blind as they would have you believe. It helps for a girl to have been involved in a healthy relationship with her father or for a man with his mother. The role of the parents in helping the child develop a positive self-image is invaluable.

Children need to be told that they are beautiful and smart. Why do people who failed their first attempts have a tendency to repeat the same mistakes over and over again? What other factors guide a woman in choosing a mate? Is money always on the mind of the woman? Do modern women still believe in the myth of a Prince Charming dashing to their rescue with shining armor? Have women lost their ability to fantasize? Have women grown smarter and more realistic? With all the agitation about women's equality, did the men become confused about what women really wanted from them? Did men get the message that it was patronizing and condescending to behave like gentlemen around women? With the latest rush by women to post-secondary education, have men developed an inferiority complex around educated women? It is not that men cannot be affectionate and loving. Maybe they are afraid of being rejected. Women's feelings have been described as similar to a wave, with ups and downs. Men typically cannot sustain the flow of affection long enough to match their partner's fluctuation. By the time the woman is ready to listen, the man is off to the next activity. Although men and women have the same need for compassion and intimacy, to have those needs fulfilled they take a completely different road. Men are good at dissecting a long conversation, extirpating the essence of it, and moving on. Most of the words are tuned out, not even heard. Women need the soothing effect of long and circumlocutory conversation.

Chapter Seventeen

Hello! Are You There? Communications Styles in Men and Women.

What would the world be like if men would listen to everything that women have to say?

According to women, getting men to listen to what they have to say would constitute the ultimate shift of power. Some women who participated in that meeting did not hide their annoyance at those who were bragging about women being the great communicators. If we are such great communicators, they said pointedly, why aren't the men listening to us? This rhetorical question deserves some careful analysis because the implications could be tremendous for all of us. "Communication is inherently ambiguous," writes Deborah Tannen, Ph.D., author of "That's Not What I Meant." This ambiguity becomes all the more evident when we start comparing communication styles of men and women. Are men capable of adjusting their direct-to-the-point communication style to the more emotionally laden, support seeking or offering women's pattern? Are women capable of giving up some of their meandering to keep their male listeners' attention? What can be so wrong about women seeking to maintain some connection in a world that has gone impersonal? Will men take hints from women and start valuing women's expertise at interpreting body language? Is the gap between the sexes destined to grow even wider? I suggest that any serious changes will start at the individual level. It is true that people around us are continuously defining who we are. We are also constantly making statements about our identity by the way we behave and communicate. The probes that we use to interpret our environment are culturally defined and by definition are based on assumptions, biases, and prejudices. Maybe the first step to better communication is to be allowed into the interlocutor's worldview. However, that is usually not possible if there is disparity, perceived or real, in the balance of power. It is even more difficult if one culture, one sex, or one group is going to assume a position of superiority over the other. Take language for example. Americans often state that foreigners speak with an accent. This statement is usually made in a derogatory way as if the foreigner had committed some capital crime. A more accurate and culturally sensitive statement would be, "This person speaks with a different accent," because from the foreigner's perspective, the English language is full of cryptic accents that are as indecipherable as hieroglyphics.

Another thing was clear from this large group of women, they were very much aware of their attributes and gender characteristics. If men were to listen, there would be fewer wars, more harmony, and there would definitely be more order. Would there really be fewer wars? There is some evidence in the literature to support this view. In a study conducted with 32 Australian students, it was noted that a much higher percentage of men believed in aggression than women did. This belief was directly correlated with the choice of war over peace when it came to resolving an explosive situation. The other interesting finding of that study was that negotiation had little or no effect on the original position. The obvious implication is that input from women should be sought more often in resolving world's conflicts if the desired outcome is peace. There seems to be a definite advantage for women's participation in politics.

The women in the group held on very jealously to their perceived privileged position as having better taste and being able to shop and dress better. If men would listen to women, men would definitely dress better. Little did they know there is ample evidence to support their view. Some neuroscientists believe that it all starts in the brain. Men use their left brain to focus on the major characteristics of their gestalt, taking mental shortcuts. Women, on the other hand, integrate information from both sides of the brain to study all of the details, including colors, shapes, and consistency, allowing them a more total experience of the situation. Maybe this can explain why women in general take so long to shop. There is just so much information to process. Professor Joan Meyers-Levy, from the University of Chicago Business School, refers to this phenomenon as the selectivity hypothesis. Ad agencies are at the cutting edge of this research and have for some time now used different approaches to attract men and women customers. Ads created for women will be rich in details while those created for men are simple and often in black and white. Subliminal messages are easily picked up by women and often missed by men. Unfortunately, there have been a lot of miscues as the ones creating the ads are typically males and cannot always hide their biases.

Chapter Eighteen

Men and Women Approach A Morally Challenging Question: Kohlberg and Gilligan revisited.

How do women go about making an important decision? Do women respond differently to a difficult situation? If so, does the fact that boys and girls would chose a different approach to come up with a no-win solution to a conflictual situation make women morally deficient? Many times, social scientists do not have such questions in mind when conducting their studies. However, the power of their voice often gives immediate credence to their findings and those findings are quickly generalized. Inferences are often made that are far from the original intent of the university professor who tested the question. In our attempt to dissect yet another layer of the complex question we posed about the nature of women, we wanted to revisit the work of Kohlberg on cognitive and moral development.

Kohlberg's work originated from a purely Piagetan understanding of the process of cognition and childhood maturation. At each level of cognitive development, the individual is equipped with different abilities to grasp different concepts, assimilate them, and reason his or her way out of difficult situations. Boys, Kohlberg postulated, are more likely to invoke what he calls the universal principle with emphasis on equality, fairness, and universal principles. It is not our intent to present here the details of Kohlberg's work. However, he seems to have taken several giant leaps.

First, although his samples included only boys, his findings were generalized to both sexes. Secondly, his stages seem to establish a hierarchical value system, as if one stage was superior to another. Finally, in keeping with the prevailing biases of the time, he concluded that boys do reach a superior level of reasoning earlier than girls.

These views did not remain unchallenged. Kohlberg's own colleague and friend, Carol Gilligan, went on to prove the existence of an alternative view. According to her research, girls and women look at situations from a care perspective. Women are likely to explain their moral choices by invoking the importance of caring about others and about relationships. Gilligan's research was quite an improvement over that of her mentor, Lawrence Kohlberg, as she matched equal numbers of males and females of specific ages in her sample of thirty-six people. However, her population was recruited from a group of educationally advantaged adolescents and adults and it is questionable whether or not the findings can be generalized to the rest of the population. We feel that the groups studied by Gilligan might have been too much alike and might have not been representative of the ethnic and cultural quilt that characterizes America today.

Without going back to the continuous nature versus nurture debate, one cannot help but wonder whether the conclusions would have been the same if the samples were selected away from the ritzy New England environment. What influence, if any, does the culture of violence and indifference we have been experiencing in the post cold war era have on our moral reasoning? As societal rules are collapsing and our system of values is disintegrating, will more people revert back, not by ignorance but by choice, to more survival and self-centered moral choices? Or will the establishment have to resort to more stringent rules to maintain order? Are we heading towards a new era of fascism? Should this become reality, who is likely to suffer the brunt of the oppressive measures? These questions obviously have serious implications for minority groups and it is worth researching them in representative samples. Does the act of stealing have the same meaning when committed by an individual who has witnessed his parents struggle to feed the younger siblings or when committed by an individual born with a silver spoon in his/her mouth? It is with all of these issues in mind that we conducted the following study.

The Population:

Two hundred eighty-five subjects were selected. No attempts were made to select one group over the other; however, the selection was not random. It included people who came to my Fort Lauderdale psychiatric practice looking for help or accompanying someone looking for help. It also included people that I came in contact with in my work as consultant to various community agencies. Some of the respondents were recruited from bowling alleys and from a drug rehabilitation program. For a distribution of the sample by age, sex, religion, and race refer to "Appendix A."

The Question:

The participants were confronted with a challenging question borrowed from Kohlberg's original dilemma, the so-called "Heinz dilemma:"[49] A man presents to the pharmacist with a prescription for a lifesaving drug for his dying wife. The drug is so expensive that he cannot afford it. Should he steal the drug or let his wife die? The participants, whether male or female, were asked to put themselves in this man's situation. They were encouraged to chose one of the two alternatives. Some of the respondents found it impossible to chose and wrote in a third answer,

---

[49] See Jacobson and Parmelee. Reference No. 40.

none of the above, choosing in essence to let the wife die. The information gathering process was far from being as elaborate as that of Kohlberg, who put his subjects through a semi-structured interview. Instead, the participants were asked to comment on their choices. The comments were then assigned to different categories in accordance to a code sheet created for the occasion. The following categories were created:

1) No comment: The first group included those who made no comments

2) Survival-oriented/Self-centeredness: The second group included those individuals whose comments reflected a focus on self and on their own survival. This group parallels the pre-conventional stage of Kohlberg, the early stages or the physiological stages of Maslow, and the physical need stage of Patanjali in Vedic Yoga.

3) Conformity to societal rules: The third group reflected conformity to societal rules. It is equivalent to the Kohlberg's conventional stage. This group exudes self-confidence and its members believe in their ability to negotiate, barter, and bribe. This group would rather face rejection than endure the pain associated with breaking the rules.

4) Altruism: The fourth group was more altruistic and its members made their choice based only on the sanctity of life over money. This group is very conscientious and is very much aware of the value of life and commitment.

5) Spirituality/Transcendental: The fifth group was the spiritual/transcendental group. The subjects in this group

saw the exercise as somewhat futile, as we should all leave it up to God who holds our destiny in his hands. This group believes in the power of spirituality and seems to attach less importance to the official ending of this life. To members of this group, death is just an event marking the passage to a better world.

To put this kind of classification into perspective, we must first agree on a continuities/discontinuities model of human psychological development rather than a purely hierarchical model. If we consider for example acceptance of death as inevitable, it might have come from the fact that the individual might have been exposed to a lot of violence or from a process of personal growth. The problem with the hierarchical model is that it is arbitrarily set and is likely to reflect the bias of the observer.

Findings:

Distribution of Subjects:

According to Sex:

Males: 44% (N=125)   Females: 56% (N=160)

According to Age:

18% of the population was under 21

The vast majority of the sample (68.4%) was between the ages of 22 and 50.

According to Race:

African-Americans: 30.9% (N=88)

Percentage of Total: Males: 11.9 %   Females: 18.9%

Euro-Americans: 49.5% (N=141)

Percentage of Total: Males: 23.5%   Females: 26.0%

Hispanic-Americans: 10.9% (N=31)

Percentage of Total: Males: 6.3%   Females: 4.6%

According to Religion:

Catholics: 23.6% (N=67)

Percentage of Total: Males: 10.2%   Females: 13.4%

Protestants: 23.9% (N=68)

Percentage of Total: Males: 10.9%   Females: 13%

Jewish: 11.6 % (N=33)

Percentage of Total: Males: 3.5%   Females: 8.1%

Other: 40.8 (N=116). No Religious affiliation or None of the above.

Percentage of Total: Males: 19.0%   Females: 21.8%

Response to Question:

Choice 1: Steal the drug: 69.5% (N=198)

Percentage of Total: Males: 30.5%   Females: 38.9%

Choice 2: Let the wife die: 14.0% (N=41)

Percentage of Total: Males: 7%   Females: 7.4%

Choice 3: No answer: 16.1% (N=46) (Could not decide)

Percentage of Total: Males: 6.3%   Females: 9.8%

Moral Stage: (According to comments)

1. No Comment: 44.6% (N=127)

Percentage of Total: Males: 19.6%   Females: 24.9%

2. Survival-oriented/Self-centeredness: 5.6% (N=16)

Percentage of Total: Males: 2.8%   Females: 2.8%

3. Conformity to societal rules: 28.8% (N=82)

Percentage of Total: Males: 12.6%   Females: 16.1%

4. Altruism: 15.4% (N=44)

Percentage of Total: Males: 5.3%   Females: 10.2%

5. Spirituality/ Transcendental: 5.6% (N=16)

Percentage of Total: Males 3.5%   Females: 2.1%

Comments:

The distribution of sexes in the sample was comparable to that of the general population. Although most of the subjects were in the twenty-two to fifty year age group, we believe that the sample was representative of the population at large. The study did not reveal any major surprises. It did demonstrate a high correlation between age, cognitive maturation, and the ability to take the high ground of spirituality and transcendentalism. Assignment to the spirituality group was more common amongst the older group. Males and females tended to be equally survival-oriented and self-centered. Although, according to their comments, females were more likely to conform to societal rules than males, significantly more females chose to steal the drugs than males. A possible interpretation is that factors other than moral values were at play in guiding the women's choice. Females were more altruistic than males by a ratio of two to one. Maybe the most important finding in the population studied was that there was no connection between religious affiliation and moral choice. One hundred sixty eight out of two hundred eighty five (59%) of the sample studied identified themselves as belonging to one of the monotheistic religions and yet close to seventy percent (70%) of the sample chose to steal the drug. This number is probably underestimated since some of the subjects under the category " other" belonged to one of the Christian religions and did not want to be designated as "Protestant." Overall, the results seem to indicate that both men and women who chose to value life over property rights did so independently of their religious affiliation. This finding, however, should be interpreted with caution. The influence of dogmatism and fanaticism when making moral decisions cannot be excluded. (Wahrman 1981) This group, however, took a very down-to-earth attitude, showing a clear demarcation between religious beliefs and the need to take care of business. In other words, connection to others remains more important than religious scruples.

At this point, the reader may be on the verge of annoyance, wondering like Bart Simpson in the Ramada Inn commercial, "Are we home yet?" I can feel your frustration because we raised a lot of questions and we were supposed to demonstrate major psychological differences between men and women. Well! Maybe the point to all of this is that for individuals who are fashioned in the mold of a patriarchal society, subtle differences about moral choices are not easily discernible. Could it be that as men are growing older, they tend to give up their youthful, macho image to adopt a more nurturing posture, blurring any remaining differences between men and women? Or is it simply that the question as presented to the participants was flawed in the first place? As the old adage goes, "Ask the wrong question, you are likely to get the wrong answer." According to Gilligan, the question as asked in the dilemma determined to a large extent the perspective from which the situation was to be perceived and every respondent was being examined from a pre-established moral code. (Kyte, 1996) Obviously, additional studies are needed. Other variables like the circumstances surrounding the individual's moral choices need to be accounted for. And to further establish differences between men and women, we need to listen to women voices directly. We will do so in the next section of this book.

PART IV

REAL WOMEN

REAL STORIES

Chapter Nineteen

Sex for Sale: Voice of a Madam

Prostitution is only a specific expression of the universal prostitution of the worker.   *Karl Marx*

They are clad in beautiful dresses from renowned Maison de Couture from Paris or wearing barely enough pieces of clothing to cover their body contours. They are on the street corners of Thailand, Rio de Janeiro, Manila, Santo Domingo, and New York City. Under the guise of massage parlors, escort services, or flash dancing clubs, under the protectorate of a madam or the tight grip of a pimp, they are practicing the oldest profession on earth. They are sex workers. According to Thomas Aquinas, prostitutes are a necessary evil as they were permitted by God to prevent males from becoming totally out of control.[50] The practice of prostitution started in the temples in the Sumerian era when women were allowed to hang around the high priests that were like men-gods. The role of prostitutes was seen as essential as they were attending to the divine needs of these men who needed to be in total harmony with nature.[51] The Industrial Revolution has brought important changes in women's roles. Wives had to follow the constraints of the Victorian Era, procreate, and be proper, while prostitutes provided men with forbidden pleasures. Needless to say, prostitution became an industry in its own right as entrepreneurs realized that everything related to sex could bring large sums of money. Organized crime became involved. Today this industry involves millions of

---

[50] See Bourke v. Reference No. 5

girls, some as young as ten year of age. The numbers are easily maintained as runaways, victims of sexual abuse, truants, and drug abusers constantly join their ranks. Health hazards to prostitutes include venereal diseases such as syphilis and AIDS, acquired through indiscriminate sex and needle sharing. Catherine A. MacKinnon, a professor at the University of Michigan Law School, provides an answer to the question, "What do men want?" Pornography provides the answer, women bound, women battered, women tortured, women humiliated.

To illustrate this subject we solicited the point of view of a modern-day madam who took her job very seriously. At no time did we get a sense that she was doing anything immoral or illegal. A formal interview could not be arranged for obvious reasons, but she was willing to talk over the telephone.

Acting on information from an ex-escort girl, I called Madam Anonymous, a lady in her mid-forty's who has been running an upscale escort service business for over two decades. Over ten thousand clients later, her enthusiasm and her academic interest in the topic have not abated. She claims that she could write hundreds of treatises about the topic, both from a purely business and from a psychosocial perspective. She felt the need to qualify every statement, explaining that her business is part of a small minority, la creme de la creme, which, unlike seventy to eighty percent of the escort businesses, insists on recruiting girls with at least some college education and have the ability to converse, entertain, and treat the clients well. Madam Anonymous has her own theories about human psychology. She sees men as capable more of a physical response, while women will display more of an emotional response. Men reacting to stress tend to become physical, lose their cool, and long to engage in competitive and

---

[51] See Lerner G. See Reference No.44

aggressive activities. If they cannot be on the football team on Sundays, they will lounge around the big screen television to watch the game and release their anger at every missed pass or jump with joy with every catch by players on their favorite team. Women generally will not understand what the excitement is all about. To release their emotion, they will chat, scream, and whine while getting everything done. Madam Anonymous sees the clientele as divided along class lines:

The White-collar type is involved in the practice of a liberal profession such as law, medicine, and engineering and often feels trapped in a marital relationship that has long lost its supportive value. It has become just another business. The husband barely talks to his wife. Such men will not hesitate to pay a small fortune (sometimes up to $ 500.00) for the company of a physically attractive, conversant, and entertaining girl. This girl is viewed more like a temporary mistress who has the ability to detoxify the man, nurse his bruised ego, and offer him an outlet for emotional release, a function that the wife Is no longer fulfilling. In Madam Anonymous' view, this is not any different from a man who goes out and spends seventy or eighty thousand dollars on a luxury car. It is an egotistical statement.

The blue-collar type tends to have much less control over the situation. They tend to become easily angered and are likely to become violent. The rate of abusive incidents tends to be much higher. This type of client is likely to find his way to the larger portion of these businesses that are not as selective as the business Madam Anonymous runs.

Why do girls get into this line of business? There are several types of workers. There are those who dream of a nice house with white, picket fences and those afflicted with the Peter Pan syndrome who seek to make their way into the heart of a rich man who will take them away and take care of their financial needs. These women are looking to become "kept women."

Other women have been raised in upper middle-class families where their needs have been met, yet they feel in bondage. They find the Victorian trappings of their rich families very suffocating. They seek freedom while being unwilling to give up their expensive lifestyle. They become escort girls.

Madam Anonymous does not necessarily see the profession as free of demands. She likens the life of an escort girl to that of a model. The girls are under a lot of pressure to stay in shape and remain attractive. Men In this country have been conditioned to equate thin with sexy. One only needs to look at the commercials for jeans to be convinced. The profession also carries the risk of early burnout. However, in Madam Anonymous' experience, the girls who enter the field with a history of a promiscuous life will probably view this as an opportunity to perpetuate this lifestyle and do not usually last past their twenty-fifth birthday. Some girls enter the field at a more mature age and view this as an opportunity to meet clearly defined financial goals. They are more able to handle their emotions, display more mature defenses, and have a much lower burn out rate.

As to the ethical and legal aspect of the profession, Madam Anonymous was careful to differentiate what she does from the derogatory, legally defined term "prostitution." She feels that she is doing a community service that has the result of relieving stress in a lot of households and that it frees men's minds so they can attend to their important functions in our communities. In fact, she states, different communities have responded differently to this kind of business. It is freely advertised in most major city yellow pages. She does not see this business coming to an end. She became involved in this business over twenty years ago. Many have come and gone, especially men who tend to be more exploitative. There have been over ten thousand and the men are still calling.

Chapter Twenty

Excluded from Participation: Voice of a Catholic Nun.

Racism and sexism are everywhere. Not even the religious orders are spared. The Catholic Church has not been accommodating at all to the needs of its changing flock. As a result, very few people are heeding the call to service repeated over and over from the papal sanctum. Many Catholic parents would not like their children to become nuns or priests. According to sociologist Richard Schoenherr in his book "Full Pews, Empty Altars," the number of American nuns have decreased from 173,351 in 1962 (the year the Second Vatican Council started) to 94,431 in 1994, a 45% decrease over thirty-two years. If the trend continues, nuns will become a thing of the past. The second Vatican Council brought a lot of hope. Contemporary culture was allowed into the church. People could speak their own language to communicate. Catholics could let their hair down and express their originality. Drums were allowed into the liturgy. This entire explosion of joy and faith has come and gone. The Church today is more conservative than ever. Once again God is a White male who understands only the culture of the majority. It seems out of touch with the dilemma facing low-income couples who have to make decisions about family size and reproduction. Humanae Vitae impositions are now thirty years old. The newer edict, Veritatis Esplendor, is considered even more retrograde. Catholic women are being forced to disobey their pastor. In spite of repeated incidents pointing towards celibacy as unnatural, the Church authorities have not budged and are not expected to. Priests and nuns are leaving their orders out of frustration. Women are excluded from priesthood. Is there any hope that men and women will be allowed to celebrate their faith in God without all the fetters of their humanity? The following interview gives voice to Maryse who was in the religious order for many years. She quit once she felt that the nunnery could no longer offer the support that she needed for a life of commitment to community service and celebration of her faith, away from racism, prejudices, and sexism.

Q: I've been researching women's issues from different angles. I think you are bringing a perspective that is very valuable in trying to understand the whole range of issues concerning women. I understand that you've been associated with being a nun, right?

Maryse: Not just associated, I have been in religious life.

Q: Tell me a little bit about your background.

Maryse: Let me start by telling you that I am from Haiti and I am proud of it. Most people don't know how to say my name, including my husband, and they will attempt to change it. I don't allow it, because it is a direct connection to my own heritage. I left Haiti when I was very young. I was 5 years old. And then I lived in Canada, in Montreal, for about four and a half years. I was in boarding school and even though I was young, I only spoke French, and so I was allowed to speak only to certain people. And it wasn't until just recently that I started to speak Creole, which accounts for my heavy tongue when I have to use it. Neither my mother nor father raised me. I was born only two years after Duvalier's accession to power and my father was trying to run away from the government. No members of the family were safe. Only recently did I start to realize that maybe it did have an impact on my life as I started to experience some nightmares. I realized that my father was in hiding with other members of the family. I remained in boarding school until about twelve until finally my mother came and got me. She was living in New York. We then moved to Chicago. Up to that point, French was the language that I spoke, but Creole was the language that was spoken to me. I had to answer in French. People find it very strange.

Q: How did you become associated with religious life?

Maryse: When I was In Chicago, I went to a Roman Catholic school called Visitation. I was very impressed. I ended up joining the same order as the sisters who taught me in elementary and high school. As I reflect now, I believe that I was really touched by the mission and the vision of the sisters. Timing is everything because I was still in Canada after Dr. King died. I think we came in 1969 and that was a transitional time. At that time I think there was a big religious exodus and so a lot of nuns had left because of the transition from The First Vatican Council to The second Vatican Council. It all happened so fast. I was placed in a boarding home where I was the only Black person. I was a kind of a curiosity for everyone. It was before the large migration of Haitians to Montreal. It was like 1962, '63. So that was an interesting perspective. Racism was rampant everywhere. The church did not offer me any protection from it. Members of the church were active participants.

Q: Wasn't that against the very teachings of the New Testament?

Maryse: I do feel the church is racist, and therefore the sisters, whether consciously or unconsciously, participate. I have to qualify that because when I talk to the sisters and I tell them that, they get very offended and they say, "Well we've worked all our lives for the people, for you people, (usually that's how they qualify it) and now you're saying we're racists." But they don't realize that's the structure. If they're from communities that are 90% Anglo-Saxon Irish, that's the only background they know. They see everything from a White woman's perspective. People from the church perspective think that because they're nice, they cannot be racist. Well, I feel like there are a lot of nice people who believe they are superior to other people just because of the color of their skin. If that is not racism, what is? So that was very hard for me as a woman religious. I knew this and like I tell people—especially women—as women, historically we've never had a voice. Therefore, I felt that as a woman, as a Haitian woman, I had the responsibility to make my voice heard. Often times, people look at me as if I'm a radical. I tell them that it is because they do not want to hear what I have to say. The truth can bring up a lot of discomfort, especially when you profess to believe in the Gospel. As I said, being a religious woman in a religious community, I felt like I had to tell the other sisters in what ways the community was racist, not excluding themselves. That has been painful because the sisters mean well and they have big hearts, however, they participate in racism.

Q: How did you go about doing that when you were so isolated?

Maryse: Their idea of addressing the problem was to appoint a racism task force. The problem had to be confronted since over the last 20 years a lot of the sisters, women religious, went beyond just their little local area or just beyond the Black community. They went down south to Central America and South America and they saw the bigger picture of the structure. I think before they didn't realize what kind of structure they had joined. Some people were brave enough to confront that, but even so they asked a Black person to be the facilitator and this particular person was a religious sister, too, but she was Black. She really laid it down straight forward. She wondered how could they participate in racism. Even from the structure, the sisters themselves feel like they have to have millions and millions of meetings about things. They write things down and you have to follow orders. She (the facilitator) was saying that that was very racist because everybody doesn't follow that structure. Do you know she was so truthful that a lot of them couldn't handle it? So then they got another Black person who was more subdued, who participated more in White structure. What I mean by that is that as women religious, we participate in racism and you have other Blacks who conform more to it. Like I said, when you don't conform, they call you radical. Well, okay, I'm just trying to live life and to have equal opportunity for people. I don't see how that could be radical, but that's how they feel.

Historically, in the church, the role of the women religious has never been recognized. Women have been condemned as the cause of all sins. The notion that women would one day be ordained seems very remote. Women have not been given full membership in the church. They stand at the margin. The Church leadership has been responding at a snail's pace to the needs of its members. Only recently have women been officially allowed to serve as altar servers. But, of course, a lot of the priests have been very progressive, they have always had young women who have been altar servers. But the church is now saying that it is okay, while in most other churches women are ordained into the priesthood. They are often ordained in defiance of the leadership. I wonder whether it makes any difference because they may be ordained, but they are still ordained into a patriarchal system.

Q: What do women religious want?

Maryse: It would take a complete change of attitude, more than the symbolic kissing of the ground in third world countries for the people to feel that their pastor is in tune with their daily lives. Just because we're given certain rights, do we want rights that continue to be established and dominated by the male perspective? These are questions I've always had. At one time, I felt I wanted to be a priest, but then I realized that once I became a priest I would still participate in the same system that oppresses, which is what the church does a lot. It oppresses people. Many of the Black women in the 20's and 30's who tried to enter into religious life had to be maids. They couldn't be regular sisters, they had first, second, third orders. Now the church is trying to get rid of that, but there are still some residual effects. Even for myself. I had to constantly have conversations about my education and how far I wanted to go and all of that. For me, I can never answer from just the perspective of a woman. I always have to qualify from a Black woman, a Haitian woman's, perspective. Some might not see me as the typical Haitian. I'm a Haitian who has been merged into a White system. I have learned to play their games, to walk their walk and dance their dance, sometimes unknowingly. At the risk of seeming odd to my colleagues, I have made many choices. My friends have asked me many a time why I became a nun because I seem odd anyway, just becoming a nun, I proclaim what I do. So regardless of whether I'm a nun, or I'm married, or whatever I do, I pronounce It, because I'm excited about what I'm doing. It is not always easy because the whole feeling of acceptance is very important all of us. I know it is to me. It's very hard, because once you make those choices in society, you are not going to be embraced. Like when I tried to speak out against apartheid or different companies that cooperated with that government, even my own Black friends could not understand why I was joining in what they saw as a White women's movement. But that is the truth...you know, slavery continues in different ways. I'm mostly out there by myself, because I think of myself as being a feminist. And again, from the Black perspective, Black women feel like that's a White woman's issue. The word feminism is a trigger word. It brings out different emotions in different people, but I use that word in the most positive aspect. I really feel for women's suffering and women's rights, and I keep a historical perspective on where we came from and what still needs to be done. I may not always remember someone's name, but I'll remember what that individual did and I'll remember that a lot of women who didn't have rights, shed their blood, took a stand, like Jesus. What he said was not popular and usually women follow in that step. So I find it ironic that women are not allowed to be priests, when in the bible they really model Jesus' lifestyle.

Q: You keep on referring to yourself as woman religious. Is that any different from a nun?

Maryse: I am glad that you ask. They often refer to any women in the religious order as nun, when in fact nuns are cloistered from a canonical perspective. The sisters are a part of the laity as far as the Vatican is concerned. It's interesting because it makes one think because it's not the same case for the priests and it makes you realize just how biased the church is. They do not want to allow women to participate. Very few people know that there have been women popes and there have been women priests. There is like an aura of secrecy that perpetuates the notion that there has been a conspiracy to exclude women. It's not heresy, I have seen documentation from my professors under whom I have studied.

Q: Does the habit have some symbolic significance?

Maryse: I guess I always tell people I wear my habit inside. In the early '60's to middle '60's there was this big exodus, which was taken from the Bible, everybody leaving and making transitions from Vatican I to Vatican II. One day the sisters would be wearing habits and the next day they wouldn't. That caused a division among women because some of the sisters decided to stay in habit and some decided to wear lay clothes. My community was pretty progressive and, in fact, if the women wanted to wear habits, they were asked to go to another community. Of course they were told another reason why they were not accepted. They really didn't allow other women to make their own decisions. Personally, I didn't want to have a habit. There I was, a person of color, without the distinctive habit. How were they supposed to know that I was a nun? That was quite a challenge. They needed to make an extra effort to acknowledge me. A lot of people had a problem with my being a Black woman without a habit that they could visualize. Another reason why I chose not to wear a habit was, first of all, it separates me from the laity, and people have a way of saying, "Oh, you're better than everybody." I didn't feel that I should be better than anybody should. I'm just living a different lifestyle than everybody. I certainly do respect the people that are wearing habits because some people from, a practical point of view, feel that it's easier to keep to their vows of poverty. I tried to live a life of simplicity, not determined by the structure of the hierarchical church, but within my own discernment process.

Q: Tell me more about your vows?

Maryse: People often talk about women married to Christ. Interestingly, I never heard people say that when referring to the men. When the men become priests, they never say they are married to Christ. They always use women married to Christ. There is something kind of morbid about that statement. I don't want to preach heresy, but when people say, "Oh you're married to Christ," I say, "I don't look at it that way. I made a commitment to being in a community with other people and God is always the focus of my life." I feel if that is the case, then people who are married, who are laity, they may have as much, if not more of a connection to God.

Q: How about sexuality? There have been so many debates about sexuality, including the inevitable sensationalized stories about women religious falling in love or being seduced by priests?

Maryse: The church tends to deal with sexuality in a different way. One of the things I found very interesting is talking to people who are "laity," who are not in religious life. They often talk to me about sex and I try to explain to them that sex is an act and it's a natural act that people do. Sexuality on the other hand involves your whole relationship, how you deal with people, how you look at yourself, how you look at life, and how you express that love. I used to be embarrassed to talk about this and, again, it's something that's put on women. I think it is more of an accepted fact that more priests were sexually active. However, more time is spent debating the question of whether or not a woman is a virgin. Society approaches the question in a very sexist way. I was not sexually active before I entered religious life. So when my other friends who joined had to confront the issue, it was quite a struggle. My struggle was of a completely different nature. I longed to have children and religious life was not going to allow it. I find it rather hard to believe that some canon law would go against something so natural as bearing a child. Another major challenge was the realization that in a community, people had different sexual orientations. Furthermore, they were scared to express their sexuality for fear of being labeled. But regardless of what a person's sexual orientation is, when they come into a community, they're vowing that they're going to be celibate, regardless of whether they are homosexual or whatever orientation a person declares herself. That just becomes a part of what we are, period. Again, that's society's lack of understanding and lack of education. There is a fear about anything or anyone who is perceived as different. I do think that in the men's community they tend to have a lot of problems talking about their sexuality and a lot of that is taken in because it's not dealt with, it's acted upon in an unhealthy way.

Q: You started to talk earlier about your feeling of isolation within the order. Can you elaborate on that further?

Maryse: That was indeed very painful. Living with women, especially with women who are of a different background than me, I felt excluded. There were many times that I had asked to live in a community. I was denied. That's one of the biggest factors why I left the community. I felt that it was hard because I was trying to serve within the Haitian community and nobody would come with me, because in a community of men, and especially women religious, we'd talk about being sent to mission and it was different from a long time ago. A long time ago, they would send women to certain missions they were assigned to certain missions. These days, we would look in the mission book and see who would take us and where we could go. We could go to our own job interviews by word of mouth and talking to different people and so that's what we did. We would find our own places. For me, I entered religious life with women so that I could have a community, a community of prayer, so that I could share my life. When I went to Haiti, and when I came back, there was no one there to listen to my story and to connect with my own pain. Often times I tried to make religious life work for me, but I guess religious life is a very archaic structure that often lacks flexibility. I needed to feel that I belonged. It wasn't there for me or otherwise they wanted me to go where there were all White sisters, and that's not what I felt called to do. Most of the years I was there, I went where they told me to and I served well and I connected with the people. When I first went to a place that was 90% Mexican, I had to go running to apartments and they looked at me strange. I had to establish myself. Eventually I was accepted in that community, but I was there like 2 or 3 years and then I had to be moved. Usually in religious life, as women, we move around a lot. That whole sense of stability was not there for me, a sense of belonging. I certainly was rooted in God, and that's what kept me going, but I needed a little bit more. I needed a sense of stability. I met my present husband right after I left the religious community. That's interesting because I always have to discuss with my husband my whole perspective because sometimes he doesn't understand my need for prayer. In the morning, I need quiet, and the first thing he does is turn on the TV. I need a sense of tranquility so I can hear what God is saying. People always think that's really odd because I talk a lot and I'm very motivated, therefore people wouldn't realize that. There is another side to me, a side that is reflective, meditative. If I do not take my hints from my daily prayer, I feel lost. My whole day goes terribly because I don't get focused. I need to have a little solitude even if I have to go to the bathroom and pray. I read from a little book called a breviary.

Q: Any regrets?

Maryse: I don't have any regrets. I feel that God has blessed me, that I've had the opportunity to learn a lot. I always felt that I was a Dominican and for the time that I was called to religious life, the grace of God followed me. It provided me longing and opportunity. The sisters from Visitation gave me the opportunity to share their lifestyle. It was wonderful in many aspects. I have tried to take what the sisters taught me in that way and share that with other people.

I still have a lot of unanswered questions. Why did the sisters have to change their names? Why do you have to give up your identity? You are no longer part of that life, in this life you will be known as "Sister Theresa." You look at all the Saints they have they're all basically all White names. The only Black person I could even think of is Martin De Pores. You couldn't take the same name that somebody else had, so you know how many people would be competing for that? And they're usually White sisters. I think that before, the only way you could live a life of service was to join an order or to join the Peace Corps. I think people look at religious as pious, because people used to always come to me and say, "I heard you make such a big sacrifice." Maybe it's because of the time I entered and the community I entered, except for the painful parts, I had a great time. Of course I had my struggles, but I didn't feel I was making a big sacrifice. I felt like my life was being very fulfilled. In fact, I feel I have more good things happen to me. I used to be a teacher before I entered and I still taught as a sister, but as a lay teacher, I didn't always eat. In the summer we didn't have any money and we didn't always get to eat. As a sister, I never skipped a meal. Even when I was living by myself, I was budgeted to eat. I think people are still looking at those mission churches. We do have sisters who go to the barrios and different places, they choose to live in extreme poverty. But for the most part, women religious, the structure is very rich. When you go into those churches they have all kinds of luxurious paraphernalia. The motherhouse where I come from was very stylish, very up to do. There is nothing in poverty about that. Personally, I didn't have my own money. We lived a common life and I really try to use that in my relationship with my husband. We come from a society that says, "I earned this money and I can do this." Life in community, however, put the emphasis on the common good, "I have a penny, you have a penny, we put it together and we can buy something with two pennies, which is more than we can with a penny a piece." I use that "our" a lot and I see I'm really having an effect on my husband because he never used to say "our money," "our car," and all that and before he would never use that terminology. I really learned a lot from religious life and so in that way I may be a little different than with people of the laity, but I try to blend in. The number of women entering religious life is not what it used to be. The community is lucky to get one or two people a year.

Chapter Twenty-one

An Alternative Perspective: Voice of two Lesbians.

" Your life is a sham 'til you can shout--out loud--I am what I am!"

Jerry Herman

Almost thirty years after the Stonewall Bar incident in Greenwich Village, New York,[52] gays and lesbians involved in long-term relationships are still waiting for access to the same legal and financial protection enjoyed by their heterosexual counterparts. Only nine states have adopted measures making it unlawful to discriminate against individuals on the basis of their sexual orientation. Many myths persist about lesbians. They are often portrayed as sexually compulsive. Frequently, they are seen as a group of privileged elite. For others, lesbians constitute a group of women who are always on a recruiting binge for their ranks. Data from both the 1990 US Census and the Institute for Gay and Lesbian Strategic Studies do not support such views. Although more and more gays and lesbians are coming out of the closet, the numbers of self-declared homosexuals have remained at 4.4% for men and 3.3% for women. The nature/nurture debate

---

[52] See Bawer, B. Reference No. 10.

about the origin of homosexuality has persisted. Claims by neuroscientists about some differentiating brain characteristics and by geneticists about a homosexual gene are far from being substantiated. The American Psychiatric Association has removed any reference to homosexuality as a disorder from its authoritative Diagnostic Statistical Manual (DSM IV) and has officially declared that there is no published scientific evidence supporting the efficacy of "reparative" therapy to change one's sexual orientation.[53] However, over 200 ministries have popped up all over the US whose only focus is the "healing" of gays. Attempts at re-defining the identity of lesbians have met little success. Monique Wittig's challenge to women to refuse the categorization as women after what was supposed to be a rallying cry, "Lesbians are not women," have fallen on deaf ears. The following interview gives voices to two self-declared lesbians who were gracious enough to share their thoughts with us. I am very grateful to them.

Q: I would like to get your reaction to Monique Wittig's statement in "The Straight Mind" of "Lesbians are not women," but tell me first about your background.

Jane: I have a Masters degree in social work. I was born to two Italian parents who lived together until I was nine. My

---

[53] See Witham L. Reference No. 86

father was a homicide detective. My mother was a housewife who held intermittent jobs. When my parents separated, I lived with my mother. I was soon playing the role of a parent. I was a surrogate for my mother. I took care of the house with her. I was the middle child and took care of my sisters. I don't know if that had anything to do with my orientation, just my personality in general, when it comes to being able to be autonomous and care for things.

Q: What kind of school did you go to?

Jane: At first, I went to Catholic school. Then my parents got divorced. The family had financial difficulty with my parents splitting, so I went back into the public schools. I've lived in Fort Lauderdale my whole life and just went through the public school system. When I got out of high school, I started going to college. I paid for it myself and continued paying for my own schooling up through my masters because my parents were broke. So I had to do it myself.

Q: How about you, Katie?

Katie: My dad was born in Sicily, Italy. My mom was sixth generation Italian from the South. My dad died when I was 12. My father owned a trash business. She was well off and didn't have to work, but she chose to go to work. I went to Catholic school, and then I went on to college. She thought it was the best for me. I had a scholarship to go to Georgetown for Pre-

Med, I went there to visit. It was too cold, it was too far away and I didn't want to go that far away so I went to Alabama. Then I finished my masters at the University of Georgia. While I was there, my mom headed for Texas. So I moved to Texas for a year and realized that I didn't want to be there, so I moved to California. Later on, I moved back to Florida.

Q: How about growing up as an adolescent?

Jane: I don't think I felt like I was struggling with anything. I was overweight from the time I hit adolescence. Was it the hormonal process or the difficulty dealing with the transition of my family splitting up? I soon became my mother's helper. As far as my sexual orientation position, it was not of interest to me. The first time I heard of "gay" was when I was 17 years old. After I graduated high school, I got a call from one of my best friend's family. Her mom wanted to know if I knew what was going on in my friend's life and if I could fix it. I had not given much thought to the question of sexual orientation. I found it quite intrusive and bothersome as a matter of fact, that this woman that was very close to me was now obviously having some affair with a woman. To tell you the truth, I didn't find it a positive thing at all. I found it really intrusive and I had my first conversation with a counselor at that point. I was just asking general questions about being a lesbian. She was a 28-year old woman who was heterosexual. She just gave me a story about her having a friend in college and stated that it was no big deal and at that point I just put it away. It might have been the first time I even thought about sexual orientation.

Q: Before that, as an adolescent growing up, you probably had to face a few crises that you needed to resolved. The usual questions, "Who am I? Where am I going?" Those questions, when they came up for you, how did you handle them? How did you handle going to the prom?

Jane: I was a strong personality from early on because of the position in which I found myself in my family: I was expected to act as an adult in the situation, although I was the middle child. My younger sister was rather immature and my older sister was rather reckless. My mother had her own difficulties, emotionally, so I didn't tolerate a lot of crisis in my life. I learned to look at things rather clearly and logically. I just took care of everything at a very young age. People thought it was very bizarre, because at 14, everybody thought I was 18, and at 18 they thought I was 26. It was always that way just because of the way I carried myself. I had a very small circle of friends and usually they were very popular and very attractive young ladies. They would go off and do their own thing and I really didn't find myself in those situations where I would be questioned. I didn't go to the prom. I wasn't interested. In fact, I went out and I drank and had a great time that night with peers that were actually older and younger. I don't think I struggled with my orientation. At first, I was very sexually interested in men. The idea of going with other women did not even cross my mind. Whether it was joking around about this or that star, "He's good looking," or cruising up the strip in Fort Lauderdale and talking to college boys. They say that when lesbian women come out, they go through phases. They first start reading everything that is available on the subject. Then they try to retrieve old memories and try to put them into perspective. I did go back and tried exactly what was said in those books. There is a need to explain strong enmeshments with women and emotional bonds with other female peers. For me, the patterns were established very early. I often joked that men could not make me cry, while my female peers made me cry all the time. If I ever became emotional, it was always about my attachment to some female peer.

Q: How about you?

Katie: It was very odd for me when I went to high school. I had boyfriends throughout. Now, looking back on patterns, when my best friend told me that she cared about me. "Okay, I care about you too," and then she said, "I love you." I was so appalled. And she went on and on telling me how much she loved me. I just thought, "Oh, my God, something must be wrong." I had such a strong aversion to it that I decided to put an end to the friendship. Now, I realize that maybe my own fear could have brought this feeling towards her. Was there something different about her? Did she have some of the characteristics of the boyfriends that I had dated? I had all that I have asked for. I was very much taken care of by my mother and if I had needs and crises, I would turn to my mom. I took on a leadership role very early in my family. I endured my share of losses. My dad died when I was 12. I was the caretaker for my younger sister. She was allowed to get into trouble, but I had to tow the mark. I did well. I did all the things I was supposed to do. As for dates, I had ten. I think my only crisis was when I was supposed to go out with someone for the junior prom and I chose not to go. I got really upset with my boyfriend for whatever excuses. I often said to myself, "I won't let that happen again." I think that it had to do with the teaching in Catholic school. Sexual issues, if discussed at all, were limited to a few basic instructions. Sex before marriage was a cardinal sin. It was unbecoming of a good Catholic girl to even talk about it. My friends from public schools were quite versed in the topic. Not me!

Q: Now, thinking back throughout that period of time, thinking about the circle of friends that you were around, was there anything about you that maybe your friends could have detected that was any different?

Jane: Again, I had a very small circle of friends and they were the most popular girls In the school, so I don't think anybody would ever have accused me of anything because of who I was hanging out with. It wasn't like I was hanging out with the girls from the softball team. I was never attracted to the typical adolescent lesbian coming out. I was attracted to beauty and to these wonderful, dynamic women. When I finally ended up in my first relationship with another woman, my best friend from high school was the first one that questioned me. And I asked her how she knew and she told me she had a dream.

Q: You mentioned adolescent "coming out." Can you talk a little bit more about that process? What are the characteristics of an adolescent lesbian coming out? What are the telltale signs?

Jane: I think that adolescents coming out feel very confused. It is enough that they have to deal with the usual adolescent crises of identity, now they have to face some uncertainty and the fear of not being accepted by their peers. They often try to disguise their inner conflicts by adopting the most outlandish appearance. The girls might adopt the androgynous look. The hairdos are like out of a futuristic movie. The belly button, the nose, and the navel might be pierced. The parents don't know what to do. They want to make their own statement. They start using certain ambiguous words to test the waters, by using the word bisexual rather than gay.   I noticed recently at a prominently gay festival, where the young ones were still going into quite a bit of androgyny before they grow into themselves and what that means to them as women and in their own feminine characteristics.

Q: What about the internal conflict that goes on?

Katie: I can tell you that I watched the conflict of my friend in high school and how attached she got to me. I didn't understand all her infatuation and attachment to me. She would get so upset if I didn't sit next to her at lunch. She was obviously struggling. Her parents began to accuse me, "You get so upset with her, I think that you're gay." I would say, "My God, me? I don't know what you're talking about." I became afraid that the story might be spread to the whole school campus. I was almost certain that the girl's mother would run to the teacher the next day. Her schoolwork started to suffer. She was always daydreaming. She's a physician now.

Q: How can you tell the difference between the phenomenon of infatuation that occurs with heterosexual adolescent and an adolescent falling into a lesbian relationship?

Jane: I don't think that one can really tell the difference. The feelings are exactly the same.

Katie: I listened to the girls in the schoolyard, the girls express their affection in the same manner.

Q: Making the transition. When you started to feel, well! This is the sexual orientation that you have. How did you deal with that, let's say within your family environment: Traditional, Catholic, Italian?

Jane: I didn't tell. No, I didn't tell at first. Absolutely not, I told my siblings. I think it was easier. I would have preferred that they guessed. I come from a family that is not that communicative anyway, so even if they guessed, they weren't going to bring it out on their own. My siblings, I talked to probably 2 or so years earlier and I talked to them following the breakup of my first relationship. They pretty much knew. They had been waiting to ask the question. My sisters find it very hip, so they think it's quite cool and they have no issue with it. They probably use me as the topic of their conversation at their own dinner parties. My mother, I explained it to her in a letter, even though some of my friends chided that it was a cop out. But she was at a distance and I found that the easiest way to articulate my experience, as well as to tell her that she had no argument involved in it. She never did argue about it, but she never touched the topic. It was never overtly discussed prior to her death. She would never talk about the issue, although she had met past lovers. It was never expressed as being a partnership. My father, I have never had an overt conversation about it. I don't find that I'm the norm. I have peers whose families are very involved in their lives. My father is very involved in partners, he's very open to meeting people, but it's never overtly talked about. But I don't think that's a gay thing because even when I was with men, he never had an interest in becoming intrusive. My father was full of boundaries, he welcomed them and that was it. But it's not a comfortable conversation when it comes to sexuality. It's just not something that he's willing to talk about. So it really becomes a rather covert topic in the house except amongst my sisters because they like to overtly talk about it.

Katie: I think that since I was struggling, I was going to get married but I still hung out with this one friend from high school. Now she's in medical school. I would see her and that was when I was 24, when I decided, "Okay let me just experiment with this before I get married, let me just try this." And I wrote about it in my journal. Then I went away on sabbatical to California for a couple of months. And my sister read my journal. When I came back, we were out one night and I had been back for maybe two weeks and she said, "Isn't there something that you need to share? Something that must be on your chest that you have to talk about?" I said, "No, what are you talking about?" She said, "Well if I told you I had read a book..." I said, "Are you telling me you read my journal?" And she said that that's what she'd read. With her I began to process and talk to her about what that was like and my experience. I don't think

I ever directly told my mom. My mom is very perceptive and she will engage in conversations in which she'll ask me things. My mother's way of asking was: "Did I do something wrong as a parent?" I said, "No, what are you talking about?" She said, "Did I do something wrong, did I make you unhappy somehow?" I watched her struggle and that's when I began to talk about it. To this day, I can do whatever I want as long as I'm happy. That's what she wants.

Q: So you really have it easy in a way because I realize that a lot of gays and lesbians have a lot of conflicts.

Jane: I have a friend who ended up in therapy. The first thing her parents did was put her in family counseling. She was 18 years old. And this was somebody who knew she was gay, she swears, since the time she was little. It doesn't appear to be what might be typical of a gay woman, when it finally came out, her coming out as a young adult. I still look at 18 as young, even though they're coming out much younger now. Her family, being a typically Jewish family, had a very difficult time with it. And the first thing was to place her in counseling. Somehow they wanted to undo what had been done. Bizarre enough, now they're probably one of the most supportive families that I know of when it comes to interacting with her partners. It's a true family environment, but they certainly did react at first with wanting to get her help.

Q: Are there stages that you could identify in the family coping with the discovery that their daughter is a lesbian?

Katie: I think that if they're ready to hear it, they're going to ask. I have a friend whose family still has not asked. She's 35 years old and she still hasn't talked to them. That subject doesn't come up and I ask her, "When are you going to tell them?" She says, "I'm never going to tell them." I say, "Don't you think that they know?" She says, "I'm not going to verbalize it until they ask me." And they've still not talked about it. She of course was put into therapy when she was 16 years old, thinking that there was something wrong with her. "My God, my daughter's hanging around with all these girls, there's something wrong with her." Never did they ask, "What is going on?" They just keep it as a topic that's closed.

Q: You said, "Putting in therapy." I have a question about that. Do they put them in therapy to cope and really deal with the problem, with what they perceive as a problem? Or do they actually believe that they could switch things around...turn things around and make them un-gay or un-lesbian?

Jane: I think that everybody, I shouldn't use the term everybody, but many people when you first come out...I've had friends of the same age, in my 20's, who thought it was a phase. I think that the family's first reaction is that somehow this is just something you're going through and by directing it and going through processing it, that's going to diminish and you're going to go on to somewhat of a typical pattern...meaning heterosexual orientation.

Q: In studying child development, we are taught that there is normal stage of chumship when boys hang out with boys, girls hang out with girls. When do you then start thinking that maybe there is more there. There is some sexual attraction there. Maybe these adolescents are gays or lesbians. The therapist is placed in the unique role of making that distinction. What are your thoughts about that as a lesbian, but with also a therapist?

Jane: The past 20 years have seen tremendous changes. It has come in different stages. Teenagers today are enjoying unprecedented freedom. You only need to listen to the teachers to find out what issues the teens are dealing with today. When I was a teen the main issue was interracial dating. Today it is same sex dating. Now same-sex dating is as open as interracial dating was 20 years ago. I think it's much more complicated today. When I was in high school, it was not as overt. It was not something that you would openly flaunt. I imagine that if I had gone into psychotherapy 15 years ago for this issue, it probably would have been more painful than today when I have the freedom to interact and open up. I don't know if I would have chosen, 15 years ago, explore that aspect without struggling through it. I had to struggle through it even at 21. Imagine if I had to do it at age 15. At 21, I had a much better idea of what I wanted and what I understood. Nowadays, it's a much different atmosphere. Children are very open-minded, whether their parents are or not. They really go and do whatever they please. I don't know if you could make that judgment call when you are 17 or 18 years old.

Katie: I don't believe everyone is always definite. I think that since I wasn't at such an exploratory stage anyway, about giving up some choices or whatever it was about. I know that when I see young adolescents in therapy that are saying, "Am I gay?" I don't think necessarily go, "Oh! This one must be gay." It is up to that adolescent to work through the whole spectrum of feeling until he or she comes to grip with whom he or she is. No one's forcing you to choose one way or another. I think that back then it was more certain that you would get stuck with that label. Somebody wanted to put you in a category to understand you. And now, because they did not go beneath the surface, the adolescent is prematurely stuck with a label. And if it turns out that this adolescent was not gay or lesbian, a whole range of gender identity problems starts. Have you ever seen those girls in school that become labeled and taboo?

Q: What about dating as an adult? What are some of the difficulties that you have encountered in the gay world in terms of dating?   Heterosexuals have a lot of problems dating nowadays, for many reasons. People are so busy, they don't take time to talk with anyone anymore. Neighbors no longer speak to each other. Are there any problems or particularities about dating as a gay person?

Jane: I think that there's a similar Issue with heterosexuals as well as with homosexuals. The bars where people tend to flock in order to meet people are full of 20 year olds. When you're 30, you don't go to these places anymore so you're kind of left with an abyss of where to meet people. I think it's probably somewhat similar for heterosexuals. Thirties is not necessarily what you find when you go out. You find more of the younger crowd going out. Meeting people is not quite as simplistic as when you're gay. You're not able to go out and have that immediate understanding that a man and a woman have when they're in the work place, or they're in an office, or wherever they are where people meet each other. It is certainly different on that level. There are a lot of stereotypes out there about the cues...they joke about the language whether it be a cultural language or a sexual language...that people begin to give each other cues so that you know who's gay and who's not. There's a lot of validity to that. There's a matter of walking into a room...and do two gay women know who they are? We do. It's bizarre. There are nonverbal cues.

Katie: It's hard to explain as to what it is. They call it gaydar, to be able to see that. "Well that person looks like a truck driver, he must be gay," that's not always true. I don't know whether it's a look or something that they say, how they present themselves, how they look at you. It's just a way that they seem.

Q: Maybe I should share with you my own evolution about the situation. When I started my practice, I could not recognize anyone. But now I can. I could say that 80% of the time my guess turns out to be right. I still cannot tell you what the basis of my assumption is. A lot of times it turns out to be true. But what is it about gays or lesbians that makes them recognizable by other people?

Jane: I've heard bizarre statements. I remember talking once to a student whom I believed was gay. It was strictly a professional interaction and then over lunch, this person started spouting off all this personal stuff. When she said, "I knew you were gay," I said, "How did you know?" She said, "A gay woman looks at you different. She looks at you like a man does." I said, "What do you mean by that?" She said, "They look in your eyes." I thought that was the most bizarre thing I had ever heard. I look at anybody's eyes when I talk, so what's that supposed to mean? But there's one bizarre perspective from one woman who says that there's a level of attentiveness that's not the same. I don't buy it. I'm not quite sure what it is, and yet there is a term that has found its way in the culture, it's "gaydar." It's ridiculous terminology, but it's thrown around and from the time you begin to get your feet wet, you start scanning around and you kind of polish this "gaydar" of sorts and it's different, I mean it's true. Rarely will you be wrong. I did also hear a friend of mine who's recovering say that one alcoholic, whether they're sober or drunk knows another one immediately. I don't know what that's all about either. Maybe It's just something that you pick up on characteristics and traits, I'm not sure.

Q: Well, if I can make an analogy, when I walk around and I see Black people, I could tell who Is Haitian and who is not. But I'm sure there are people who are not Haitians who do not have that ability to really find about the Black people who are around because they say that all Black people look alike. They say that all White people look alike. There are a lot of things that people say in an attempt to stereotype people, but some of it has some validity. And we just can't put our finger on what it is. Attraction! What makes a person attractive? Let's say the canons of beauty, if you will, about a lesbian person.

Katie: I believe that beauty is in the eye of the beholder. What is attractive to me is not what is attractive to some other person. It's chemistry. Why would I like someone else, but not that person? I really don't think it's conscious. It is like asking, "What did I like in men? What did I like in anyone?" What are the similarities? I think a lot of it has to do with my chemistry. Whether I like them as a person, whether our Interests are the same, whether I just like them, or my heart begins to flutter. I don't know. Your first love. How did it happen?

Q: Is there a classification for gay people In terms of types?

Jane: There are stereotypes and then there are classifications within the culture itself, like any culture. The same phenomenon happened with the Black culture. At one point they were subdividing themselves into shades. There was a lot of bickering going on. In the gay culture, they pin against each other at times. You see them on the talk shows hollering at each other.

Q: What do they call them?

Jane: Well, obviously, the two on the list here. You have butch and femmes, although I don't hear the word femmes used much anymore. There is a whole nomenclature out there. It seems that one cannot open a magazine without discovering a new designation. Gays and lesbians have been called dykes with dicks, queer butches, aggressive femmes, lesbians who like boys, bulldaggers, transsexual lesbians, dyke mommies. This descriptive terminology is designed to capture the wide range of sexual experiences available, but could also be as an attempt keep one step ahead of anyone who try to label the group. I think the words in the 80's and 90's were "lipstick lesbians." There was also a radicalization of the movement. When you read the writings of the 70's, it's frightening because women felt like they needed to be like bulls in a China shop. They had to barrel their way through.

Q: Why do you think they did it?

Jane: I think there was a radical movement of just feminism in itself. So they had feminists who felt they had to present themselves as warriors. They were like women that went back to their adolescence. They felt that in order to assert themselves as women, they had to take the androgynous appearance as if it would give them the ability to fight the man's world. Lesbians did the same thing. The movement took on in the seventies like a giant wave. Everyone jumped on the bandwagon. I think by the 80's and 90's...I'm very lucky to be in this generation. I think that women had pretty much come to the realization that they could keep their polished appearance, that they can magnify their femininity, and still make choices about sexual partners, about lifestyles in general. The 90's have seen some further transformations within the culture itself. The women who went through all the fight were being pushed aside as no longer relevant. One could see them with some appearance reminder of time passed. They held on to the style like a memento as if to say, "I'm here and you're not going to judge me." With their background, thank goodness for them bullying their way through, now we can come out in a less abrasive way and affirm ourselves. But I can still be a woman and I can still choose these things and within the culture right now I guess that's what their terming them right now, "lipstick lesbians." Women that can maintain their femininity yet have choices. I'll be the first one to admit that there are important issues yet to be resolved.

Q: Lesbians are often portrayed as more aggressive, more forward, more assertive, less soft. Any validity to this or is it just another stereotype?

Jane: I don't know if I would use the word assertive. When I use the word androgyny I mean taking on maleness in order to punch their way through and demand that their presence be known and demand the respect. I don't think that we need to demand anymore. It can be done in a much quieter way by just carrying yourself in a certain way.

Q: It's not unlike the general feminist movement in the sense that there was some classification as to men had the pants and that allowed them to open the door in terms of being able to go out and get the jobs that were well-paying. And men think the "women" with less muscle mass "weaker" and the low-paying job, etc. Maybe it's a similar phenomenon. Because you see a lot of jobs that were traditionally "men's jobs." You see some women in there with an androgynous look, like putting up wires for the telephone company and you automatically think, "Maybe this person is a lesbian." But I don't know if there is any validity to it.

Jane: I know that in certain areas, if I go to New York or if I go to California, you can see a different culture within the culture of gays. I know that I have peers who came from New England where androgyny might be necessary. If I go to New England or if I go to North Carolina, sometimes I don't know who's gay and who's not. There's a level of androgyny just in their cultures where women just tend to, I mean they're walking around in plaid and boots and they live in the mountains and this is what they do. I couldn't say who's gay. This area is a little different because it's not quite as androgynous. Do you know what I'm getting at?

Katie: I have a friend from Massachusetts and she said that even for her she could pick them out anywhere. People that you think they are. They're not, because that's just their way or their mode of dress and you can get caught up in that. I do believe that there are cultures within cultures. When I was in Provence town all the women that I saw, it was like, oh, my God! I don't see those kind of women down here where they fit that androgyny role or they look like boys or their hair is cut short and just the outfit that they wore. They just fit in differently.

Q: Is there an increased incidence of psychological problems with people of this group? If so, what could be the reason?

Jane: There have been times when one might say that there was an increased incidence of psychological problems. Gays have lived under tremendous stress. They become depressed. Relationships are very unstable at times. Hopefully, as the culture changes, I think that we're less apt to see psychological problems related to the gay issue. Problems of adjustment are common. If you are born White in this country, you are part of the majority. When you are gay, you suddenly find yourself in a minority group. It can be quite a shock. It's different when you're born Black and you have to deal with that issue your whole life. But when you're 18 and you're all of a sudden realizing, "Oh, my God, I believe I'm something that my family is going to turn away from, my peers are going to turn away from, I might get fired from a job, I might get refused housing." It becomes overwhelming. At some point you have to sit down and figure out who you really are. So many gays end up in support groups, where they have the opportunity to work through the problems.

Katie: That's an adjustment in itself. You really cannot go quietly through the motions without some serious questioning. You are deprived of the usual validation of your experience as provided to the heterosexual. You don't go around flaunting and making a statement like: "Oh, you wouldn't believe this gorgeous and sexy woman that I met." You sit quietly and eat your words. So you just learn to adjust in a different way. How do I fit in without saying those things and how do I fit in readjusting myself?

Jane: All your life, I have worked on improving myself, I set up goals for myself and I reach them. I have high standards and I treat other human beings with respect. Suddenly you find yourself sitting with bigots who insist on putting you down because you are a lesbian. You find yourself having to put up a steel armor. Your defenses are up. Your interactions with other people are seriously affected until you become able to go beyond that. Life goes on. Another day, another bigot, another battle fought and won. Bigotry, whether directed towards Blacks or towards gays and lesbians, is still very ugly. The jokes go on and on. Ellen's got a show now or because it's an open topic as people talk, their ignorance about the topic is so apparent and you have to sit in on that. Imagine that if I was a bigot and I was going to put down Blacks, I wouldn't do it in your presence because it's obvious that you're Black. But if people don't know I'm gay and they sit around a table, they begin to go off about these tangents. Yet I have to sit and listen to that. Then I have to take it all in, put things into proper perspective, and control whatever feelings the situation might trigger in me. You have to display a lot of courage, because the barrage of negative comments about gays is unrelenting. However, everyone has a breaking point where you start having doubt and wonder: Is it worth all the aggravations?

Q: There is a myth that relationships within the gay and lesbian culture do not last and tend to be shallow. Lesbians often have to face the pains of breaking up and starting over. How do they go about looking for help? How about the notion that only a professional who is going to understand those issues should be sought?

Katie: Well they probably look into special women's books or they look in the gay resource books that are out there, the gay magazines. There are certain ones in which they advertise.

Q: But isn't that excluding other people that might be culturally competent about that issue?

Jane: Sure. It would be no different from people coming to you because you're Haitian and that you have some expertise about the Haitian culture. I don't know, for some that might be an issue, for some it might not. Again, your perception in looking at these questions and meaning them to be as general as possible. Is the breakup of a lesbian woman different from the breakup of a heterosexual married couple? I don't know. Are the emotions different? I don't think so.

Q: Well, I could tell you the issues I've encountered in dealing with this population because I have had a lot of lesbian and gay patients. I don't find it any different from the issues that a heterosexual couple would have. Some times it's so obvious that the issues are the same, that I will borrow examples from heterosexual scenarios to illustrate a situation. Every region in the country has its own area where gays and lesbians tend to congregate and hang lose. In this area there is the South Beach crowd. It has been described by some as a jungle. Yet a large number of gays and lesbians have made it into their haven. They have claimed it as their own. I don't know what your experience has been in terms of feeling comfortable in certain areas of the city.

Katie: I think I probably wouldn't go hang out in Liberty city. I probably wouldn't feel comfortable there. I look at my own safety when I think about comfort. I have friends who love to go out with me and love to go to gay bars because they find them much more fun, much more liberated, and much less stuffy than the regular straight clubs. So they like them. When they come to visit and they ask me to hang out and I'll say, "OK, I'll go to any of the bars with you." So I'm comfortable with being in a bar. And they say, "I don't want to go to the straight bars. I want to go to your bars." And they would rather go there, even though they're straight. Because anything goes. You can leave your attitude at the door. But when you look at people in general, at the people coming from the straight clubs, they don't look happy. And when you go to a gay bar, anything goes and people are much freer.

Q: That festive mood, is it real or is it artificial?

Katie: I don't know whether it's real or if it is artificial, but it just seems more relaxed. I can just be who I am and I don't have to hide it. To the rest of the world I sometimes have to hide who I am. So it's just a more relaxed atmosphere in general. And the only time you might feel uneasy is if you feel uncomfortable when someone of the same sex makes a pass at you instead of taking it in strides and say how flattering that is.

Q: Are there any issues that you feel are particular to the times we are living in with regard to lesbians and gays?

Katie: Probably for men it would be AIDS. When you walk into men's bars, they hand condoms out. Condoms are everywhere. But why don't they hand them out in straight clubs? HIV disease is not something that only affects gay men. They are very much more aware of their sexual vulnerability.

Jane: I think that for women, becoming mothers is one of the most important issues now for lesbians in the 90's. They're having babies. The culture is polishing itself. They're becoming more comfortable with themselves, with their own sexuality, with their own similarities with heterosexuals. Lesbians want to raise families, to be women. And they're willing to confront those issues now. Women are having babies all over the place and raising them with same sex partners. The judicial system will have a lot of catching up to do. More and more, the judges will be confronted with issues like custody and alimony initiated by divorcing/separating gay couples.

Q: Do they do it through surrogate fatherhood or through adoption?

Jane: I think adoption is still a problem in Florida. I have friends that are looking into adopting a child from China or Japan because it's easier. But I have two women friends who have two babies through artificial insemination, although the donors were peers: a male, one father of both children who is going to be somehow involved in the family. So I think it is becoming more and more a viable option. It becomes the woman's decision on how involved she wants the male figure to be in the baby's life. It's nice to see that it's an open issue and it's openly talked about. It's not necessarily looked down upon within the culture, as well as outside of the culture. Again, the culture has struggled with its own viewpoints on what it is to be gay, whether or not it is a cop-out to integrate into regular heterosexual beliefs and values. Personally, I think that it is very nice that there is integration now. I'm a gay woman, but I have all these issues that are similar...and if I want to be a mother I'm going to be a good mother. I could send my kid to private school and be part of the PTA. There's a level of integration, whether it be on the level of physical androgyny and getting comfortable with femininity, to the point of getting comfortable with your own desires to raise families, as that feminine aspect of having children and maternal aspects of raising them.

Q: Are there any legal issues pending?

Katie: I know that in New York, I could have a child and my partner could legally adopt that child to be ours. In the State of Florida it doesn't work that way.

Jane: There are sad facts about the law still today. I can remember in 1992 when we couldn't get the equal rights amendment passed. I don't I think that people really understood what they were about to change. It was next to nothing. But they didn't pass it because it was presented as a gay issue. I remember as a young adult, being very saddened by it. I just couldn't fathom that people were voting not to let me enjoy job security. They did not want the law to protect me against arbitrary dismissal from my job on the basis of my sexual orientation. Imagine people calling a boycott on Disney World because the company was willing to offer insurance to same sex partners. It's pathetic. I remember when we went through the whole vote in the early 90's, they had made a comment on a show about how if they had voted to give Blacks rights in the 60's it wouldn't have passed. They didn't vote on it, they just made it so, because people are so ignorant. Had they had voted on it, people would have voted no because of their fear of change and of the differences between people. So when you look at that ignorance, it's amazing how prevalent it still is. We are still giving these options to people without educating them about the issues they are voting on. I can't fathom that we're still giving people the option to discriminate.

Q: Gays and lesbians have been portrayed as always engaging in proselytism and trying to bring recruits into the fold. Is there any validity to that?

Jane: I think they're getting more vocal...and good for them. It's sad because I think that people tend to think that those who are the most vocal are the ones who fit the stereotypes. I followed the whole Degeneres' controversy with a lot of interest. Was she trying to push her sexuality in people faces? Was she trying to recruit new members? Or was she simply saying: "Enough is enough. Ain't hiding any more!" Are there some narrow-minded gays and lesbians that believe behind every heterosexual there is a gay person waiting to come out? The answer is yes and it is unfortunate. If every gay person is a recruiter, they must be doing a very poor job. The number of gays and lesbians has not increased. Last night when I turned on the show and I saw them put up a parental notice before a sitcom because it had to do with these two women. They're so terrified that a child might turn on the television and see two women interacting. We're not talking about sex, we're not talking about nudity, and we are not talking about violence. Yet they're going to warn that this is adult content because it deals with two women who went on a date. It's amazing to me. There's that culture that thinks that what she's doing is catching.

Katie: Well, they forget that we get raised in heterosexual homes. If we could just watch it and become it, then how come everyone doesn't just stay in that heterosexual orientation.

Q: But America has all of those gay shows. I could just think about celebrities having affairs. In some other countries it's common knowledge that some of the presidents had a mistress and out of wedlock children. Yet in this country, they bash about some possible innuendoes about a celebrity. It's not just about gays and lesbians; it's about anything that doesn't fit that puritan philosophy that is running this country.

Jane: Your initial question about radicals, personally, I'm certainly not radical and I'm not out beating a drum and flashing myself as flag bearer of a culture. But I do respect the radicals who are out there because I think that throughout our time it has been the radicals who have moved us forward. So I respect what they're doing. Whether or not they're representing who I am or representing just what they believe is another question. Take those teenagers, I remember treating teenagers ten years ago. Their parents were losing their minds because of interracial relationships...and they were pounding their fists saying, "I don't care. These are people with whom I interact and this is who I'm going to be." The same radicals are going to push us through the 90's and bring us somewhere else. Whether or not they're portraying a stereotype or a myth that I don't agree with, it's the radicals that are going to move my generation and bring in the next one, I welcome it.

Katie: That's true for any group or any minority: It's always going to be the radicals who will be blamed or given credit for whatever happened.

Q: Anything else you would like to add?

Katie: I just think it's sad that for a culture that's so diverse and different, to think that we're so culturally sensitive and we really want to understand. But when it comes to something that we don't understand, we get fearful and our fears are what control us. So, we don't decide to get educated or to understand or to meet people. But there's so much out there and we only limit ourselves by our fears instead of understanding or getting close to each other.

Chapter Twenty-Two

Courage Under Fire: Voice of an Abused Woman

A recent report in the annals of Internal Medicine found that one in three women disclosed that they had been victims of domestic violence. Of the 542 homicides reported in Detroit in 1994, 162 were linked to domestic violence (Philadelphia Tribune, Roberts 1995). A woman is beaten every 9 seconds, 1.3 women are raped every minute. Approximately 30% of pregnant women suffer physical abuse during their pregnancy. The rate of sexual assault in the United States is the highest of any industrialized nation in the world.[54] In 1991, the final year of the old Soviet Union's existence, there were over 5000 women murdered. In 1994, more than 15,000 were killed in domestic violence incidents alone. More than four million families in the US are directly affected by domestic violence at any one time. These assaults are likely to do long-term psychological harm to the victims. According to the Crime Victims Research Center of the National Victim Center, about a third of all rape victims developed rape-related Post-Traumatic Stress Disorder at some point in their lives. Battered women are 4 to 5 times more likely to require psychiatric

---

[54] See Violence. Reference No. 83

treatment than non-battered women are and they are 5 times more likely to attempt suicide.

The interview that follows is a tale of courage. It also illustrates the internal dilemma that abused women face as they are torn between their natural inclination to nurture and rescue and their need for safety.

Marilyn: I got married right out of high school and I was a housewife for most of that time. I could do what was expected of me in the early 70's by staying home with the kids and being a housewife.

Q: How old are your kids?

Marilyn: Now they are 26, 24, and 22. We were together about 13 years. We had split. He just saw me as the person at home, like his mother: stay home, watch TV, then when the kids come home, clean house, not necessarily cook for him. So anytime I tried to branch out, or to go to school, he would find fault with it. He would complain that I was choosing a career or a job over the family. It was agreed that after I had the kids, I would go to college and go to law school. He went back on his word. He claimed that I was too sick and that I couldn't handle it. And if that didn't work, he would just act out.

Q: How would he act out?

Marilyn: He would stay out, run around with his friends. He is a native Floridian, came from a very dysfunctional family. I know that now. The mother and the father just stayed together just because they were together. They didn't necessarily like each other or talk. When it came to the kids, their upbringing was never discussed. He just kept running. He kept finding fault with me and running. His idea of a relationship was that he would take care of me and keep his freedom. I should be content and not even question his whereabouts.

It was frustrating. He kept promising and I kept thinking, "As soon as the kids are settled, I'll do it anyway. I'll go to school." Things were really out of hand. I just could not take it anymore. One day, I just packed up my stuff and moved to an apartment.

Q: How was it for you to live alone?

Marilyn: I had been the manager of the house, of the finances anyway. Of course, he thought because I didn't go to work that I couldn't work and make enough money to take care of my kids. He thought it would only last a short while. He said, "Oh, you'll be back."

Q: What was he doing all of this time?

Marilyn: Basically, losing everything we had. He just lost everything: the house, the cars, everything. He didn't pay for anything. He didn't keep up. He just ran around and partied so he didn't pay for anything.

I stayed alone for about five years. I basically didn't think about anything other than working and the kids, trying to keep them out of trouble. It's a handful, raising 3 kids as a single parent. Then somebody said, "I have a friend I want you to meet, a nice person." He seemed to be a pretty nice person. Actually, it was his mother across the hall that had said it. And I had seen him before when he wasn't in as good a shape. I was surprised to see that he was doing well. He had been kind of like a homeless person before, but he really wasn't.

Q: Was there anything in particular that you were looking for in a man?

Marilyn: I looked for compassion. People who feel like I do about other people...about the community. What really attracted me to him was my son was seriously hurt and was in the hospital. I was going back and forth and I was very upset when I saw him the first time that evening and I wanted to go back to the hospital. But I really couldn't handle it. So he went with me. And he took such good care of my son, not even knowing him. He had had an operation and had not been able to get up or take a shower. Nurses do really help you do too much.

He was across the hall and I was talking to his mother about how my son had just come out of surgery and how they wouldn't let him come home. I was really upset and crying. She said, "You're too upset to drive. He'll go with you and he'll drive." And he did. He just seemed very concerned and very nice and when he got there, he just did so many things for Kenny to help him. He was so compassionate and helpful that I saw him in a different light. I had been ignoring him before. I ignored him because before he had been a rowdy type of person. Not really my type at all, kind of wild. Like a party/drinker type person. Loud. Between the time that I had first seen him he had gone into a program to stop drinking. He couldn't handle it and he had gone into isolation to restructure his life. So he was totally different from what I originally knew. His wild, boisterous, and out of control lifestyle frightened me. I hadn't seen him in a while. He wasn't pushy and we did things like visit my son and take time with the other one and do things that you get used to doing things on your own like fixing your car.

Q: How long were you together before you started to realize that something was wrong?

Marilyn: I saw a little bit about four years into the relationship. The first time, we were not living together, but we were together all the time. He lived across the hall. So many other things were happening with my kids, I seemed to be preoccupied and I didn't pay enough attention to him or I didn't want to go to all the places he wanted to go or something. And I could just see little things coming out. He was annoyed and I could see a little meanness. He would say things like, "You don't have enough time for me. You pay more attention to the kids than me." He would bring up real petty matters. He seemed to have less patience; didn't want to hear what I had to say as much, didn't value my feelings. So, I broke up with him. Then he kind of regrouped, calmed down. I think he was a little out of control, going back into his old habits. Then he just seemed to stop, because I said, "Forget it. I don't need this."

Q: During the time that you were breaking up, what was his reaction?

Marilyn: He didn't believe me. He kept trying to talk to me and then he wanted to know why. I was telling him, "I'm seeing behavior that I can't deal with." I had a lot of things going with the kids and I couldn't handle him cutting up. So, I just had to say, "I have to let you go."

Q: Was there any indication of physical abuse at that time?

Marilyn: No. He was always around, even though we had broken up, but he pretended to be around because he was concerned. If I opened my door, he opened his door. That means he was just there watching. When I'd come out, he'd try to talk to me. This went on for about 6 months. Then he went back into his first mode. The way he was when I first started going out with him. He seemed to calm down a lot and go back. I just assumed that he was under some sort of stress before. I had been under a lot of stress, so I figured that maybe he had something in his life that stressed him out. He's the type that comes to your rescue when things are overwhelming. After six months we got back together. Then we became engaged. For a while he had his son down here for the summer. I let him and the son stay with us, because it would be more convenient for him. His son was 12. He was okay for two months and then he went totally out of control. I found out later that it was because he had started back with the drugs and drinking. Cocaine. That lasted for a few months. I said, "you can't do this. You have to find a place to live, as soon as your son goes back home, you'll have to leave." He didn't believe me. He thought he could turn on the charm and whatever, and that that was enough. He was very charming and a lot of fun. What got me with him was that after just working all the time, here comes somebody to take you away from work and to do fun stuff and to travel and do things that I had never done. It was a lot of fun for me. So that didn't work, because I had seen too much of him. Actually, at that time he was drinking. He hadn't gotten back into drugs until he got his own place.

Q: When did the first episodes of actual abuse start?

Marilyn: I knew that he was slipping back into drugs, so I was trying to get him help. Trying to be supportive, not just dump him because he was having a relapse. I went to bring him something to eat instead of giving him money. He was always asking me for money. So, I wouldn't give it to him. I took him food. He just totally went berserk, because he was following me. Here he calls me to do something, but he's around following me to see where I'm going. He was paranoid. He said he'd seen me somewhere with someone else. He would call me over and over again. He would always call me at home constantly. I would talk to him, answer whatever it was he wanted, hang up, and he would call right back. It was just crazy. I wasn't looking for it so I didn't know he was always out there lurking.

The first time he hit me, I went to take him some food when he told me he was hungry. I said, "I'll bring you something." Actually, I took something home for my son first. By the time I came back to his house with his food, he had gone looking for me. I was there waiting for him with his food. I didn't think, because he was so animated and comical, I thought he was playing. I said, "Where have you been?" when he came back to the house. He was totally out of it and he said, "I saw you. I saw you come out of that guy's apartment over there." I thought he was playing. He wasn't. He got really nasty. He grabbed me. I said, "You know I'm going to leave now because you're not in a good mood." He said, "You're not going anywhere." He just started throwing me around. And he really wasn't hurting me.

He kept hitting me, but he wasn't hurting me and I thought, "I know he could hurt a person if he hit them intentionally." But he was hitting me and holding me. He wouldn't let me go, but he wasn't hurting me. When I got tired of him, he wouldn't let me go. He wouldn't answer me; he was just talking crazy. He started choking me. He wanted me to shut up. That's when I knew he was serious. It just seemed like forever to try to get away from him. Every time I thought I was away from him, he'd grab me. I couldn't get out of the apartment. Nobody would do anything. I was screaming and he was choking me or he's just grabbing me and pulling me back. It frightened me. Nobody had ever hit me. Nobody had ever acted like that before. I finally got away from him and went home. I called the police. He had ripped my clothes and was chasing me. Some people came out and some guy stopped him from catching me. That's the only way I got in the car and got home.

I called the police. They didn't do anything. They said that because I left where it had happened. So I said, "That's it." He tried to call and apologize and say he was sorry, and that he was going into a program. But then he was just following me and bothering me and calling me and threatening me. It was very hard to keep the kids from retaliating against him.

Q: What kind of threats did he make?

Marilyn: That he was going to kill me! He said, "I'm going to kill you. I'm going to kill your kids if you don't come back to me. You can't dump me like that." I kept saying, "You need to get some help. I understand it's a problem you have. I kept being understanding when I should have just been cut and dried. But I kept trying to help him and get him into programs and get other people to help him. He couldn't figure out why his family wouldn't help him. Why weren't they more supportive?

Q: How long did this go on, from the first incident, the stalking and the threats?

Marilyn: About 3 months. After numerous phone calls and police reports...or the police not doing anything. I was always with somebody. My kids would always be with me or somebody was always with me. I was afraid, because whenever I was by myself, he would always come and grab me and try to take me somewhere, or he would cry and try to make me feel sorry for him. One morning I thought everything was okay, because I hadn't seen him or heard from him. I was going out to get into the car to go to work. He was out there and because he didn't see anybody with me, he just sneaked up on me and kidnapped me. He just pushed me in the car. I ended up headfirst on the floor and just took me away in my car. I was trying to get out of the car and the more I tried to get away from him, he would either hit me or choke me. I had a gun in my purse. I knew he knew I had a gun that my sister gave me. He just wouldn't stop. He was just driving like a fool through the streets. And I was screaming, but because my head was down, he'd put his hand around my throat. He took me to his apartment. He threatened me and he took all my clothes. Here I'd always been able to talk him out of anything before and I thought, the more excited I get, and the more he knows I'm afraid, the worse he gets. I tried to calm down, even though I was afraid. I was trying to talk to him and he was very scary. He had all these knives. He kept saying, "I'll kill you if I can't have you. I'm not going to let you go. You don't have to do that, you have to come back to me. I'll get help." He was very scary because he was so deadpan and just weird. He had a knife. I kept trying to get out of the apartment. There were two doors and they were both locked. He had locked the door from the inside with a key so when he came in and locked the doors, he took the keys so I couldn't get out.

He brutally raped me that time. He said, "I can do anything I want to you and you can't do anything to me. If you call the police, I'm going to kill your children." The way he was lurking around all the time, I just knew I had to be calm, even though I was hysterical. I had screamed my head off and nobody did anything. So I was just quiet. I didn't say anything. He just kept talking and started making all these plans. He said, "I'm going to take you home, and you're going to call me, and you're going to come to my house after work. We're going to talk about getting married. We're going to live here. I'm going to get help." He had all these plans that he thought because I had stopped fighting him that it was okay. But I stopped fighting because the more I fought him the more he hurt me. The angrier he got, the more he threatened me. He had knives all over the place.

Q: Did you get injured physically?

Marilyn: Yes. He kicked me a couple of times. I was all bruised up and scratched up. I don't really think he wanted to physically hurt me; he wanted to frighten me into not leaving him or breaking up with him. He was just doing whatever he did to make me shut up and be still, I guess.

Q: How did you leave his apartment that night?

Marilyn: He just said, "Everything's okay now. I'm going to take you home and when you're done with work, call me, or I'm going to call you. We're going to work things out, but if you call the police, I'm going to kill your children." So, he took me home. He got out of the car a block away from my house and he said, "I'll talk to you at 4 o'clock." He was so calm, he thought everything was okay.

As soon as he got out of the car I drove to my driveway and was screaming. Before I got in the house, I remember my older son running outside. I just went straight to the telephone and called the police.

Before they had always said, "There's nothing we can do." This time, some guys came out. I had been down to the State Attorney's office. I had filed a restraining order. I had made all kinds of complaints. When I was talking to this policeman, when I told the dispatcher what happened, she sent out a different team, the sex crime team, or something. They were totally different from the regular policemen who came out.

Q: Did they take you to the Rape Treatment Center?

Marilyn: Yes. They asked me if I wanted to press charges and I said, "Yes." I knew that I had to because he was threatening me and he was threatening his family. He was threatening everybody if they didn't help him to get me back. Everybody was hysterical. When I talked to his mother, she was hysterical. His sister was hysterical. He had been over there threatening them. He was going to hurt somebody.

Q: Did he have any history of hurting anybody before?

Marilyn: Yes. I found out much later. He had beaten people into a pulp. Just went totally crazy and beat them, but he had never been arrested. People had always been afraid to call the police or had been talked out of it by his family.

This time, they arrested him after I gave my statement. The man at the sexual unit basically said that they weren't sure if I was going to follow through because I guess they get so many people who don't. But he called me from jail to tell me he was going to kill me when he got out. Then he called his mother and told her that he was going to kill me. So his sister called me and told me that he said he was going to kill me. I went to the State Attorney and I told the judge that he couldn't get out. I went over everything that had happened and I didn't understand: What were they waiting for? Why did it take so long? Why did it have to get to the point that he could do this to me and get away with it? I was just horrified that he could get away with this. I asked them what they wanted. Did they want to wait for him to kill me? They thought I was going to sue the county or somebody because they never followed through.

He was in jail. It just dragged out for two years. We kept having court hearings. They kept changing lawyers so we kept having bond hearings. But I personally thought if he dried out from drugs and alcohol, he would be better. But every time I saw him in court, he was worse. He kept screaming out. He was scary. He was never released from jail. The State Attorney protested. I had been before the State Attorney before and they hadn't done anything; they sent him a warning letter. After all those threats, they didn't arrest him. Even though he'd beaten me, even though the policemen saw the prints around my neck. They wrote in their report. The judge couldn't figure out why they didn't do anything then. He admitted that he did and they didn't do anything. But I wouldn't let it go. I said, "You can't let him out. He's telling everybody he's going to kill me and kill my children." They just kept him in, and they kept trying to find witnesses. His family would come down and tell tales. But he had told other people what he was going to do. Critical people like the minister of the church. People kept volunteering to go down and tell them, people from the hospital where I worked wanted to testify about all the threats, about the harassing calls, about flattening my tires. So, they never let him out. We kept going to trial, but either his lawyer would quit and he'd get another lawyer...until I let them plea bargain because it kept taking people who were testifying for me away from work. So, I plea-bargained with a few conditions.

The plea bargain was seven years of mandatory psychiatric treatment, drug treatment. If you're really good and you earn all this time, then you can get out on probation really early. He could have gotten out for time served because he had been in jail for two years. That he'd at least have to serve more than the 2 years. I don't care how much he'd earned.

Q: How long since he has he been in jail now?

Marilyn: About four years. There's a possibility, State Attorney's office said there's a possibility, he's coming up for review. He had completed everything; he had been a model prisoner. But he had earned so much time, gained time, that he was coming up for review. He had completed all the requirements.

I feel like I know that he will come directly to me wherever I am. I left the hospital where I used to work. I moved from where I used to live. What else can I do?

Q: Are you scared?

Marilyn: About coming face to face with him? Yes. Last time he was at a court hearing, he was wild. He didn't care what they did. As soon as he saw me he just kept trying to come over or say something. He just wouldn't shut up. He wouldn't stop. I don't think he'll ever stop. I don't want to come face to face with him.

Q: What are you going to do? How has it affected your ability to have a normal life, to relax and possibly get involved with someone else?

Marilyn: I see a lot of what happened with him as being my fault, because I didn't know when to stop. I kept thinking, "Well, he's not all bad. All he needs is help. Nobody else is helping him so I can't abandon him." I kept letting him get away with too much, letting him apologize and charm his way out of things. Basically, I just wouldn't give up that he could be that bad. I kept thinking that if he got the right help, if I could help him, he would be okay. Not necessarily for me, but at least for himself. Once I saw the ugly part of him, I didn't want him. But I didn't want to leave him to be on the street or totally bare. People kept saying he's no good. People just kept badmouthing him. People did not help him, like his family. As long as he was doing okay it was all right, but as soon as he needed help, nobody wanted to help him. I didn't think he was a totally bad person. He was an abused child and he was still suffering abuse at the hands of his parents as an adult, just trying to win their favor. They were totally abusive. I couldn't believe it. So, he acted out on other people. He wasn't able to just cut them off because they were hurting him. I could see the pain, and my plans with him were gone, but I couldn't just kick him to the curb because he was weak. I've been able to see weakness in other people. I guess it is the narcissism in all of us. We always think that we can go on a rescue mission. Often times we come up empty. It seems like I'm attracted to that type of person, one that needs help, people with faults. While other people might look at what they can get from others, I don't. Is it some kind of flaw in my character?

Q: Is there anything in your childhood that might account for this soft side of you?

Marilyn: Before I came to Florida everything was fine. I lived with my grandparents. At that time I didn't know my natural parents and I didn't miss them. I had a nice life with two people who took care of other people. They always took care of other people who were not able to help themselves. Just because you had, you didn't look down on anybody else. You're not better than anybody is. If there's a person in need, you have to help them. This was the philosophy. This is what I grew up with. I grew up by myself so I had everything. I had a lot of friends who didn't.

Q: How about your natural parents?

Marilyn: I didn't know them 'til later. My mother and father weren't married. My father went to war and my mother was embarrassed so she left me in New Jersey. I didn't think about being abandoned when I was little because I didn't know the whole story about it. I didn't know why I was where I was, but I was happy I was there. I couldn't have had a better childhood with people who adored me. They played with me and taught me important values.

Q: But you were like a cherished and prized doll then?

Marilyn: No. They made me help other people. You did your time. I was not a cherished doll at all. I know they adored me, but they wouldn't allow me to be mean to other kids. Somebody could really get on my nerves, and at no time did they allow me to think that I was better than anybody else was. I couldn't be a brat.

Q: What do you see for yourself in the future? What's going to happen to your ex-boyfriend?

Marilyn: Hopefully he has been rehabilitated. Hopefully he can come out of it and have a normal life. I pray God that he did learn something from the experience, that he did grow stronger. I hope that he will be able to stand tall and rise above his entire ordeal. He needs to get to know his children and be something positive in their lives. No children should have to live in fear of their father.

Q: Do you really think that he's getting psychiatric treatment in jail?

Marilyn: I am not too optimistic about that. It is just too bad; the cycle of violence is likely to continue.

I have to admit that I'm not typical. I have always been independent. I wasn't dependent upon him for my livelihood. It was not like he took care of me, like the other people he was involved with. He got away with so much. I think I was a lot stronger than other people were. I'm not afraid to go out on my own. I was not afraid to care about him and say, "Yes, he needs help. But I can't stay in this relationship; I have to go. But I can help you, regardless, I can try to help you." Should I come across him again and if he needed help, there is no doubt in my mind that I would try to help him. That's just the way it is. I have to try. Does that put me at risk? Absolutely!

Q: I'm speechless. There you are! A victim of a serious crime. Your life was put in danger and yet you are still thinking about others. Where do you draw the line and think about your own self?

Marilyn: I did. That's when he had to go to jail. When I no longer felt that I could get some control in his life, I decided to take action. When I started to feel threatened, I followed through. I was able to see beyond the façade of charm. I'd never witnessed a person who was charming one minute and an absolute maniac the next. But I could draw the line. Don't threaten me or my children or my family. Don't even threaten another person. If there is some hope that helping him or another person can make a difference, you've got to do it. You can't just kick a person to the curb, anybody.

Q: Now that you've gone through this and you are showing a lot of magnanimity. How can you be thinking about other people while you are going through your own feelings and fear and apprehension? What would you tell other people who are caught in similar situations?

Marilyn: You have to think about safety. You have to get out if you are afraid. You have to follow through. The court system is used to you dropping charges and not following through, so they'll let it go. But then you can end up dead. I could have ended up dead because I kept trying to help him. I kept being suckered into his basic needs, "I'm hungry, I'm alone, I'm sad." It was just by the grace of God that he didn't really hurt me. I thought that he was going to kill me. I was really afraid. You have to be strong. You have to think, you have to look beyond your feelings and know that you can't always help everybody. You have to know when to stop. You have to know how to push the legal system in order to try to get that person help.

Sometimes it seems as if you are fighting two enemies, the legal system and the perpetrator. The legal system makes it so difficult that you feel like dropping everything. On top of that you have your own internal dilemma. You know that underneath that abuser there is a human being begging for help.

It is easy for someone else to say, "Why do you care?" But you have to care. How can you not care? How do you stop? It's not like he was somebody I didn't know. I have a problem not caring about people I don't know if they need help. So if there's somebody that I know, somebody with whom I can associate positive things, somebody who's shown me caring, shown the people who I love caring, I feel obligated to help him. I know that I was lucky, so many other people have died in similar situations.

Chapter Twenty-Three

Escaping the Stereotypes: Voice of a "Welfare Mother"

Thirty-four years ago, at the height of the Civil Rights movement, a President of the United States, Lyndon B. Johnson, dreamed of a great society that would be free of poverty. He created the AFDC (Aid to Families with Dependent Children) otherwise known as welfare. Instead of eliminating poverty, the system has created "a web of dependency" for its 4.6 millions recipients. From both sides of the aisle on Capitol Hill, guided by myths and misconceptions, liberals and conservatives alike have vowed to put an end to the abuses and put a screeching halt to welfare, as we know it. Several bold steps have been taken in that direction, starting with the Family Support Act signed by Ronald Reagan in 1988 and followed by the sweeping Welfare Reform Act signed by Bill Clinton in late 1996, just before his re-election. Since then, there have been many claims of success, but both the myths and the hurdles persist. Not all welfare recipients are teenage uneducated Blacks, mothers of three who inherited their dependence on welfare from the generations before them.   Not all welfare recipients are healthy, young individuals who are just waiting for a forceful nudge to get off their duffs. In fact, the majority of long-term welfare recipients are Whites and Hispanics.   Nine out of ten are women.55 Twenty-five to forty percent of long-term recipients have handicaps that prevent them from holding a full-time job.56 Two-thirds of them have not graduated high school. Thirty-one percent of those in public-assistance programs had one or more psychiatric disorders in the past year. More than half of the welfare mothers have been victims of domestic abuse. About sixteen percent of the welfare mothers have significant substance abuse problems. The above statistical data illustrates the challenges that the policymakers are facing in their attempt to reform a system gone awry.

The following interview gives voice to a welfare mother that defies all the stereotypes, but gives a human face to a controversy that is likely to take us well into the new millennium.

Q: Cassandra, what I am trying to do is to confront the myths that have been presented to the public throughout the media. Women receiving public assistance have been seen as Cadillac queens, they have been called lazy, unmotivated, and other derogatory names, but the one that is most widespread is

---

[55] See Whitman D. Reference No.87.
[56] ibid

"welfare mothers." You do not seem to fit any of the stereotypes. Can you tell me about yourself?

Cassandra: Well, I have two brothers. I have one in the Bronx. My mother was employed throughout my childhood. My father was very ill, he was an invalid. We lived in the South Bronx. We were very poor. We had a lot of, we had a very, very big family, of cousins and aunts and uncles, which we saw frequently, but my parents, we were the poorest of the family and my father especially was embarrassed. And so he would never ask for help.

Q: What is your father's ethnic background?

Cassandra: He was a first generation American. His parents were from Italy. And my mother was a first generation American. Her parents were, well at that time it was called Russia. My mother's parents met here. They came when they were young adults. And I believe my father's parents, too, met here. As a matter of fact, my mother's family and my father's family lived across the street in the Bronx and that's how they met. My father was ten years older than my mother was. My mother was 19 when she married my father. My father had been married before, but it was annulled. Apparently, the woman that he had married never had gotten divorced from whomever she was married to. To an Italian, the idea of divorce was very humiliating. My family had many secrets. I think that had a lot to do with why my father didn't seek help with the family, whether financially or, my mother always felt so overwhelmed, she didn't want children. She, it wasn't at that point, because we were White and we lived in a totally Black neighborhood, it was just almost impossible to get any kind of help. When my father got ill, I was about eight. My mother had a hard time getting any kind of help. But my father, like I said, always seemed very against, I think, letting anyone know what happened in the house. It was really imparted on us kids that whatever happened in the house had to stay in the house, don't ask for help, don't tell people anything, and that really affected us. I was the youngest.

Q: What was it like growing up in that family? How did you manage to get your education?

Cassandra: I have two brothers and one was about 4½ years older than I was and the other was about 18 months older. I have a master's degree in special ed. from Hunter University and I have a bachelor's degree in psychology from Fordham. I went to a professional Art and Design school in New York. I was in college when my father finally died. He lingered on for many years. I had left home soon after he died. I had my own apartment. I enjoyed being on my own. I moved out of the county. My parents lived in the Bronx; I moved all the way to Queens. Things were a little difficult between my parents and I.

Q: What do you mean?

Cassandra: Looking back, I think I was suffering from depression. I had a lot of problems. I became very introverted and kept away totally from people. I blamed every thing on my parents. I was emotionally distant. It lasted for many years.

Q: What about getting married and having children?

Cassandra: Well, I met up with a very controlling man. It was my very first serious relationship. I hardly had any boyfriends and I married him. I don't think either one of us really loved each other, I think it was more of a convenience. And it didn't last very long, I don't know, maybe it lasted 15 months or so, but we got an annulment. Unfortunately, I met another abusive man and after about, probably about a little more than a year, I had gotten pregnant and so we got married. We stayed together about eight years. I started to attend some women's groups, and we broke up.

Q: Were you trying to break away, or did it just happen?

Cassandra: By the time I became enmeshed in this relationship, I was convinced that I was the abusive one. I blamed myself for everything. I had three children by then. I stayed with him because I thought in my head of the child needing a father, no matter what. And I thought it would be better for the children. One day, I called the abuse hotline and they sent somebody out to meet me. The woman was really very supportive and after about ten months she convinced me, at least

I finally saw that I was co-dependent. How could that possibly be happening to me? In the course of the treatment, it suddenly dawned on me that maybe I was abused myself by extremely critical parents.

Q: What was your work experience?

Cassandra: I started to work when I was 14. My mother had made it clear that she would no longer support me. My other two brothers had left home by then. Since I wanted to go to Art and Design High School, which costs money, I went to work at the same place where my mother worked. She worked at a collection agency. I really enjoyed working; I took on a lot of initiatives. I was a good worker. I worked for Woolworth for several years. I worked my way up to floor manager and I wanted to go into the assistant managing program, but I was told the position was not for women.

Q: Did they say that it was not for women?

Cassandra: Plain and simple! Women were not allowed in the assistant management program. So, I left and I went to a private organization. By then, I was living on my own and I worked full time and went to school part time. I convinced the man that I could do the bookkeeping and he hired me. I learned it on the job. I had gotten my teaching degree. A friend encouraged me to get into teaching. I applied for a teacher's license. New York was going through a financial crisis and there was a hiring freeze in the public school system. I did finally get a job in a private school. It lasted only a short time. I was too outspoken for my supervisor. One day, there was a bus driver there who was drunk. He had to transport the children. I refused to let the children go on the bus with him. I got fired. I then landed a job with the Department of State of New York. I stayed there for about two years. I really enjoyed that job because I worked for the employment agency, Department of Employment for New York State, and I liked helping people get jobs. I really liked interviewing people. I liked hearing about different ways that people earned a living. I wanted to get back into teaching. I learned that there was a position in South Bronx, my old neighborhood. I convinced the director there to hire me.

Q: Are you saying that you always had to convince someone to give you a job, even though you were qualified?

Cassandra: Well, he didn't think I could do the job because he said that it was a totally Black neighborhood, I was a White woman, single White woman, and this was a school for youth with a criminal history. It was a school for children who had already been in jail and were making the transition back into, on the street, or back into prison if they goofed up. So I had to convince him that I was going to do the job. He finally accepted me. I loved that job. I thought it was the best job I ever had. I loved the kids. There was just a lot of political junk going on and that's when I met my first husband.

Q: What year was it, then?

Cassandra: Let's see! It must have been, I was born in '53, so it was probably about '75 or '76? And it was tough. Fortunately, I had a car at the time. I had a little Volkswagen. I was still living in Queens. It was a great job.

Q: It must have felt like a great accomplishment.

Cassandra: Yes, it did. I really enjoyed the kids. It wasn't just a teaching job because the children there really needed more than teaching. They needed support and guidance. They needed someone to talk to, someone to help them make the transition back into the real life. That was my best job. And I stayed there for about two years. Like I said, I met my first husband. He was an attorney. I was not in love with him, but it was an opportunity to get out of my poverty. I expected him to treat me well. I did not know that there was going to be any abuse. So I thought. And we left New York and moved to Florida in February 1980. We moved down here. I finished my Masters up in New York and soon after that we moved down here. I guess that things were really never good from the beginning. Unfortunately, we bought a house. He was not ready for commitment, he moved out. There I was, stuck with the house and the mortgage. It was poverty all over again.

Q: Were there any settlement or divorce proceedings?

Cassandra: No. He, we got an annulment. Even though his name was on the mortgage, I could have walked away. I could have probably, legally, forced him or tried to force him to pay half, I knew I couldn't make it. I knew it was going to be for nothing.

Q: Why?

Cassandra: Because I knew no court would even do it. I mean, when I was single and I graduated from my BA, I got hooked up with a guy who was abusive, we moved in together and I walked out with my suitcase. I lost everything. And he kept saying to me, you go into court and I will tell him you're just a tramp who lived with me and I knew that was true. I knew that no judge was going to listen to a poor White woman.

Q: So you did not feel like going to battle, you felt defeated from the start?

Cassandra: There was not going to be any battle, it would have been death. I would have faced sure death. It just wasn't worth it. And so I really struggled with a very high mortgage, cause those were the times when interest rates were sky high. It was 14% or something. It was unbelievable. I became depressed. I didn't really do anything or go anywhere. I had gotten a second job. I had frequently, throughout my career, had gotten second jobs when I was on my own. It's not that I was a big spender. I didn't have fancy things or expensive clothes. I didn't go places. I didn't travel. It wasn't that I was wasting money, it's just that I was living. I was paying for my rent, paying for my car, paying for my food, and paying for my education. I also had to pay student loans.

Q: Didn't you have any children from the marriage?

Cassandra: No, I had three children by a second husband. Thank God we didn't have any children.

Q: So, when did you start seeking psychiatric help?

Cassandra: It was very soon after, I had, before I broke up with my first husband, I had went for counseling. I was, at that time, extremely depressed. There had been lots of periods in my life where I had went down to where I didn't know where I was or who I was. So, I wasn't sure what was going on. I was very physically sick.

Q: Was there any alcohol or drugs involved?

Cassandra: Not with me, no. No. I was very sick with my stomach very frequently, lots of problems with vomiting. I always thought it was because I never had enough money to eat.

Q: How did that affect your children?

Cassandra: They never knew. They couldn't understand. The health professionals would just pump me with drugs. Most of the time I didn't go to the doctor. I wouldn't have health insurance. I just, I knew it would go away. One time a family doctor, he was the only one that was of any value, and he really didn't talk to me, he just kind of just treated me. He treated me for colitis, for anemia, he was the one I went to when I first went for, when I was a kid, I was maybe 17 or 18, I went for birth control. But he never talked to me. You know, when I went for the birth control, he just gave it to me. When I had said I had something, he just gave it. He never asked what was wrong; he never asked what was happening in the house. No one ever really did. They just thought I was weird or I was, high-strung I was called.

Q: You got married again?

Cassandra: Well, I went to counseling. I had been to counseling for a couple years. It was a woman. Unfortunately, I guess I wasn't ready to really accept counseling. And I met Bob soon after I broke up with Jack. We kind of just hooked on to each other. He was very, very, very different from my first husband, from Jack. It was like night and day. And I had sworn to myself that I wasn't going to deal with somebody like Jack. I mean, Jack was the attorney with the suit and he was the only guy I had ever dated. He was from my own background. I'm Jewish. And that was probably the only reason why I married him. And so I got Bill, who was blue collar, who I thought was more my style.

Q: Down to earth?

Cassandra: Right! This time, he was not that uppity guy whose mother was worried about my telling others that I was from the Bronx. I should tell people I was from Queens. Imagine people's reaction, when they found out that my ex-sister-in-law was married to a Black man. We could not find anyone to hang out with. So I think, I really feel that had a lot to do with us staying together, because of that. So after about a year or so with him and we had talked about getting married. We were in Fort Lauderdale. We both had our own homes and I didn't realize at the time that having our own homes was like our shelter. When we got annoyed with each other, we just went to our own homes. We sold our separate homes and moved in together. That was a major mistake. By then, I was pregnant again. I thought that the clock was ticking. Soon, I would be unable to bear children again. So, I decided against having an abortion. He relented and we got married.

Q: Did you feel supported during the pregnancy?

Cassandra: As time went on, he became more and more resentful. I had to stop working because it turned out my son was very sick when he was born. I just spent all my time going to doctors. No one could figure out what was wrong with the baby. My husband got more and more resentful. He often stated that I wasn't pulling my own weight. I wasn't taking care of things; I had burdened him and things got more and more difficult. So, when the boy was two, we met a neurologist and she said oh don't worry, this was going to go away by the time he reaches puberty and has hormonal changes. We didn't know at the time, well she said he had ADHD. It wasn't until he was four, after we already had a second child, that we found out he had Tourette's. So, and he had some physical problems and he had to have surgery. When he was little, he had GE reflux, and he had a real problem with eating, throwing up, and he had epilepsy, which wasn't diagnosed until he was about six. So he had a lot of things that people didn't realize, because I guess it was so much, you know, the symptoms were like so crazy. So we had Judd, really just because we wanted a normal child, you know, it was so stressful having a sick child. I think Bill was very disappointed at having a sick child.

Q: Was the second child as difficult?

Cassandra: It was almost as difficult. His feet were disjointed. He should have been in braces, he wasn't. About a year later, no, not even, about six months later we finally put him in braces because I kept going to the doctor telling him there's something wrong and he kept saying don't worry about it. I had, but by then I had experience with first son that when you go to the doctor and he says don't worry, you find another doctor. So, I was literally spending 24 hours a day with two sick children. Judd also had GE reflux with throwing up and Judd then also, as

Judd got older, I noticed right away that Judd had a problem eating and something was wrong with his mouth, but I also knew by then that doctors just don't listen to you. First off, they don't listen to a woman. They think every time we go to a doctor it's like, you know, you're overreacting. You're being hysterical. You take things to heart too much. And I had learned that from years and years and years from when I was a kid. So when, unfortunately, when the second boy was about six months old, I got pregnant. I did not want to abort it. I had really wanted a daughter. I guess I convinced myself the third one would be a daughter. Statistically the third one was supposed to be a daughter. She wasn't. It was a boy with, guess what? Medical problems.

Q: So, the three kids have medical problems. At what point did you start going for assistance, public assistance?

Cassandra: Like I said, I was brought up that you don't ask for help. As I mentioned before I did have some experience with system, I had gone on unemployment years earlier when I was in college. I had gotten food stamps at that time for just a month. They would only give me food stamps for a month because they said I made too much in unemployment. So, they gave me emergency food stamps. I didn't like being on unemployment because it's torturous. I didn't like getting food stamps because people look at you funny in the stores. People are not helpful;

people look down at you. People who go there, you have the feeling that you have to look junky, that you have to look disheveled, because if you go there looking like a real person, they'll say to you what are you doing here or you shouldn't really need this or things like that. That was in New York. Then I came down here, well, again, when I was living down here and I had the three children, Evan was six months old and I went to New York. And the boys were very sick and I couldn't find anybody to help, I went to New York. When I was there, the school system there told me why don't you apply for assistance. And I kept saying well, I don't know, I don't know, I don't want to deal with this, I don't want to do this. And they kept pushing and pushing, and they were the ones that found out that Judd did not speak and that he needed therapy. He was mute, he needed help, and they were just so helpful, just so helpful. They really cared. They would call on a Friday afternoon. Five of us were living in my mother one-bedroom apartment. My husband was down here in Florida. They were just so helpful; Friday afternoons they would call me and say have a good weekend, try to be strong because, you know, it was very bad with the kids. The baby, he was literally suffocating to death and I couldn't find a doctor that was giving right medicine, Christmas Day I left. I came back down here and went to a doctor that day and he said he would have died in two more days. He couldn't believe it.

Only then, I decided to apply for some assistance. I can do this on my own. I got disability for two boys at the time. I didn't apply for the young one, I just didn't think that he deserved it. I eventually did apply for the third one and I got disability for all three. Periodically I got food stamps, on and off, throughout the years. I don't know why, but, I mean, just very haphazard food stamps. But like I said, I don't know, it just seemed hit and miss. I don't know how they figure out, they will not tell you how they figure it out. They will not give you any information. You don't have any clue as to what you're supposed to utilize. Like I didn't know that you can use your telephone bill as a bill until I had a friend who was on assistance, AFDC, and then she told me you're supposed to bring your telephone bill. So, I said okay, so next time I brought the telephone bill. I said you're supposed to count this as a bill.

Having to deal with the bureaucracy was like torture. I don't wish this on my worst enemy. If I did not have all those medical problems, I would just give it up.

Q: Tell me about the procedures when you go for AFDC, you say it is torturous.

Cassandra: It is, it's like a maze. You are on your own. If you're not there on time for your appointment, you might as well go home. If you get there on time, you have to wait. Well, every single time you're there, you wait, but if you happen to be late, that's it. You say no, no, and then they say. "Well, you have to bring or send it to us." Well, the first time that happened to me, I said, "Okay I'll mail it to you". Well, apparently, I mailed it. What I did not know was that there was a time limit. That's it.

Q: Have you ever made a formal complaint about the dehumanizing treatment that you receive?

Cassandra: No. Oh, are you kidding? Argue with those people? It's like arguing with the Gestapo. No way! There is no way! You go in there, you shut your mouth, you stay in line, and you wait. You don't talk unless you're spoken to. It works out much better that way. You just go, sit down, and let them do the talking. I mean it's like, you know, how do you do, come in, and they're facing the other way. They don't look at you in the eye; they don't shake your hand. Government employees used to pride themselves about being courteous and well mannered. Not any more!

Q: They are overwhelmed?

Cassandra: Yeah. They are. But none of it, like I said, I was there once late, they canceled me. If your paper work is one day late, they cancel you. I had to reapply. Because all it was, she said, well you were like two days late and I didn't receive the paperwork. I was like, who knew? You didn't tell me that that would happen. You didn't even tell me I had to have it in by a certain date. She would say very nonchalantly, "Oh just said send it to me within a week or something like that." And they make you feel like they're the ones that are paying you. I applied for unemployment about a year or so ago, about 1½ years. And I was shocked. That was my first, initial encounter with the new laws. I applied. Government office of environment used to be very friendly. When you walk into an office, you no longer feel like the employees are there to serve the citizens. You feel like you have been stripped of your humanity and identity at the door. You become a tiny part of this giant amorphous mass that has been branded with the dreadful words "welfare mothers." You are not human; you're not an individual. To illustrate the point, everyone in the room that morning gets an 8:30 AM appointment. You all sit in the waiting room and then they say, unbeknownst to us, they gave all of us 8:30 appointments, so they call out, "Anyone with an 8:30 appointment to come in line." Well, everyone stood up. The whole room! And everyone was looking at each other wondering what was going on. A lady came up with the demeanor of a drill sergeant. She talks to us as if she's talking to one person. You know, put your name on the top page, yada, yada. We're all like looking at each other and no one said a word. No one said a word.

Q: You wouldn't dare?

Cassandra: No. You wouldn't dare. A poor woman came in flanked with two toddlers. It was a few minutes after the appointed time; they wouldn't let her in. They rescheduled her for another day. I mean, what was the big deal? It was a whole group and the woman was talking to everyone at the same time. What was the big deal that the woman was a few minutes late? No one understood what she was talking about anyway. I didn't know what she was talking about, but I didn't care. I just filled out whatever I could fill out. There was a couple of men who were like, "I don't understand, can you help me?" And she kept saying, "Be quiet, be quiet." The men looked even more confused. You know, women are used to it, you go into those places you shut up, you do what you're told, you fill out whatever you can, and that's it, you walk out. So, and then finally a second person came, but all she did was pick up the papers and they said they would contact us. Well, they denied my claim. I got one check and then they refused me unemployment. They blamed me for getting fired. That's it.

Q: No recourse?

Cassandra: That's it. There is no recourse. That's the end of it. Well, I don't know about anybody else, but I'm pretty sure the employer would always say it was the employee's fault. I don't know about that. So again, I went. I got some food stamps and again it was just torturous with the food stamps. It's a different office. You go to the office. You are back to square one. The officer asks you the same questions again and again. You sit in these plastic uncomfortable chairs. People come in. Their grooming is awful. They wear torn clothes, dirty clothes, matted hair, you feel totally out of place.

Q: Did they make a requirement that you would have to find a job?

Cassandra: For unemployment? Yeah. They had, as a matter of fact, they had told me, or told all of us, that if we didn't have, I think it was five contacts, and we'd have to prove contacts, we had to have name, address, and the name of the person.

Q: What kind of jobs did you look for?

Cassandra: So, I went and typed up some resumes and went to some private schools and gave them the list of the schools. That was my five contacts.

Q: How difficult was that for you to follow the process?

Cassandra: Well, I didn't really want to, how could I go back to work with 3 sick kids? The kids were still getting Social Security. I had just gotten off a legal battle with Palm Beach County school board. I had sued them for failure to provide an adequate education for my first son under PL 94-142. I had to put the kids in a private school. So, I worked at the private school and I got reduced tuition for them. So, it was kinda like, I had to get him out. He was being really abused there. When I left there, I took the kids out of private school and I put them back in public school and once I did that, it was very hard because I had the kids in two different schools, two different times, two different schedules. There were two different ones who were in elementary and the first one was in middle school and I had to constantly, there was always a problem at school. The school expected you to show up for the IEP's (Individual Education Plan), whenever they ask you. It was impossible. There is always some confusion about the school administering the different medications to three different children. I had tried in the past to get someone, but most of the time if I had a baby-sitter, it would be in-between their medications. So I really didn't want a teaching job because every time I went for an interview, it was too many hours. Jack never took care of them, but when he was gone, it was even harder because of the medicines. They're not the types of children who can come home and be latchkey kids.

Q: How old are they now?

Cassandra: Don is seven, Joe is nine, and Karl is twelve. And still, at 12 years old, Karl cannot be trusted. I have to have him here. I had to pull Karl out of school; he doesn't go to school now.

Q: How different do you feel that you are from a typical welfare recipient woman?

Cassandra: Well, I kind of feel offended by that statement. I don't feel different, okay? Maybe I'm a different color from the "typical welfare recipient," but I don't think I'm different. I think a lot of those women are a lot smarter and a lot more with it than they pretend to be. I think they are pretending a lot because they know the system. I think that they have been, you know, like I said, I was, the reason why my family was so anti getting help was because they want to keep the secrets in the family, the abuse. I think other people, I think most people who go for help really need the help. It's not that they are doing it because they don't want to work or they just want to stay home, I think most people, I mean, I've met other people who applied for assistance and I know a few who didn't really have to apply, but did. But you know something? Even those people, they, you know, if you've got small children and you've got, I think this woman has an alcohol problem, and she, okay, she didn't have to apply, but she did and she got it, and she learned little tricks. But at least, so she was on it for a few years. She helped with the kids. Now she's not and she's working. Is that so terrible? So, she got a little extra food stamp than normal, so the children benefited. Was that so terrible? So, they're healthy and strong and now she's back to work. I mean, I don't get it. Why is that so terrible and yet it's not terrible to buy a screwdriver for $500,000. You know, I don't understand. And they compare it only because it's women. You know, when I go to Social Security or I'm also under CMS, Children's Medical Services. It feels so much different when you walk into an office, and you are treated with courtesy and respect. Women should not have to be treated without dignity, just because they happen to be poor. And you know what? A lot of time the government employees who are mistreating the clients are women themselves. Women, I don't know, women are very hard on women, very hard. You men have a better system of bonding. As soon as little girls are placed in a social situation, they feel that they have to give up their spontaneity to enter into competition with one another.

Q: I know you have shown tremendous courage in face of adversities. If you had a message for the system or for other women, what would you say?

Cassandra: There's nothing to say to the system. I don't think they're going to help us. To women, I'd say don't rush into getting married or having children. Get yourself a support system first. And women who are already there and understand, to reach out to other women and be supportive. You know, don't look at them as competition; don't look at them as trying to take away their man. Look at other women as your sisters in arms.

Chapter Twenty-Four

Escaping Prenatal Selection and Burdened By Destiny: Voice of An Indian Woman

The official number of deaths in India in retaliation for failure to deliver promised dowry is on the rise. Most deaths go unpunished. Consumerism has been blamed for the increase in deaths. It is estimated that 97% of Indian wives have been beaten at least once in their lifetime. The legal system has been very sluggish in protecting women.[57] The root of this problem is ingrained in Hindu religious orthodoxy. Dowry is derived from the ancient Hindu custom of kanyadan, where the father of the bride presents his daughter jewelry and clothes at the time of her marriage, and varadakshina, where the father of the bride presents the groom gifts of cash and other material items. Traditionally, these gifts were presented voluntarily, but more recently these customs have become coercive. A report published by UNICEF officials in India revealed that as many as 50 millions girls might be missing from India's population due to the systematic sex discrimination and the abortion of female

---

[57] See Pratap A. Reference No.68

fetuses.[58] Sex diagnosis through ultrasound and amniocentesis has made the elimination of the unwanted fetus even easier. Birth attendants are often given the job of killing the infant girls for as little as seventy-five cents.

Meanwhile most of the political parties have been competing with each other to take a stance favorable to women at least in their manifestos. A recent bill to reserve one third of the seats in Lok Sabha (the Lower House of the national parliament) was heading for deadlock. India is a country of contrasts, a phenomenon captured by Thomas Homer-Dixon in the title of his book, "The Two Indias." Many Indian women have sought relief by migrating out of the country. Very often however, they cannot escape a tradition of oppression and abuse.

The following interview gives voice to an Indian woman who can still hear the cries of her sisters as they echo from the motherland.

Q: Why don't you start by telling me a little bit about your background?

Tara: My parents are originally from India. They both were born and raised in India, but they, for better opportunities, had moved to Africa and that's where I was born and raised. At the

---

[58] See Iredale, P. Reference No.37

age of 15, for education reasons, they decided to send me to England, so I went to boarding school for four years in England.

Q: Isn't it somewhat of a pattern, that a lot of Indian women from India would go to England for their education?

Tara: You are right. Strangely enough, in spite of a long history of colonialism, many Indians feel some strong emotional bonds to England.

Q: How does that make you feel, as far as your identity is concerned?

Tara: I think you might lose your identity, but if you go back to India I think you have learned a lot of things from different cultures, I would say, because you were exposed to so many different things that you could go back and learn and teach.

Q: What are some of the good things that we've learned? Have you kept enough of the cultural background from India to call yourself Indian?

Tara: It all depends on what kind of a family background you've come from. If you've come from a very strong family, I don't think that you would lose the cultural identity. Indian women are very good in keeping the cultural heritage together. That is my area of interest.

Q: That is what I really want to get into because it's fascinating when you read all of those different things about India, about Indian women, and sometimes it's confusing. Tell me some of the main characteristics of the Indian culture that make it so unique.

Tara: I see that they, Indian women, are very tolerable. They will put up with a lot of hardship or whatever to get what they want or to achieve. Above all, they will try everything that they can to keep the family together.

Q: Right, is that good or bad sometimes?

Tara: Sometimes it's bad. Especially, say for example, in my case, in living in the United States, I don't have that many Indian family background friends, so trying to teach or keep up with it is very difficult. And yes, the American culture does have a lot of good things that many Indians have adopted and assimilated into the Indian culture. But it is hard to make the distinction, sometimes.

Q: Let's talk about marriage. In America, the bride's family will spend a lot of money on a very lavish wedding ceremony, but there is no comparison to the kind of pressure we often hear about dowry. What is that all about anyway?

Tara: In the golden years, a lot of families would not accept a daughter unless the daughter's family gives them a dowry when they're getting married. As my grandfather explains it, the dowry was supposed to be a send-away gift. It was like a guarantee that the daughter will not live in the in-law's family in time of hardship. The bride's father wanted to insure that her daughter would not be condemned to a life of deprivation amongst strangers. Greed transformed it into an opportunity to get rich off the sweat of the bride's family.

Q: How much of a hardship is the dowry to a father, to a family.

Tara: In terms of numbers, basically, say an average family is only earning say $15,000 to $20,000 a year and they are asking for almost $50,000 to $100,000 as a dowry. They don't have that kind of income. Basically, it was a way for the upper caste to keep control over the lower caste. They are just basically from my background; my parents were just farmers. They just grew everything on land and they make their earnings from their living.

Q: Where would they get that kind of money? Okay, but how is it enforced though? Is it something that is forgiven?

Tara: In Indian society, a woman who remained without a husband is an outcast. Very early, your parents have to secure a husband for you. The marriage is arranged. Unless your parents have X amount of money for dowry, the daughter will not get accepted.

Q: What if the marriage is arranged, and the family cannot come up with the money. What happens in this relationship, what happens to these women?

Tara: Well! The parents keep trying for another family to marry the women. Or sometimes a lot of people do commit suicide because of that. And not only will the daughter do it, sometimes the parents will go that far because they just don't know how to face the world.

Q: How much support can the women expect, before they reach the point of committing suicide? What are some of the problems the women encounter on a day-to-day basis?

Tara: A lot of things, it's like we're all living in a village. The prospective groom might be living right next door. Before you know it, the news is all over the town. Gossips abound. The family feels humiliated. Sometimes, they end up killing themselves.

Q: What about domestic abuse? I have heard that almost every Indian wife has been victim of one form of abuse or another at some point in her lifetime. Is that too much of a generalization?

Tara: Domestic abuse is a serious problem. Even when the situation does not end up in bride burning, dowry harassment is not uncommon. I personally haven't experienced it, but if you are living in the Indian community, it is hard not to encounter a woman who has not been abused. On the other hand, harsh treatment by males is not always recognized as abusive. Women have a much lower status in Indian culture. Their role in the running of the affair of the family is not seen as very important. So I feel that they don't get to voice their opinion as much as they should.

Q: Is this domestic violence viewed as an offshoot of this inferior status? Is that carried over to the country of migration? Is there as much violence in an Indian family living let's say in New York?

Tara: I really don't think so. After a while, Indian men realize that they are living under different rules in America and that they might face swift penalty.

Q: Is it because of education or the acculturation process?

Tara: They have picked up the good things from moving out of India and then try to keep the good parts of what they were taught.

Q: How about your own experience?

Tara: First of all, as a child, my marriage was arranged, so I'm going to tell you my experience. As a child, my parents taught me not to date, so I never thought of having a date, and we were not exposed to television or parties or stuff like that, so it never bothered me as a child. And the way it works is that my parents will look for a family that they think has good background. In the older days, they may even see if they want dowry. They'll find out if they are looking for dowry because some families might make it known that they only want a girl if they have X dowry or whatever. So my parents looked for a family that had good background. To them, that was the most important factor. And then they found out more about the boy in the family that they were trying to match me with. And once that step was completed, it was officially announced. A meeting is then arranged. In my family, I would not even think of challenging what my parents would say. I don't think I would have said no even if I didn't like him. They did give me a choice. My parents didn't have a choice. So it has changed already, that one generation.

Q: Tell me if you can, how your personal experience turned out? After all, this man was a complete stranger that you did not really fall in love with...

Tara: Very difficult. I don't think I would want my daughter to go through it. Because first of all, I was brought up in Africa, like I said, and my parents found this family in America for me. First, I had to change countries. I didn't know anything about America. And then they got me married in a month after I moved to America. Before I could get acquainted with my groom, I had moved in with him.

Q: How old were you?

Tara: I had just turned twenty. And I didn't know how-to live-in America; I didn't know his parents. First of all, we all lived together. Soon after the marriage, I had to follow him. The son always stays close to his own family. To this day, I live with my in-laws right now. There I was, living in a totally different household with different parents. Everything I did or said was scrutinized. Who was that strange girl who came in their family to steal away the heart of their beloved, cannot-do-no-wrong son? You don't know how they're going to behave with you. If your family made an error in investigating your husband's family background, you are doomed. You pay the consequences. It was very difficult for me to communicate with my husband because I really did not know him.

Q: How long have you been married now?

Tara: It has been fifteen years.

Q: How have things progressed over the years?

Tara: I would say that the first four years were spent getting to know him and the family and getting used to the idea that this is what it is all about. And then I think I slowly started accepting him and loving him the way he was. But it took time. And this is what I meant when I said that Indian women are strong.

Q: To be able to put up with it?

Tara: To put up with this, right. From my experience, I feel that if it was a woman from another culture in my place, she probably wouldn't have put up with what I did.

Q: When you get in a relationship, you have expectations. What were yours?

Tara: In my case it was difficult because as I was growing up, my parents never really let me think in that direction, just go to school, learn, etc. etc. And then the only thing that they taught me was that you were going to get married and the husband was going to take care of you. So I never had expectations that I was going to be a doctor or lawyer or whatever. Whatever my family made me do is what I was supposed to do. But it has changed during the fifteen years.

Q: And you feel that you have a fulfilling relationship in all aspects? Do you know what I mean? I understand you are an accountant?

Tara: Can a relationship ever be fulfilling? Professionally, I'm a bookkeeper, I would say that I am fairly happy.

Q: How common is it for Indian women to engage in extramarital affairs when they feel stuck in a relationship they had no control over?

Tara: I think it is a matter of choice. The opprobrium that a woman would bring upon herself and her family is always a consideration. Most women will try to accept their husband the way he is. You accept and love the good parts about it. You have to start forgiving what you don't like. You keep on going. You hope that the marriage will last without going through the trauma of an affair or a divorce. But things are changing. I mean, I personally have heard a lot of families having problems like that. The rate of divorces is on the rise.

Q: Let's go back to what you said before about the fact that when you are born a woman in India you are doomed and will be perceived as inferior.

Tara: Right now, I have only two girls and my husband has never said anything like that. I don't think he believes that my daughters are inferior. I cannot say the same about the way my in-laws may feel. Maybe, they would have been happier if I had another boy. It just shows that they are still thinking in the old ways, that girls are inferior. They believe that a boy will probably carry your name. I have to agree, many people think that women belong in the kitchen. That's the culture we are living in.

Q: I have read some awful things about the way female fetuses are systematically destroyed as soon as sex determination is completed. Do you know about this practice?

Tara: Like I said, I haven't stayed or lived in India for a long time so I can't tell you what's happening in India, but I have read and I have heard that, yes, it does happen.

Q: How about the caste system?

Tara: That's the thing. I told you how my parents went to look for me to get married? They only looked for a boy who was in the caste. If, for example, I was westernized, I would say to my parents, "Okay, no, I don't want to marry what you chose, I want to marry this person that I met." Even though he's Indian, but he's not from my caste, it will not be accepted.

Q: How many castes are in your culture?

Tara: I think about 70 or 90. There is a lot. And if you're an Indian, you can, by the way they talk, the way the dress, you can tell what kind of level from the caste system they are.

Q: What is the basis for the caste system?

Tara: It is originally religiously based. The caste one is born into depends on one's karma. Karma is the total of good and bad deeds that one accumulates in his/her previous life. Of course, since India is a very religious country, your religious standing determines your social standing and your social standing determines your economic standing. If you are born a Brahmin, you have got it made. It is the highest of the four main groups. This caste has dominated all aspects of Indian life. But if you are born an "Untouchable," you are condemned to a life of abject poverty.

Q: Who are the untouchables?

Tara: They are considered the lowest caste basically. These are the people that do dirty work like picking up garbage. In this world everybody has to do something. That does not mean that that person is lower than the other person is. But in India, the caste system will make you feel that way.

Q: And what is the highest caste?

Tara: One of the highest ones that I consider and have known is called the Brahmins, they're like at the priest level, in the Hindu religion. And they are considered the cleanest. They have dominated everything from the economy to the reins of political power.

Q: So where do they live?

Tara: They live in the same neighborhoods, believe it or not, but they just have a different job. They go to the temple. They have an ascetic life. They believe in the principle of ahimsa or reverence for life. They have a vegetarian diet. As to the untouchables, they will eat whatever they can find, including meat. The higher is your level in this caste system, the closer you are to the one Hindu god, Brahma, the creator. Actually, Brahma is one of the divine trinity that also includes Vishnu, the preserver and Shiva, the destroyer. It is contradictory when you think about it. How could God classify you in different levels? The Brahmins enjoy their status and would not let you see it any differently.   They don't want to do anything with the untouchables.

Q: So the untouchables are like pariahs of society?

Tara: You could say that.

Q: So the religious system itself, the way it is now, has a lot of inequalities and contradictions? But is that any different from Christianity?

Tara: You are right, the class system seems to exist in every religion. Even though when you read the Jewish Talmud or Jesus' teachings in the Gospel, you have to conclude that God wants to see everyone as equal. I went to a convent school for two years in Africa. So I learned a lot about the bible. And when I look at it, I look at it in the same way as my Gita (short for Bhagavad-Gita).

Q: What is the name of it?

Tara: Bhagavad-Gita. It's considered our holy bible. It's basically an episode of the Mahabharata, a poem of 100,000 couplets, the longest ever written. In this book, Lord Krishna, the incarnation of Godhead Himself, spoke to his friend and devotee Arjuna. He teaches us through his words in a field where they are having a war between brothers and he's teaching us all about religious way, you know, like how to live, how to be honest. The world is seen as a place where harmony has to prevail between purusha and prakitti (person and nature).

Q: Can you tell about the meaning of the bindi and the different outfits?

Tara: I personally can only tell some of them, but if you lived in India, I'm sure with experience you would be able to tell. Like in the different areas, they wear different kinds of robes. You've seen my mother-in-law wear the sari? That you can automatically tell that she probably comes from this section of India. There is also the forehead mark called bindi. Women put that on and it's usually red, but today everybody does it for fashion. They put all different shapes and colors and everything to match their outfit, but originally that's what it's supposed to be for being married. And it would tell the other party, "Don't touch me, I'm taken." And I think that keeps a lot of problems from being, about having affairs and passing comments or anything like that. It really does make a difference.

Q: What about mobility in the Indian society, in terms of politics. Do you know of any women living in India who consider themselves to be "successful?"

Tara: The situation has changed significantly over the years. My mother got married at the age of 15. She never had a chance to go to school. She basically didn't have any expectations. I would say in the next generation, because of what the parents went through, they learned that education is better. They were able to get away from farming. They might be able to do something better for themselves. So they were forced to go to school. Today in India, more women go to school than ever before.

Q: Over the years, I have had the opportunity to meet a lot of Indian women in the fields of nursing or medicine. They seem to be drawn to the health care field. Any reason why?

Tara: Oh yes. I would say maybe not that many families are drawn to this field, where they could easily make a name for themselves. Let me put it this way, some families from some parts of India are more professional because they don't have any kind of business, they don't have any kind of land, so they only have their profession. So like if they come from a professional family, so then they are going to guide the children to go into that direction.

Q: Maintain the tradition within the family?

Tara: Exactly! My parents had a farm, so what did they do, or their grandparents had a farm, so they made sure that the daughter or the son knew how to cultivate so they get them married and then the next thing they knew they're just doing things on the farm. So it depends what kind of a background they're coming from. But I feel that yes, there are a lot of women who are in a lot of different kinds of professions.

Q: What about politics?

Tara: Politics? I'm not too much exposed to that in Indian women, but yeah, if you look at Indira Gandhi, she made it and I think she was a very powerful woman.

Q: Major changes never come without a revolutionary movement. Was there somewhat of an Indian woman movement or how did that come about?

Tara: There have been many movements in India. The whole Mahatma Ghandi movement has gone beyond the borders of India. It has been studied in universities around the globe. He is both admired and despised. His message of resistance with non-cooperation was to be non-violent. However, others portray Ghandi as someone who did not want to rock the boat and saw him as condoning the violence against women in a brutally patriarchal and oppressive society. They saw his movement as thwarting true revolutionary drives that would liberate the masses. His movement facilitated the transmission of power from the British colonialists to the Indian upper class without significant changes in the life of the masses and of women. The social movements of Ram Mohun Roy and Ishwarchandra Vidyasagar started up the first real fight against oppression of women in India. Widow re-marriage was made legal.

One cannot talk about politics in India without mentioning the impact of Indira Gandhi, who benefited from the political stature of her father Nehru.

I'm not much into politics in India, like I told you, I wasn't brought up there so I haven't kept up much with it. I have not abandoned my cultural and religious heritage, however. It is all around me.

Q: When one thinks about an Indian woman, one has the mental picture of a workhorse. Is it myth or reality?

Tara: I do not know about it being a myth. Indian women usually wake up at four o'clock in the morning. They go through some personal hygiene rituals. They clean themselves thoroughly because it is very important in our religion to take a bath. Then, they have prayers before sunset and right when the sun is rising. And after the sun rises, I think the religious part is over basically and then the day begins in India. In a typical village town, would be to start taking care of the house, prepare milk, lunch, and dinner. The first meal is served at about ten o'clock and then they all go to work. And then they would probably come back from the fields about three, four o'clock and they'll make dinner then and then they'll have prayers of the evening.

Q: What about raising children? Whose job is that?

Tara: As you probably guessed, it is basically a woman's duty to raise the children. The mother does it all.

Tara: So you are basically the keepers of this tradition, but when you don't like what's going on. How much pressure are you under to really keep things going in the same way?

Q: The pressure is tremendous. You just do it. You grow up and see your mother doing it all the time. You feel that you have to continue the tradition. Dad went to work and Mom was home with five of us. I come from a big family, and Mom was always there, taking care of us. My dad never participated in our care.

Q: So the women stayed home and take care of everything and everyone?

Tara: Oh yes. Nothing much has changed. They would come home from work and the table is ready for dinner. The wife will serve dinner to the husband and then she will sit down to eat. In India, the wife will never sit down to eat dinner with her husband, she has to make sure the husband is fed first and then she will eat.

Q: I have heard that if something should happen to the husband, say for example, the man takes sick, has a heart attack, the woman will get blamed for it. Is there any truth to that?

Tara: Oh yes, they feel that the woman brought the bad luck. They might say that maybe the woman was not the right person for that man, that she has failed in her duty to take good care of the man. There is also an element of superstition. It might be due to bad luck. And then if they are kind enough, they might say maybe it was just an accident.

Q: And then what happens to the widows?

Tara: This is the worst situation that an Indian woman might find herself in. Widows are thrown around, rejected. They are not treated properly. It is the same both in India and the States. Widows are not given the respect and attached to her status when she was a married woman. She is treated as if she was victim of a crime.

Q: And is there any such thing as a support group for widows?

Tara: I believe there is today, but I don't know how far that is. I believe they have support groups there in India now. But if you go into the villages, there's not much change. You'd have to go into a city to find any help.

Q: Do you have any hope that things will ever get better?

Tara: Yes, I think it will. Personally, if I had the means, I would go back and make changes in some families, using my own experience.

Q: If any changes are going to happen, it will be one person at a time? You do not foresee any major upheaval or revolution or anything like that?

Tara: No, not at all.

Chapter Twenty-Five
Intimidating, Attractive, and All Alone: Voice of
a "Single, Educated White Woman"

Women are staying home alone in record numbers. Both men and women are afraid to make a commitment to an enduring relationship. It is not for lack of trying. New strategies are being developed every day by date brokers to place interested people in each other's path. Single bars are out and cyberspace is in.[59] More and more women are choosing safety over spontaneity. Men are being asked to show how much brains they have before they have a chance to display their bulging pectorals and flattened abdominal muscles. The use of personal ads is on the upswing. Women are not afraid to say what they want. The list of requirements seems endless: Honesty, compassion, good communication skills, a sense of humor, ambition, status, and resources. Men value physical attractiveness and youth in a mate. It used to be a time when all a woman wanted was a hard working man who could take care of her material needs. He was expected to be a breadwinner, a craftsman, a husband, and when called by his country, a soldier. Women are now playing all these traditional roles, earning less than men do, but well over the 59 cents that prompted protests in the height of the second wave of the women's right movement. Increasing numbers of women are bringing home the bacon and earning much higher salaries than their husbands. Women no longer feel they have to seek refuge under the financial umbrella offered by a man. If the golden rule (the one who has the money makes the rules) still applies, women will soon be making all the rules. What a man wanted was someone who could take care of his culinary and laundry needs while he still had some degree of freedom to seek romance and adventures somewhere else. Men are intimidated by women's displays of success, education, and money. Today, although the vast majority of children continue to be conceived the old fashion way, daring alternatives are being taken. Single women, lesbian couples, and infertile women are experiencing the joy of single parenthood through artificial insemination and surrogate motherhood. The number of children being raised without the participation of a father is alarmingly high. On the other hand, fifty percent of marriages will end up in divorces.[60] An estimated three million couples are living together unmarried, yet this has had no positive effects on the divorce rate. According to a recent article from the Los Angeles Times, a sexual phenomenon that has known a period of lull due to the

---

[59] See McAllester, M. Reference No. 53
[60] See Sandroff, R. Reference No. 80.

AIDS epidemics is back, swinging. Swing clubs[61] are using the Internet to publicize their wild sexual parties where couples freely swap partners according to their own established etiquette. Women are calling the shots. To the estimated 3 millions members of those clubs, sex is a hobby, a sport. To them the freedom of polygamy is "mankind's natural state." This phenomenon is far from the monogamous and conventional sexual practices described by the authors of "Sex in America: A Definitive Survey." Many women are either not lucky enough to land a partner or not daring enough to attend swing clubs. They prefer to do it all alone, using a wide choice of love paraphernalia. In "Women Who Love Sex", Gina Ogden reports that 64% of women could reach orgasm without any physical contact.

The following interview gives voice to an educated woman. She is White, attractive, and successful, but she is single.

Q: Sarah, I've been on a quest about women's issues. I would like to hear your perspective about dating and relationships in this changing world. Would you tell me about your background?

Sarah: Background? Okay. I was born in New York. I lived there for 13 years, moved down to Florida at the beginning of

---

[61] See Maher A. Reference No.50

high school with my family. I have lived with both my parents. I have an older brother. I went off to college for four years, went on to graduate school for a year and a half. For the past twelve years, I have been working at a small private clinic as a social worker. I recently got my license as a mental health counselor in between. I am also in private practice.

Q: Quite a journey you have had! How has it been for you as a woman seeking knowledge and education, defining a career?

Sarah: Well, I think growing up I was encouraged to go on as far as education. It was just kind of expected that I would graduate high school and go on to college. It was never anything that I considered, to not go on. My family, my parents, had some college background. My mom is the oldest of her family, her younger brother and sister are college educated, so it was just kind of, just figured that that's what you would do, you would go on to college so I followed that path. I did enjoy school and I enjoyed learning. I was very into my books. I didn't hesitate to choose a field where I had to go on to graduate school in order to do anything with my degree. I have a degree in psychology because I was always interested in finding out about many things. That's just the way I've always been. I always wanted to be knowledgeable and just further myself as much as I could. I actually started out knowing that I wanted to get an advanced degree. I wanted a doctorate. When I got my masters, I was satisfied and decided to stop.

Q: Did you at any time feel that your choice was between the pursuit of a career and becoming a traditional woman with husband, children and a house to manage?

Sarah: Well, I think it had a lot to do with my family background.   Even though, it was a traditional Jewish environment, nothing was ever forced upon me. If you wanted to become an independent person and do your own thing, then that was fine. Personally I never really, I never met anyone that I was that involved with that I wanted to marry, choosing the career path was therefore easy. I was okay with that because that gave me my independence and made it okay that I didn't have to have a husband or a serious relationship to depend on to support me. And then I just kind of grew more and more independent. The more I was able to accomplish, the more empowered I became, saying to myself, "Gee, I can do this alone!"

Q: I notice, I cannot help but take notice, that you are a very attractive woman. Does that tend to intimidate people, the fact that (a) you are very attractive, (b) that you are educated? Is that a turn off to some people?

Sarah: Absolutely! I think that when men meet us, they expect that if you're attractive that you're not going to be educated. They imagine that they can have you around, that they can show you off to their friend. You're going to be hooked on your pager waiting for their call. They expect you will do exactly what they want you to do and to be totally dependent on them. They can take total control over your life. It's very difficult to meet men who want someone who is as independent as I am. They're very intimidated by that and they don't want someone who may be more educated or smarter than them. A lot of times, I find myself dating men who are in my professional circle. They're not as intimidated by someone who is as educated and attractive. Some men could not care less about the woman's lack of education. All they want is an attractive woman that could be used as a feather in their cap, to boost their fragile ego.

Q: Do you take offense to that?

Sarah: Of course! I think it's very sexist. I think women should be independent. I think women should be able to do what they want. I think that guys should not expect that some woman is just going to want to get married and have children and just want to rely on someone else. You would think that, from their perspective, a woman who wants to hold her own weight, have a job, and make a living would be valued. I think that some men just want to perpetuate the idea that women are property like in ancient times.

Q: It is a male dominated world. The old idea of women being fragile and weak, unable to stand on their own is still with us, isn't it?

Sarah: I think it starts with their own self-image and how they see themselves as men. If women can take care of themselves, what is there for the man to do? They almost feel emasculated. They feel useless and threatened, knowing that you have the education or that you have the skills to survive on your own. Maybe they were raised in traditional families thinking that women don't have those kind of skills and that they're brought up to get married and be in the husband's shadow, raise children, stay home, and keep house. And I think a lot of it is just the way you're brought up, traditional views.

Q: So it's been difficult to really find...No, let me turn the question around, what would an ideal man for you be like?

Sarah: I actually don't have the mental image of an ideal man. In fact I don't look for very much. Education is important. I mean, I'm not the kind though that if someone tells me he didn't go to college I will right away say, "I don't want to talk to you." I certainly look at people as who they are, not what kind of degrees they're carrying or what kind of job they have. I am not looking for a bum. Basically, if they at least have a job, because a lot of men down here in Florida I meet are very transient, a lot of them don't even work. They are just loafers.

Q: Are you likely to meet those guys in bars?

Sarah: Not always, you meet them everywhere. They have many lives. A lot of them you meet in bars. They might approach you while you are having dinner in a restaurant. They are just hanging out. That's it. That is their lifestyle. They just come and go.

Q: Would it be stereotyping to say that they go around on the beach hoping that they will be picked up by some rich woman? Are they modern times' American gigolos?

Sarah: Some of them are, yes. And I think that Florida attracts a lot of that just because of the climate here and also it's a lot of transplanted people, so you have a lot of people from everywhere coming and going all the time. It's not like up north, like in New York. A lot of the upstate people are born there, they stay there, and there are not too many people coming and going. I think Florida also attracts a lot of transients. Everyone is a transplant.

Q: But how do those people support themselves?

Sarah: I wish I knew. I mean, wow, how do they not work and they're surviving? I don't know. I personally think a lot of them must be into illegal stuff cause there's just no way you can survive down here without having any sort of income.

Q: Would you say that dating patterns have changed a lot recently?

Sarah: Well, obviously, traditionally the man would ask you out, the man would pay, and it was, they just kind set the pattern for a relationship. I think now its, you can be more conservative or you can ask a guy out or you can be more independent in a relationship, you can pay your own way or offer to pay his sometimes, you don't feel like you're insulting them if you do that. I know personally, I don't want someone who's going to always pick up the tab. It always make me feel like I'm obligated to them because I think then, in their minds, that in some way you are obligated to them when they do that. Going Dutch suits me just fine. I don't even mind paying the check sometimes. It is more acceptable that way and guys don't look down on it like they used to. I think they see you as liberated and equal in their eyes when you are able to do that.

Q: Have you ever been in a position where you asked a guy out?

Sarah: I've been in a position to, I don't necessarily to it. Should you ask them out, chances are they'd say yes. You better know what you are getting into. You have to feel comfortable doing it. If it was someone I just met, I probably wouldn't because I don't know that I would like that rejection.

Q: Have you ever been in a situation where you just knew that a guy was interested in you, yet would not ask you out? And what happened?

Sarah: This is the most unusual situation. Sometimes I might try to encourage him. I'd strike up a conversation or at least show I'm interested or I might just be too chicken and not do anything. I have blown many opportunities because of my own timidity. I would rather lose out than do something that I might end up regretting. So I just try and talk with them or give them some sort of sign of encouragement that I am interested so they don't think that I'm not personal.

Q: Would you characterize yourself as a typical single, educated, White woman?

Sarah: I think...Nah! I think I'm pretty typical. When I think about my friends, I think we're all the same in the sense that if we see someone we're interested in we might either ask them out or at least let them know that we're interested. We're not like traditional where we sit back and wait for the guy to say something. If he doesn't, oh well!

Q: Does that mean that you have to be yourself and do not hide the fact that you are educated?

Sarah: I think that it is a pretty much accepted fact that guys are intimidated and do lose interest when they find out that women are educated. Remember now that we are living in an era when women are outnumbering men on the college campus. Some men will not hide their resentment and might be frankly hostile.

Q: Do you think women of minority groups are experiencing the same problems? Let's say for example a Black, educated woman? Do you know?

Sarah: I know that it is the same. I mean, I've known plenty of Black, educated women that I've gone out with socially. I think it's the same exact situation for them. I think it's an education thing, not so much the culture that's intimidating for them.

Q: Why are women encountering all these problems all of a sudden?

Sarah: I think that it has to do with the feminist movement. Things have started to change. Women are being told to be stronger, to stand up for themselves and to be more independent. It all starts with education. How are women going to break the proverbial glass ceiling if they are not educated? Women understand that, while men are being complacent. The world has always belonged to them. They do not feel that they have to do a thing. The business world will belong to the educated person, male or female.

Q: How do you check yourself with your value system, if you will, as you are out there all exposed to this jungle?

Sarah: I'm very leery. I don't trust people I meet right away because I think there is a lot of characters out there that are very shady. I certainly will not reveal a whole lot until I feel comfortable. I wonder if it's someone that could be trusted or if it's someone just looking to scam something. I would say something like give me your number and I'll call you or I might give them my work number where it's a safe place to call me. I don't have to worry about being bugged. Because you just hear terrible stories and I don't trust people that I just meet if I don't know them.

Q: Can you tell me some of these tales?

Sarah: You would not believe the number of stalkers out there. Some of them are complete wackos. I've known people who have been stalked. It is very scary. Especially if you are living alone, you don't want somebody to show up at your door. A lot of times you go according to your gut feeling. I mean, I have a pretty good sense when I meet somebody whether or not I should proceed. I give myself some time. I like to at least get to know them. Besides, if I meet somebody and go out with them, a lot of times I might meet them somewhere neutral rather than have them come pick me up. If it turns into a disaster, I don't want them knowing where I live.

Q: Do you feel you have to walk around with your armor on all the time?

Sarah: Yes. A lot of times, I do. Well, I think the armor is always up at the beginning. As I get to know the person, I might want to take it down one layer at a time. I feel safe in a group, but when it comes to maybe having a one-on-one contact, that's when I have to be guarded and be careful.

Q: How do you support each other?

Sarah: That is where women are at a definite advantage over men. We women are not afraid to sit at the beauty parlor or at the club and scream loudly that life sucks sometimes. We are not afraid to meet and commiserate. My friends and I, we're all one big support system for each other. We feel that we are all in the same boat. And it helps a lot; just knowing that I have friends who are there for me. And we always, our mentality is just to go out and have a good time. If you go out thinking that you are going to meet someone, you're setting yourself up for disappointment. So you go out, have a good time, and if you meet someone or whatever, that's great. If not, at least we had a good time and were together. That was our goal in the first place. Dependent women feel that they have to meet somebody, they do not feel that they can exist, let alone survive, without somebody in their life.

Q: Is a South Florida man any different from men around the world?

Sarah: I have met men from other parts of the world while on vacations. Guys from other places do not seem as superficial and are not as intimidated by educated and independent women.

They seem to treat women with a lot more respect than the men I meet here.

Q: Whatever happened to the traditional South and all the chivalry that has been immortalized in movie classics like "Gone With The Wind?"

Sarah: I think Florida has been receiving people from everywhere. It's open gates. If the men were not exposed to their father treating their mother like with courtesy and gallantry, no way they are going to be able to display such qualities toward other women. A lot of those men have a lot of hang-ups. They would need to deal with that first. They don't have jobs or they're here for a while and then they're leaving or they're coming back, or they just don't know what they want. They don't have any direction.

Q: Where do you see things going?

Sarah: Some young women still go to single bars, although it seems passé. I really do not know where we are heading. People are meeting on the Internet. The newer bookstores are coming out with meeting and reading rooms, coffee terraces. I guess it will be the new popular trend.

Q: And then, there is the hunk factor. Some women do not like men who are into the intellectual stuff. They like men who just look good?

Sarah: Well, what I've seen from those situations is that those men aren't the same in the sense that they are looking for somebody and they don't want to have to be in the bar scene and take their chance with what they meet. They want someone that they know is interested in meeting someone, someone that's probably stable and educated and looking for the same things that they are.

Q: Isn't it the truth that if you are looking for a date in a library, you are likely to find nerds? Those men are probably interested in books, poetry, literature, and so on and so forth. Usually women don't go after those kinds of men. Women would go after the muscular, athletic, hunk type kind of men that one would most likely be catch on a beach?

Sarah: I think when you're younger that's what you look for. I think as you get older you look for different things and, well, you don't want someone nerdy, but you want at least somebody who does have other interests besides hanging out on the beach and lifting weights. So you want someone who does want to read or do something cultural rather than just hang out and do nothing and be cool all day and look good. I mean, it would be great to have all of the attributes in one individual, but chances are you're not going to get that.

Q: Are women around the world having the same problems?

Sarah: It is probably the case. I read like a lot of magazines that are geared toward women not necessarily single like Self, Glamour, Mademoiselle. The problem seems to be the same all over. But these magazines foster independence, empowerment, and self-actualization.

Q: Isn't it taking away the freedom of these women that chose to remain traditional and like their roles as mothers, housewives? For some women, hasn't feminism become a dirty word?

Sarah: I do not think women should give up their roles as mothers, but it should be by choice. Women, for the most part, remain responsible for educating the boys. If we give up, the next generation of men might even be much less sensitive and more superficial. Even so, I do believe that men do get better with age and embrace more of the nurturing and mothering qualities. I guess that they no longer feel that they have to hold on to their façade of bravado and machismo so characteristic of young, adult males. They're more tolerant of women who are independent and they realize that what they want is companionship. With maturity comes a lot of understanding.

Q: Let's talk a little bit about the stereotypes. How do you explain that women are usually described as easily confused, sensitive, very chatty and emotional? The word hysterical, for example, refers to an organ of women and I have seen some hysterical men during my career, yet the world refers to part of a woman's body. What do you make of that?

Sarah: I think for the most part is still very stereotypical that men do expect women to be exactly what you say. They are the products of their upbringing. Someone who has been raised in an environment filled with prejudices will have a hard time not espousing those views.

Q: It has often been said that the best wife that one could have would be a woman who has had a very good relationship with her father. What do you think about that?

Sarah: I don't think that only these women would be the best wives. But it certainly helps to have had such training. At least you learn how to get along and treat each other with respect. I think men are starting to be more accepting of a female being the equal partner in a relationship or marriage. I think that's probably the ideal and what people would like even though there are still a lot of people stuck in the old way.

Q: Do you see this plan toward more equality coming from legislation or do you see it coming from educating the masses, getting society to change?

Sarah: I think it is going to be from a combination of all the approaches. There is usually no legislation without some form of social activism. If the public is not educated, it will not support the right legislation.

Q: Affirmative action was designed especially for Blacks; women were included as minorities. Now it is being attacked from all angles. Is there any fear that some conservative group might attempt to reverse the progress earned by the women's right movement?

Sarah: That's a good question. The worst thing that could happen would be for women to forget how they got where they are today. The new wave of feminism should build the movement forward, not knock it down. Neither should the movement exclude the younger generations that might have different priorities and concerns than the less young guard. I think that the more educated people are, the better chance they stand of having their rights respected and their needs met. They can be part of the planning instead of having somebody else's decision pushed down their throat.

Q: The number of educated women is still relatively small in comparison to the large masses of uneducated women, isn't it?

Sarah: They're still a minority, yes. I think there are also a lot of women now who are older who didn't have that chance when they were younger. More and more women are realizing the benefits of education. I know a lot of women who are going back now and trying to get a degree because they don't want to be left behind. They want to seize every opportunity to better their life.

I know that a lot of barriers are yet to fall. Women are up against a giant wall. Everything that we learn is presented from a man's perspective.

A lot of the places are still very traditional. Some companies will still not allow women in some positions. And if they do, they often offer a lower salary to women. The rules of the game are set by men. Men decide what is normal, what is sick. Very few women are allowed to participate in research. They are excluded from trend setting positions. The bottom line is, women still have a long way to go before reaching equality.

Q: Any words of wisdom for a young White woman who is finishing high school and is about to embark into college life?

Sarah: I basically tell them that they need to stand by whatever it is that they want, that they shouldn't let people persuade them to do something differently. Do not shortchange yourself. Nothing of value comes easily. It might mean staying away from the "in" crowd. Tomorrow belongs to the educated.

Chapter Twenty-Six

Endangered and Fighting for Survival: Voice of a Black female Psychologist

There is major catastrophe in the making amongst Blacks. Although more African Americans are going to college today than at any time in America's history, Black men are lagging behind[62]. This can have very grave consequences. Black men will not be able to compete in the marketplace and will depend even more on women to raise the children and bring home the bacon. The landscape of the Black family will continue to deteriorate. Today, there are over 300,00 more women enrolled in college than men. Blacks, in general, earned fewer Master's Degrees. In 1992, Black women earned only 313 doctorate degrees in the field of education. Black men are seen as more of a threat than Black women are. When it comes to degrees requiring more interaction and competition with the traditional all White male cast of faculty members in Academia, Black women do not fare well at all. The odds that a student will see a Black face at the front of the classroom at the thousands of predominantly White institutions are about 50 to 1. Black women holding a doctorate in psychology are often kept out of the mainstream of research and are given little or no chance for advancement. The absence of Blacks in decision-making positions is particularly alarming since research on the population the Black doctors represent is likely to be conducted under the leadership of a White male professor whose agenda is not always clear and is seen with suspicion by minorities.[63]

Let us turn to the story of Dr. Carole Vincent, a Black female psychologist:

Q: I have been told that you are a rarity. How do you react to such comment?

Dr. Vincent: A rarity? That's true, there aren't very many of us, I think, and you probably have all the statistics on how few Ph.D.'s are awarded to Blacks in the United States, let alone Black women, and, even smaller than that, Haitian Black women. So there are just a handful of other Black psychologists, including Haitian women, that I know in the South Florida area and even throughout the country that I know of.

Q: It must take a lot of guts and a lot of effort to get there. Can you tell me a little bit about how you got there?

Dr. Vincent: Yeah, I don't know if it takes so much guts as perseverance. I mean you have to always believe that the time you put in is worth more than if you stopped in the middle. Like

---

[62] See Slater Robert Bruce. Reference No. 83
[63] See Goldsby R. A. Reference No'29

it doesn't pay to start something and then not finish it. So, I think the biggest thing is being able to stick with it and having a belief that pursuing the Ph.D. is something that's important, that it will give me flexibility. Once I finish, I can use my skills to help other people.

Q: Before we get into the making of a Ph.D., of a Black woman, Haitian, Ph.D., why don't you tell me a little bit about your background and maybe that can help me understand how you get to embark on such a difficult journey.

Dr. Vincent: I was born in Haiti, but I left Haiti when I was very young. I was three years old. So I have a lot of memories. My parents had difficulties with the Duvalier regime. Which educated professionals didn't? They fled the country and they left my brother and myself behind with some relatives. I have a brother who's about 18 months younger than I am. And they moved around a lot. They lived here in the United States, then they moved to Algeria, Africa. We later joined them there. I have vivid memories of the situation. We were all worried that the regime would take reprisals against us, because our parents had left the country and did not come back. In that era, it was an act of defiance to abandon Duvalier's revolution. We lived in Algeria for about three years or maybe until I was like six or seven. And then we came to the United States. I remember when I first came here I experienced what you would call a culture shock. Even as young as I was, it was extremely difficult. I didn't know the language. It did not take long for me to master the basics of the English language. I was finally able to play with the other children on the playground. I watched a lot of television. I received my share of discipline from Catholic school. Of course, I always wished that I could go to public school because it always seemed like much more fun and freedom than Catholic school was. I was always very intelligent and so I always felt the responsibility to do something with that. People would tell me, "Oh, you should be a doctor," or whatever and I thought that I wanted to go into medicine, but I couldn't stand the sight of blood. To this day, I still consider myself a bit squeamish. Whenever I see a cut or some kind of injury or someone getting stitches, I get very light-headed and I pass out. So, even during one of my internships in psychology, I was in the hospital doing a pediatric rotation and I had to assist a child who was going through a spinal tap. Well, he did fine and I fainted. I didn't think it was realistic for me to go into medicine. But, being Haitian, you don't really hear very much about psychology and psychiatry. I mean you hear about people losing their mind and labeled as crazy, but you don't hear about anybody who does anything about that. So that, it would never even have even entered my mind to really follow that as a, to follow this as a career, you know, when I was young.   I never heard of psychology or psychiatry until I was in high school and a friend of mine went to, my friend's older sister was going to college and she was majoring in psychology and I'm like what is that? Why did she major in psychology? And so she told me about it and she was saying that you learn about what makes people do the things that they do and I was like, "Hey, you know, I always wanted to know why people did the things that they did." So that was the first time I ever heard of it and was interested in it, but I still didn't know anything very much about it. I didn't know what it took or the ins and outs of what was involved.

Q: What are the ins and outs?

Dr. Vincent: Well, you have to dedicate a lot of years to getting the degree. You know that you have to write a dissertation, take a lot of courses, and do an internship. Those steps that I was unfamiliar with. And even when I went to college, I majored in psychology. Actually, I didn't start off majoring in psychology, I started off majoring in biology, but then I took a psychology course as an elective and I liked it. It was like, wow! This is very interesting. They've done all this research and have figured things out about what makes people do the things that they do, what makes people act the way they act. So then I decided to major in psychology and that's when I found out more about the requirements of, you know, what you would have to do if you wanted to have a career in psychology.

To become a psychologist, you had to go to graduate school with a bachelor's degree in psychology. One cannot do much with a bachelor's degree, except working as a mental health technician in an inpatient hospital and things like that. But at the time I was graduating from college and I was tired of school, so I just didn't think that graduate school was in me. How was I going to write a dissertation? I can't write a book. Like, it was beyond me. And I just didn't want to go to school anymore, I wanted to work and make some money. I got a job working in a lab and I used to work nights. That was interesting. I worked the 1 AM to 9 AM shift.

Q: The graveyard shift?

Dr. Vincent: Yeah, graveyard. Doing lab analyses on blood and other specimens. At first it was quite an interesting experience but soon it became boring because it was pretty repetitive. So that's when I started thinking about well, maybe I should go to graduate school.

Q: Did your family pressure you in any way? I understand that your father is a physician?

Dr. Vincent: Yes, he's a pediatrician. And I think that that influenced me. They really valued education. I don't think any of us could get away without a professional education. So I became confident that I had the capabilities and that I should put my talents to good use.

Q: So how many years did it take you to get where you are today?

Dr. Vincent: (Laughter) I'm still getting there. It wasn't like a continuous trajectory. I started at one graduate school. I took courses here and there. I went to something else. And then finally I had received a program from the University of Miami program about pediatric psychology. I became very enthusiastic. It was about the time when there was a lot of talk about Hale House, Mother Hale, that lady who had taken in all these babies born to drug addicted mothers. These children were having all kinds of developmental problems. I felt pediatric psychologists could make a difference in the life of these unfortunate children. I had found my calling. There was no looking back. I had been involved in different research projects when I was an undergraduate in New York at Columbia and also at NYU working with the kids with special needs population. When I saw the brochure about the pediatric program, it sounded like exactly what I wanted to do. I applied right away and got accepted. I took two years of course work. I mean the graduate school experience was hellish. There are no objective criteria for measuring your success. It's all very subjective; it's all very political. You are at the mercy of a faculty member who is typically White and male with all his prejudices and biases. You have to really fit into some kind of ill-defined mold of a Ph.D. You have to be let into the ranks, a White male club. It was hell.

Q: Was it particularly difficult for you because you are a Black woman?

Dr. Vincent: Absolutely! The faculty members were, at the very least, insensitive to racial issues and, at the very worst, downright racist. When I first entered the program they had only graduated like three Blacks from the program, from the Psychology Department at UM. So in the class that I came in there were two other Blacks. That was like the largest group of Blacks that they had admitted ever into the program.

Q: So what did that affect you in terms of peer support or faculty support for that matter?

Dr. Vincent: Well! It didn't, it didn't affect us much. As far as the other students were concerned, it was fine. I had had plenty of opportunities through college and high school to interact with White students. In fact I felt that I was more comfortable around White students than they were around me. I lived in the dorms on campus and there were floors assigned to graduate students. We got to know each other very well. As far as support from the faculty, I think the Black students that came in were ignored. We were just totally ignored. It felt almost as if, the Black students were allowed in the circle because of funding opportunities. The double-edged sword of affirmative action was having its effect on us. Since fellowships and scholarships were available for Black students, we were accepted. At least, that is how the White students and faculties make us feel.

Q: But they are also using you to boost up their census?

Dr. Vincent: Sure. It makes them look good to benefactors that they have Black students attending their school. In their mind, they were doing us a huge favor. A White professor commented once that I was fortunate and that I should take advantage of the opportunities extended to me. As if we were getting away with something for free. Believe me, we earn every little bit of the degree we received. Once you complete your courses, your troubles are not over. You then have to meet research requirements, teaching requirements. You have to have the practicum experiences, complete your master's thesis and dissertation and do an internship. After all of that you finally get the degree and then you have to beg for licensing. It never ends. There is always another hurdle to overcome.

Q: As a Black female psychologist, do you find yourself having to prove that you are indeed qualified?

Dr. Vincent: Well, you have to fight. You have to constantly bring to people's attention that you are being pigeonholed into working only with one type of population. So if there's a variety of clients that are being seen, then you'll see a variety of clients.

Some bigot who will see you as only capable of engaging in ethnic-specific counseling program. It is up to you to resist.

Q: This poses a real dilemma. If those clients didn't have you as a Black psychologist, wouldn't they run the risk of getting lost between the cracks?

Dr. Vincent: It's a struggle to balance my empathy for Black clients, especially for Haitian clients, who are not used to the system. They are less likely to get adequate services. I have to struggle to balance my empathy for them and my so-called professional neutrality. We are tempted to overcompensate for the deficiencies of the system. The Haitian client expects his doctor to touch him, to listen to his heart, to take his blood pressure, and to advocate for him. A psychologist might feel limited by the need to keep professional boundaries. It is a balancing act.

Q: What about developing a clientele?

Dr. Vincent: This is extremely difficult. White clients are not as likely to spontaneously choose to see a Black therapist. It is an uphill battle for most Black psychologists to generate a referral base, to have a steady flow of private practice clients. I know of very few Black psychologists who are able to make a living on full-time private practice.

Q: How about the notion that the whole field of psychology is based on or has been based on data gathered on the White, middle-class population. When you try to apply the findings to Black population, don't you feel that you are betraying your own people?

Dr. Vincent: I feel very ambivalent. On the one hand I feel that research is important. In theory, it's an important concept. Unless we, as Black people, participate in and are in charge of the research, we will have to live with whatever findings some unscrupulous, tenure seeking, faculty member concocts for us. So I feel that I have the responsibility to stay involved in it. At least with some involvement in research I will be able to monitor, to the extent that I can, what is being said about people that look like me and probably feel and behave like me.

Q: But isn't there a risk of being used as a token to secure funding and then being discarded?

Dr. Vincent: Absolutely. That happens every day. You are a token. Very few departments will hire two Blacks in the same program. So I'm hired as a token and I am expected to play the part.

Q: Do members of the dominant culture pay attention to what you have to say?

Dr. Vincent: I think that that's an everyday reality that I'm not taken seriously because I hold a minority viewpoint or I'm female or I'm Black or I'm Haitian. There's always an asterisk next to any opinion that I give because it's colored by that world's view. People generally hear what they want to hear and so when you are trying to tell them something that is universal, something that is common across people and situations, they tend to hear it as, "Oh, that is just her complaining."

Q: How much, in looking at a Black person, can you tell how much is universal and how much is color? Or is that the right question to ask to a psychologist?

Dr. Vincent: Wow! That's really interesting. In my point of view a lot of it is color determined. That the color we are really shapes our worldview because we experience different things being Black than we would if we were of a different race. There are a lot of commonalties of experience among humans, but the differences that are there are reinforced by the color differences.

Q: Give me an example.

Dr. Vincent: Well, let's see. Just the way that people react to a certain, to different events. For example, a parent is told that her child is not doing well in school. A Black parent who hears that hears a lot of other things besides just the fact that their child is not doing well at school. They have to wonder if the teacher racist. Is the child being given the same opportunities as the other children? What other things might be causing the child not to do well in school other than just his academic inability or a weakness in a certain area. A White parent might not automatically raise the same questions. When I hear the news that a Black person has done X, Y, or Z, I have to wonder, "Hmmm, is it really true?" It would be foolish not to question the information because there is so much mistrust. It has been said that it is the normal defensive attitude for a Black person to be paranoid given the amount of racism that over the centuries that Black people have been exposed to. If you don't question reality or you don't question facts that are put in front of you, then you're really being naive or in denial. You see that for the same offense a Black child will get ten days suspension and a White child will have to stay after school one day. You see that the police are more defensive when faced with Black teenagers than they are with White teenagers. You see yourself experience getting pulled over or stopped because you're in a White neighborhood at night or something like that. So until you experience it and you see how unfair and strange racism can make people, then you don't really understand it.

Q: What do you say to young men and women who might be thinking about following your steps?

Dr. Vincent: You really have to be able to delay gratification. You incur a lot of debt while you're studying and the financial payoff is way down the line, if at all. I think that there is a need for more Black psychologists, definitely, because a lot of Blacks that do get psychiatric or psychological treatment are being served by others who have no understanding of our culture or the different reactions that may or may not be pathological. There is a lot at stake here. Our communities are facing so many problems and we need to be able to offer some fresh understanding and figure out some solutions from a culturally competent perspective.

Q: Isn't it true that we always know them better than they know us?

Dr. Vincent: Absolutely! As a Black professional, you have to be bicultural. You have to be able to operate within the Black systems that you grew up in, but also within the White systems because really, going into a professional degree, what you are doing is entering into something that they created. Especially in the academic circles, it's really an ivory tower that they allow some one or two people entry into it. So you have to learn their game. They don't have to learn the rules of our game because they're not interested in entering our system.

Q: Should we then say that you are like an endangered species?

Dr. Vincent: Endangered? Yeah! Probably, probably! I don't see many more people registering. I don't know if the world has changed so much that people are not embarking on such an uncertain journey with undetermined outcome. Maybe they are out for something quicker. I just don't see a lot of people making the same choices. Not Black women at any rate. I mean, there's still, the graduate schools aren't going to go out of business because there are still plenty of others that are interested in doing that, but I think it will continue to be just a very few of us who go through it.

Chapter Twenty-Seven
Beating the Odds: Voice of a Woman Executive

Esther is Director of Nursing in a mid-sized, private hospital in South Florida. She is White, educated, and attractive. Maybe that is all she needed. Not by a long shot, Esther had to work every step up the corporate ladder. It is true that she displays all the attributes that are valued by the patriarchal system. She is forceful, independent, and assertive. She is a born leader who can take initiative, give orders to a large crew of middle management personnel, show support to a frustrated nurse who is threatening to quit, while displaying the logic-based skills necessary to see a project through from beginning to end. Esther has not given up any of her more traditional attributes. She is very coquettish and her makeup is always impeccable. Even though women have been shown to be better planners and to show better general cognitive ability, (the so-called G factor), and higher degree of motivation, only two percent of chief executive officers of major U. S. corporations are women.

Let us turn to Esther whose voice is about to tell us a tale of energy, motivation, and breaking away from sterile expectations.

Q: What is it about you that made you a success story, where many others have failed.

Esther: Looking back, I think that it is my ability to consider the whole picture while paying attention to details.

Q: Okay! That is very good. Tell me first a little bit about your background.

Esther: I have been a nurse for 18 years. I started off as a staff nurse. I got my degree in Nursing and then worked my way through school. I've been going to school my whole adult life. I have gotten two Masters, one in Education and the other in Counseling. My original interest was to teach and educate women since it was primarily a female dominated field at the time. I wanted to empower women. Quite a few of them were single women with children. Education was their only way towards independence and self-reliance. I wanted them to take on the challenge. If their male siblings could pursue higher education, why should they have to stay home with the children? I saw myself as the person that was going to enable them to move forward.

Q: I understand, but why a Master's in Counseling?

Esther: Because I knew that would go hand in hand with education and I needed to learn the skills to be able to teach and have an impact on women's life in a very non-threatening way.

Q: Tell me about the kind of support you received from your own family.

Esther: Initially, I did not receive a lot of support from my parents. By age 21, I was already married for about 1½ years and attending school. Soon I realized that I had gone into the marriage for all the wrong reasons and that I had to get out. My family was devastated. My parents were very old fashioned. They were typical Europeans. No one in my family had ever been divorced. No one! I was the first.

Q: What is your background?

Esther: I am Jewish. My parents were foreign born. I was born in Germany. The women in a foreign, European family are seen and not heard. That is not what Esther was about. So they told me that if I left or got divorced, I would be an outcast. So here I was with no money and a small child, divorced, ready to face the world, alone. I said, "See ya!" This is what I need to do for myself. They didn't want me to go back to school. They didn't want me to be educated. My brother is a doctor. Yes, he wanted to be educated; they wanted him to be educated, but he's a male. Males in our society are treated a lot differently than females are treated. I moved forward and on my own I left my family for about six months and proceeded to continue my education. I worked hard. I got some food stamps. My family had money. I was cut off. I was without a car. I took my daughter to school on my bicycle and dropped her off, took the bus, and continued my education. Eventually my parents came back into my life. They bought me a car. They can be very controlling.

Q: They also wanted to associate themselves with success. By then you had started to become successful?

Esther: Right, but they were ashamed that I was divorced. They were ashamed of me and they were ashamed of themselves. I had to show them that they didn't need to be ashamed, they could be proud of me that I didn't need to necessarily be married with the traditional family – husband, wife, two children – to be successful in life.

Q: Wait a minute. You are saying that you don't need to be the traditional husband, wife, and children. What's wrong with that?

Esther: There's nothing wrong with it, but at that particular time, it did not seem right for me. I felt that I needed to be my own person and my own boss. I needed to make my own decisions on how I was going to raise my daughter or run my life. I would rather be alone and grow by myself and learn and make my own mistakes. My life didn't stop because I was divorced. My life didn't stop because I had a child to feed.

Q: Let's talk about tradition. You said that your family is very traditional. Can you expand on that for me?

Esther: Yes. Everyone in my family, my parents are European. As I said, I was born in Germany, my brother was born in Russia, and if you know anything about European men, they can be extremely very bossy. They make all the rules. There is no talking back to a father, they just look at you crooked and you just sit there.

Q: And melt?

Esther: And melt. There is no bartering. There is no talking back. You don't say, "Don't tell me what to do," like kids do now because you would have got one backhand and that would be the end of that. My father really didn't hit me that much because I was a good child, but I had a behavioral problem as a child. English was my third language so I was passive-aggressive. If I didn't want to follow the teacher's instructions, I would pretend I didn't understand what she was saying to me.

Q: So you spoke German and...

Esther: I spoke German and Russian and Yiddish, which I still speak fluently. And English was my third language. And I had an older brother and English was his third language as well. So it was a little hard for us when we came here. But little girls were seen and not heard. You just did what your Mom and Dad told you to do. You came home from school and you had your chores. I couldn't go bike riding and I couldn't go roller-skating, I couldn't do any of those things that little boys do. But behind my parents' backs I did it and I always got caught and I was always punished and I was always in trouble because I was a little tomboy. And I would ride my brother's bike, he was four years older than me, and I would steal his bike out of our basement. I would go in and break the lock off. He didn't even know that I was picking it and I would take his bike and I would ride for hours and nobody knew until I got caught. And then I got into trouble.

Q: Girls were not supposed to engage in these kinds of behavior?

Esther: Exactly! You were not! You were supposed to be in a nice, neat dress. I went with my parents wherever they went. My brother could be off doing what he wanted, but I could not do any of those things. Girls in my family were not allowed to engage in sports. If I got B's in school, it was okay. They expected my brother to get A's. And my parents thought that I didn't understand what was going on. I was a rebel. I would defy my mother instructions not to jump off the twelve-foot fence just to show everyone that I could do it. I constantly had to prove that I could be just as good as my brother. It was so unfair.

Q: And then you made it all the way out of college and two Masters...

Esther: Yes, with straight A's!

Q: And then, and then what? Obviously getting degrees is not all there is. You have to make it to the corporate ladder. You have to make it to the day-to-day routine of work. How was that for you?

Esther: When I first worked as a staff-nurse because I needed to support my daughter, I went to school full-time. Six months after I graduated from nursing school, I got promoted to assistant head nurse. They saw leadership qualities in me. They saw communication abilities. I got along great with the physicians. I loved taking care of my patients. I was a little bit unique in nursing. I liked spending time with my patients. So I was immediately promoted, then I went to work in a critical care setting for about two years, and then I became a director in the operating room, first of one service and then of three services and then of the whole operating room. And then I did some supervision. They asked me, "Would you like to work one weekend as a house supervisor over the whole house?" I said, "Well, I don't know." They said, "Well, we'll give you an orientation." They spent about an hour with me and then I went to house supervision and then I just decided to apply for an administrative executive position in another facility. In my mind I thought I could do it. I had my fears. I got the job and I stayed there for about five years. And that's when I just kept climbing the corporate ladder. Headhunters were always calling me. But I never really had to look for a job. Jobs always came my way.

Q: Being a nursing director involves a lot of politicking.

Esther: Yes, in most places where I have worked it involved a lot of politicking. It involved a lot of nose rubbing against powerful people, men and women.

Q: Tell me how that has been for you.

Esther: Well! I made it a point to stay on top of the advances in my field. When it came time to participate in clinical discussion with the doctors and other members of the team, I could give my input. So I make sure that my clinical skills stay current. When you are ready to participate in all codes and remain comfortable in a crisis situation, you earn the respect of your colleagues.

Q: But not every director of nursing that I have met, male or female, not every director of departments that I have met, male or female, had to have that much qualification.

Esther: No, they don't. I am a very energetic person. If one can combine knowledge plus motivation, your chances for success are multiplied manifold. Nurses cannot afford to look shaky and uncertain. This can only perpetuate the stereotype of the nurse who dresses to kill but has little knowledge about anything.

Q: What do you mean?

Esther: Well, I think physicians think that nurses are not logical thinkers and that nurses tend to be disorganized. Physicians have called nurses names like "birdbrain", "empty-headed", and all kinds of horrible things. Nurses are the backbones of any hospital and they get no respect.

Q: But I've never known of any unit of any department run by physicians without the strong support of a well-trained nursing staff.

Esther: Okay, and that's a wonderful thing to hear from you, but unfortunately, this is not what you hear from most physicians. They know that they need us, but they get angry very easily with us. Whenever something goes wrong, the nurses are the first to be blamed.

Q: What I hear you say is that you needed a lot of qualities. You need leadership qualities. You need a lot of self-confidence to know that when you are talking, you are talking as an expert, but you also need to be able to set limits on people.

Esther: Absolutely!

Q: How many women, how many nurses would accumulate all of those qualities together?

Esther: Not many! I think that some could do the first, could have the leadership ability and they certainly are smart, but you said one key word and that's self-confidence. Nurses often let the male physicians intimidate them. Often they see the physician as a father figure and they are just ready to melt in front of him. They could know everything from A to Z on that patient and they all of a sudden go blank. Their self-confidence goes down the tubes as they get frightened. Rarely will you see a nurse stand up to a doctor and set some limits.

Q: So are you telling me what's happening on their unit, the interaction between that physician and that unit, is a mirror image of what's going on out there in society.

Esther: You are absolutely right. It's not any different from a situation with a male teacher, a male supervisor. My father owns a business in New York and I can talk about his male workers and what their attitude toward me was.

Q: What could be their attitude towards you? You are the daughter of the boss.

Esther: Exactly, and the daughter of the boss is so pretty and "Hi," and we just say hi to her and she's so pretty, "Oh, you look so nice today." The daughter of the boss doesn't have to think. The daughter of the boss can't be, you know, she probably just stays home and counts Daddy's money. She can't have a brain of her own. But the son is a doctor, you know, the son, we know what the son does, the son is definitely a doctor. And even my father and very often this would frustrate me as a child where I'd be going to school for my Masters and my father would say to me, "You finish with another degree? What exactly do you do?" But he knew exactly what my brother did, but did he know exactly what I did? No, he didn't. Was he interested? Maybe, but she's just a woman, why does she keep going for all these degrees, how smart do you want to get? So he...

Q: So there is a glass ceiling as to how smart a woman can get, is that what you are saying?

Esther: Exactly, where's my glass ceiling pin? I don't have it on today. I have one.

Q: Oh, you really have one?

Esther: Yes. Well, for very many years, this is a good time to tell you, I was very much in the feminist movement and I marched in Washington on nursing issues very often. I was very, very verbal about my profession and my career. We were unionized when I was in New York. I was the union leader for a year for the New York State Nursing Association. I was often involved in disputes and conflict resolution. I was very successful usually in helping the nurses keep their job.

Q: I know that there has been a lot of attrition, a lot of burnout, what do you attribute this problem to?

Esther: I think there are many things right now. Nurses are being asked to take on different tasks. Staff is being cut back. I think nurses are expected to do much more in terms of paperwork and they have gotten away from the bedside and that's very frustrating to them. I think nurses want to nurse. I think nurses want to be there for the patient. And even though documentation is important, we are somehow, because of reimbursement purposes, if we don't have the documentation, we don't get paid, we are taken away from the patient and the needs of the patient and that is very frustrating to people that go into nursing. That's number one. Number two: Patients, physicians, family members, colleagues, and administration abuse nurses. How long do you think we want to sit and do that for? When we don't get, and what you hear most of the time is the lack of support from administration. Any nurses who want to leave are invited to meet with me. I go carefully over their situation and make some suggestions to improve it. Often times they end up changing their mind. People who are not in the field have no ideas how hard nurses work. When these women get home, they have to be mothers and wives. Can you imagine?

Nursing is no longer that profession that people want to go into. The glamour is gone. The pedestal has been kicked out from under the nurses' feet. Women are finding out that they can get into a less demanding career and have as much, if not more, financial rewards. Women are educating themselves much more; there are more women in medicine and law than ever before. When I was growing up, it was very rare. I worked in a medical college part-time; there were hardly any women in the program at all. Hardly ever did you see Jewish women in this field. Jewish women don't go into nursing.

Q: Where do they go?

Esther: They go into medicine. Jewish women go into medicine and law. They go into – they're not taught to clean and scrub and – No, no, no, my fingernails! No, Jewish women need to make reservations. I mean, all of my relatives, I'm the only nurse in my family. I am the only nurse in my family. For a long time my family looked at me with pity. "Esther the lowly nurse," while everybody else was super duper professional. Now, I inspire respect because they finally see me as successful. I have the title of Director of Nursing; I have a beautiful house in Boca Raton. I drive a nice, big, new Cadillac. I have all the material signs of success. Suddenly, it is okay for me to be single.

Q: I know that in a large institution Nursing is like a block out of many to create a puzzle. To make it all fit, there needs to be interaction with the other blocks. How difficult has it been for you as a woman?

Esther: The relationship has been very positive. Other members of the executive team have been extremely receptive. Pretty much I can do what I want. I have the latitude and the freedom to go out and see physicians if I need to. I can up someone's salary, I can lower it, I can keep, fire, hire, bring in an extra body if I need to, and I sit on committees where I have a voice and that's important to me. I don't have to say (in a small voice), "Excuse me, may I offer my opinion." I don't have to do that here, the physicians are receptive to me, and the medical exec committee is receptive. I sit on a surgical case review committee that reviews the management of cases by physicians. I'm the only nurse that's allowed to sit at that meeting so I feel very fortunate and I feel very good about moving in the direction that I would like to move in.

Q: When you go to regional or national meetings, do you get a sense that other nurses in similar positions are having it that easy?

Esther: No. They have problems communicating, primarily with getting physicians to see what is the...How can I say this positively? They don't feel like they're part of the team, I do. I feel like I'm part of the team. Like they'll ask for their help and input, but it is just a formality. They do not really want to listen to what nurses have to say.

Q: Those qualities that you are displaying, should we look at them as female's qualities? Are they a leader's qualities? Are they sex-related at all?

Esther: No. They are people-related.

Q: They are people-related? Not borrowed from males? They are not specific to one sex or another?

Esther: No. I'm not borrowing them from the male and they are not specific to women. They are human qualities. Both men and women have shown them in different situations. It is society that has attributed them upon one sex or another. Usually, that's how we learn them. But, I have some traditional female qualities and I have some "traditional male qualities."

Okay, I'll tell you. What's easy for me is because people are very open with me. Some people find me extremely domineering and they go, "Oh, you're just like a man. You're bossy, you're domineering, you're cold." I've had people tell me that and then I've had people say, "You are the softest person I've ever met. You're so easy going. You're just like an angel," and they'll describe me in a very feminine way, "You're the angel from heaven," etc. So I have a combination of qualities that I don't consider male or female, but people have said things to me like, "What do you want, to wear the pants in this family?" and things like that. But, you know to be strong and to make it in the world, you have to have all those qualities and you know the only difference between men and women (laughter) is that men can be a sperm donor. That's the only difference between men and women that I see.

Q: But you could be an ovum donor?

Esther: Exactly, so there are no differences. We always look at women as nurturers, dependent, caring for people, and we never recognize them as strong, bright, articulate, educated, and strong people. We see them as, again, dependent, leading, being led. In my profession, women have always been in charge. That too, might change as gender roles are getting more blurred nowadays. More and more, you are seeing men less afraid to show their soft and nurturing side. My mother was quite tough. She survived the premature death of her parents. Often, as a child, she found herself in the fields alone, fending for herself. She followed the American Dream and she made it. I owe my strong personality to my mother, not to my father. Yet my mother cooked my father three meals a day, cleans the house. He would say to my mother, "Where's my dinner?" and she'll gently respond, "I'll be right there." I used to protest and tell him, "Where are your two hands? Get up and make yourself dinner!"

Q: How old were you then?

Esther: Young, young. My father would yell, "Be quiet!" He would have my mother do all kind of chores. It was so unfair, she ran the business, and she could not say a word. "Oh, be quiet," were his favorite words. When they go to the restaurant and my father would turn to my mother and say, "What should I get?" I always felt like saying: "Can't you make your own decisions about what you want to eat? Why are you asking Mom what you want to eat?" My parents did not see me as assertive. They saw me as having a behavioral problem. They took me to the doctor.

Needless to say that school was difficult. My teachers didn't care for me much. My parents were called to school many times.

I was always in some kind of trouble. Cooking did not interest me. Home economics were boring.

Q: Well! Now that you are a mother, don't you have to teach the same boring routines to your daughter?

Esther: You are probably right. Well, my daughter just graduated with her BSN from nursing school. She went into social work first. Now she's a nurse. Could she have gone into medicine? You know, when I think about it, yes, she could have. She was not as driven as I was. She was happy with C's and B's. I did not push her. So she went to nursing school and she was a straight A student. She's very strong and very bright and very articulate and I see her following in my footsteps. As a mother, I do not want her to be intimidated by me. I have to admit. It is not always easy. Sometimes, my blunt demeanor embarrasses her. If you want to see results, you have to take the initiative. Do not wait around for someone else to do it for you. Good looks only are not going to cut it. One day, we were riding the elevator together, she said, "You know they told me I wasn't smart enough to be a nurse. With the problem that I have, I know I could never be a nurse." My response to her was: "Don't say that, you don't know." I said, "I sat with a dunce cap on my head once when I was in third grade," and I said, "My mother came to school and they never thought I was going to amount to anything and they came to school and saw me with my dunce cap on."

Q: What is a dunce cap?

Esther: A dunce cap is a specially made cap they used to put on your head to ridicule you when you did something wrong in class, like chewing gum. The teacher would repeat or have the class repeat: "You're a dunce!" The whole class would laugh. I was humiliated. And the teacher would call me "Angel Face" because I didn't like her and she would talk to me and I wouldn't answer.

Q: You have learned to survive a lot of adversities?

Esther: Yeah, both my parents are survivors of Nazi Germany. My father almost lost his sight, because he did not have enough vitamins due to lack of foods. They were just deprived of every human comfort that you could possibly imagine during the war. They migrated to the United States and even when my brother was born, they had no food for him. My mother wanted to breastfeed him and there was nothing there. And they went through a lot of suffering. As a result they were very protective of their children. So my brother and I suffered particularly because they wouldn't let us do anything that normal kids do. I survived and I am grateful to be where I am today.

Chapter Twenty-Eight

Recapturing her Soul: Voice of a Voodoo Priestess

"Thinking automatons, moved by divine hands," such are the words that Voltaire used to describe mankind. Our fascination with the great beyond dates back from the beginning of time. Our collective memories and our museums are replete with artistic representations of this fact. As human beings, we have not been able to escape our need for adoration and meditation as we try to connect with some supreme power that always seems to elude us. Religion as a supra-individual belief is inevitably bound to our culture and the historical context of the time.[64] Some religions have been more successful than others have at keeping prejudices and biases out of their canonical laws. British author and ex-Catholic nun, Karen Armstrong, wrote, "The authentic test of a religion is not what you believe. It's what you do, and unless your religion expresses itself in compassion for all living things, it is not authentic." Feminist theorist, Luce Irigaray, sees it in a slightly different light. In order to achieve substantial modification of women's subjectivity and identity,

---

[64] See Peseschkian, N. Reference No.68

women should develop a feminist philosophy of religion, Irigaray suggests. I argue that New Age religion, a syncretism of superstition and spirituality together with indigenous religions like Voodoo, are as far as women can go toward the creation of a "feminine divine." Every woman that enters the temple is seen as possessing within her the essential attributes of a goddess. This feminine divine is made necessary by the fact that there is no female equivalent in monotheism of a father god who serves as a guarantor of man's identity. The New Age participant, just like the Voodoo priestess, is in the flesh with all its human attributes. She is woman, spirit, and logos, just like Isis. The feminine divine is by no means a supernatural, inaccessible goddess. She lives amongst her peers and is attentive to their every need. The Voodoo priestess can invoke as many different spirits as needed by the participants.

Q: Nice to see you again! When I heard your story, I said to myself, "Wow! She is a self-actualized woman, a person who went after it and really did what she set out to do." What a model to offer to other women! So, why don't you start by telling me about your background?

Monique: Well, I was born in Haiti in 1950 and I lived with a large family. I had my grandmother, my parents, my mother, my aunt, and my uncle. I watched everybody getting married, everybody dying, everybody surviving. And caravans of family from out of town, from the countryside, it was always a big parade at the house. And it was very interesting. So I went to Catholic school from kindergarten to high school. And in my family, my father was the son of an American descendant. My grandmother was of African descent. On my mother's side, there were more like the Haitian bourgeois with the high society mentality. The family had the pedigree. The family was quite poor because they had lost everything, but they had the name. My mother's side of the family had access to all the exclusive places. She took me along.

Q: You were in with the upper class crowd?

Monique: Yes, the upper class. And my grandmother took me to the other side. So I felt comfortable between both worlds. And I was more attached to my grandmother because she more people-oriented. She was a very caring person that was always ready to give a hand to people in need. She was more in tune with herself, and she had traveled a lot. I left Haiti, I was 17 years old, and went to live in New York City, chased by the political regime. My family could not live in Haiti because of the Duvalier regime. They were persona non grata. So we all left, my father, my mother, my brother, my grandmother, and my aunt. We all went to New York. I was looking forward to going to New York because during that period, everybody went to New York. We were escaping a very insecure situation. So we went to New

York where I spend a year and a half. I met my husband, Paul, and got married.

Q: How old were you when you got married?

Monique: Nineteen. And I really got married because it was the thing to do. The family expected you to get married. When you meet somebody that was nice, although I did love my husband, but he was more like something to do, when I look back at it. I don't think Paul would like to hear that though. So I think that was what I was supposed to do, to get married. My concept of marriage was very idealized. I thought I was going to be the perfect wife, the perfect mother, and I was going to do all those wife things. So I moved to Philadelphia, that's where my husband was doing his internship, and spent a year there. I had graduated from medical assistant school in New York, but I realized that I did not like it. I put it aside. I did not work in that field. Soon thereafter, we had a son. I was not satisfied with where I was in life. So we moved to Texas. The first thing I did, I applied for college. I said well, I'm going to go to school. I have plenty of time. I'm staying married, I'm going to raise my children, but I'm not going to stay home and wake up 20 years later and say, "What happened to me?" So I was disturbed. When I was a child, I was extremely inquisitive. I always asked questions. I would ponder about the future. I would continuously dissect things until I fully understand all the aspects.

Q: You are very analytical?

Monique: People always tell me, "Monique, you don't have to be that far." I hear that often. I always become intensely involved in everything that I do. My husband did not support the idea that I would go back to school. His argument was that the children were growing up, that they would need their mother at home to take care of them. I was pregnant with my second child and took the SAT exam, passed it. I enrolled in a psychology course. So I ended up with two more children. I love children. I would have had a house full of them, if it were up to me. My husband was doing very well financially. I was able to have a maid to help me in the house and I was able to go to school and come back, do my homework, and get help. And that was important. Life was good. My husband never took an interest in my studies. When I was going to school, he would laugh and poke fun at me, saying, "Oh, you are going to learn nothing, these colleges are like a mill. There are really preparing you how to work in a factory." He was always putting me down. I decided that I would press on with my own plans, since I could not count on him. When graduation time came, my husband was in shock. He never really believed that I had the will to carry my plan through. He never once asked how I was paying for the tuition. I had a part-time job at the University, in a counseling program, I paid for my school, got my books, got pregnant, had the kid, went to school, did my homework. So I did it. It was a challenge but I had fun doing it. Soon after I obtained my Bachelor in Psychology, I started to work on my Masters. I was embattled. Nothing was going to stop me now. I did a year and a half and then I moved to Florida. When we came here, there was a gap in my time. I went to real estate school. I almost did not make it to the final exam because my husband, Paul, did not want to stay with the children. He thought a license in real estate would be a waste. I then resumed my Masters at Nova University. I graduated and became licensed as a mental health counselor. I have been working with the School Boards part-time for 11 years. I always felt a big void inside. I never could tell what it was. I was quite successful. Something was missing. I couldn't say I didn't have a soul, because I had a soul. It wasn't marriage. It wasn't the children. My husband's practice as a surgeon was doing well. I had more than most people that I knew.

I found out that I had cancer of the uterus. I underwent surgery and I never thought for once that I was going to die. People were more worried for me than I was for myself because I knew I wasn't going to die. I did just fine. Then it struck me one morning. It was God that was missing. I realized that all this time, I was pushing myself and I never acknowledged his role. I never made room for Him in my life. And although I appeared to have a lot, but he wasn't there for me. The Catholic teachings were no longer responding to my needs for spirituality. I needed an inner life. I needed internal peace. I felt like the Catholic Church had too many taboos.

Q: Like what?

Monique: Taboos about sexuality, about the role of women in society. They have not kept pace with the world around them. The authorities are out of touch with their flocks. How are they supposed to shepherd them? Look at their views on issues like masturbation, oral sex, homosexuality, and premarital sex. Why would any religion want to interfere in the harmony that has always existed between mankind and nature? Those religions have too many bans on too many things. Not enough efforts are made to include all God's children. And I said, my goodness, this is ridiculous, life is not supposed to be so complicated. I felt that there had to be more to life than being threatened with Hell for just being human. If there were Heaven and Hell, I could not imagine myself being in any other place but Heaven. I was invited to a psychic fair. There I met a couple. They belonged to a New Age church. It was very interesting. For the first time, I heard about past lives. I learned a lot about stones, crystals, energy fields, auras, and healing by touching. They seemed to know a lot about the Bible. The whole atmosphere was so casual and non-threatening. The participants seemed very relaxed. It was quite an experience. I attended their gathering for quite some time. They made every participant believe they were special, that they were divine in their own way. I was still in search of something closer to my own background. I was longing to go back to my own roots. One evening, they spoke at the New Age church about people possessing within themselves a hidden treasure that needed to be tapped into. I just knew that it was true. I was in this country for a long time. I knew no one. One day, my aunt gave me a letter to take to Haiti to a friend of hers. The man was full of charisma. It turned out that he was a voodoo priest. His house was designed like a temple. He was very polite and very nice to me. I was mesmerized by his self-assured demeanor. He simply said, "Oh, I knew your grandmother, I knew your family very well." He started to tell me things that I didn't know. He made me feel welcome. He stated that I could come back anytime. That same evening, a cousin of mine took me back there to a voodoo ceremony. I never felt pressured. I could barely recognize the temple. It was decorated with voodoo flags and packed with people. Everyone seems quite agitated and was in a festive mood. It was like a huge party. I remember seeing a guy dancing with fire in his hands. He was moving the flames all over his half-naked body.

He did not seem to mind the heat that was emanating from the torch. He invited me to join him in a dance. I was frightened. Noticing my hesitation, he offered some reassurance, "Don't be afraid, Monique, no harm will come to you!" He put the fire over me and I was really scared at that point, I said, "My goodness, this is going to burn. I'd better be careful there." " No, not you!" he insisted. The fire was all over me. I did not get burned. How did that happen? I did not know. He later explained that that my family was protected by the spirit of fire, Canzo. After that evening, I had very strange dreams. I would see a lot of scenes that were very unfamiliar. I felt very isolated. No way was I going to share them with my husband. He was not one bit interested in all that voodoo stuff. In fact, he was very much against any kind of voodoo practice. He was Paul, the surgeon, raised as a practicing Catholic. I was able to finally confide in my father. The memories that he had were about the persecution that voodoo cult members suffered during the American occupation of Haiti between 1915 and 1934. Stay clear, he warned, you do not know what might happen. How could I possibly tell the old man what I was about to do?

Q: And what was that?

Well! I had my mind made up that I would go back and study about the Voodoo religion. Whatever subterfuge I had to use, I was going to do it. I had some suspicion that voodoo was practiced in my family, but everyone was discrete about it. It was almost shameful to be affiliated in any way with such practices. My escapade was made easy by the fact that my husband never asked me any details about my activities. I could spend a week away and he wouldn't know where I was. He was not the kind of husband that would be all over me.

Q: He gave you some space?

Monique: Some space. And I think it was more his personality. He really did not go out of his way to try and give me space. And so I went there, and I'd been going for two months, three months. I would go, spend a week, and I went through the whole process of being initiated little by little. It involved a lot of soul searching.

Q: Can you tell me about the initiation?

Monique: It was very interesting. I didn't know what to expect. The only thing I knew, I could trust someone. I was not harmed. A man was there with his wife. It was well organized. My family knew him. I could not remember him, but he claimed that he knew me as a child. I felt that I was in good hands. So I went to him and said to him that I wanted to go through the process. Interestingly, he first tried to dissuade me. He said that I was born spiritual and that the whole process was unnecessary. You don't become something that you already are, he insisted. You have everything you need, Monique. Seeing my persistence, he relented. "OK," he finally said, "we'll do it." He was very nice. At no point did I feel that he was trying to dominate me, or show his power.

I was invited to enter one of many small compounds that seem to have different functions. From the outside, you could not have imagined that it would have so much space. The only way in was through a small door, not even tall enough for a 4-foot person to walk in. One almost had to crawl. Inside, it was another story. It was a very eerie feeling. There lay a tombstone with all sorts of decorations. There were a couple of tombstones and large pieces of uncut marble. I guess the décor was there to symbolize the process of birth and death. I was instructed to lie down on one of the stones. There was another woman inside dressed just like me with a long, white, cotton dress and a white kerchief holding her hair together. Her face was covered with white flour. Over the next five days, she was going to be my silent companion. We were instructed to talk only when spoken to. We were brought food and water several times during the day. The meals consisted of porridge made of coarsely grated corn. It was delicious. We were also fed grilled chicken. Everything tasted so good. It was prepared very naturally. The condiments were all grown on the premises. Coconut oil was used to cook the food. The woman that stayed with me was remarkable. The voodoo priest would come in the room and ask me if I slept well. He was particularly interested in hearing about my dreams. He brought me books to read, about the voodoo religion and about philosophy, and other spiritual matters. I was finally allowed to ask questions about the process. We had no other conversation. A girl gave me a bath, using all kinds of oil and leaves. I was led out of the room walking backward, the head covered with a white sheet. I guess they wanted to protect me from the sunlight. It felt so relaxing.

On the fifth day, there was a ceremony which I thought was the most beautiful ceremony I have ever participated in. It was called, "Cheri Ayisan." Large branches of palm are braided together while invoking the spirit of the oldest woman, the grandmother who is supposed to be the keeper of all the wisdom, all the knowledge, and all the virtue of mankind. Participation in this ceremony sealed a pact by the initiated to use whatever knowledge she receives only to do good deeds. The whole process goes on while the drums are accompanying a group of dancers in their immaculate white dresses going down to their ankles. The whole ceremony emanated so much purity, that it would be sacrilegious to even think about doing harm to anyone. I could not help but feeling mesmerized by this overflow of support that I felt all around me. They were singing and twirling all around me as the whole ceremony was in my honor. I felt like a queen, that I was being accepted into a huge family that was as old as the world, and that would likely last for generations to come. I would not trade that feeling for all the gold in the world. I felt that I belonged. When I went back to sleep that evening, I had the most beautiful dream. Someone that looked like an older woman with a face full of wrinkles gave me a golden key marked with the number 9 (nine). There must have been some occult meaning to this dream, because the voodoo master seemed very pleased. It felt very powerful. I also dreamed that my great grandfather came to water the garden in the back of my home. Another time, it was my grandmother's turn to visit me in my sleep and present me with the most beautiful embroidered dress that one could ever see.

Q: Wow! Everyone was taking care of you?

Monique: A very nurturing dream, indeed. During the following months, I read everything about voodoo that I could put my hands on. So I went back again another time. My husband was becoming more annoyed with my repeated absences. Our relationship was under a lot of strain. My husband stated that I was completely out of control and that I had lost my mind. He still did not know anything about my involvement with the voodoo religion. I had found my niche in the New Age church. Paul made it clear that I had to stop going to that church or else he would divorce me. Until one day, he got into an argument with my father. My father told him that it would be stupid to divorce his wife over her participation in church. He followed me to church one day and left his business card on my car windshield. One day, while I was in Haiti he packed all my belongings and placed them in the garage. I was not surprised, as the maid had advised me of what was happening. I was too involved with the second part of the voodoo initiation to let that bother me.

The second phase was all about practical learning. They taught me how to mix herbs and prepare healing potions. They demonstrated how to "boule zin,"[65] the art of preparing small packets dedicated to the different spirits to secure their protection. And good grace. I was taught survival skills, how to kill large animals using a dagger. I learned about different plants and their healing virtues. They even showed me how to extract oil from Palma Christi and from coconut. I learned about the different songs and dances. I became able to call the "lwas" or voodoo spirits. I had become a "mambo" (voodoo priestess). I could now lead the voodoo ceremony from the beginning to the end. The lessons were all about leadership and survival. A woman cannot say that she would never kill an animal. The survival of her whole family might depend on it, whether it is to

---

[65] Initiation to fire. The initiate becomes a "medium" for the spirit of fire " Kanzo" and no longer feels burning sensation when touching hot surfaces or fire.

defend her children or to feed them. This what the cave woman had to do. Women always took care of the family and tended to the farm. They always toiled. As a woman, when confronted with the situation, whether it is a bull or a goat, I have to be ready.

Q: It's more of a communal life.

Monique: Yes, communal life! It was all about sharing and helping. People could just come in, tell the voodoo priest their troubles, and they would get help. It was the art of healing in its essence, without any interference. The whole experience was very uplifting.

Q: Now that you had acquired that new way of looking at life, how was your life changed?

Monique: I felt like I had another lease on life. I felt rejuvenated. It was as if I had come back from the dead. It is a feeling that no words can describe.

Q: You know what I'm thinking?

Monique: Tell me.

Q: The process that you went through reminds me of psychoanalysis. You reached deep inside of yourself. You confronted your demons, you demystified them, and there you are, feeling on top of the world.

Monique: Yeah, that's right! I thought so too because all the time I saw it as a psychological process because I had a part of myself that I was not aware of, I had a part of my culture, my background, my experiences, that I didn't know about. I had things in my life that I thought were right and society told me they were wrong. By the time it was all over, the confusion was gone.

Q: How did that affect your family life, your children?

Monique: I did not keep them completely out of the process. They knew all along that I was going through a very profound process with far reaching consequences. I told them.

Q: But you didn't tell your husband?

Monique: No, he was not ready. My children were very curious and would bombard me with questions whenever I would come back from Haiti. They understood that it was part of their cultural heritage. In 1985, I even had the opportunity to take them to a ceremony. My husband was going through difficult financial times. He had filed bankruptcy. He had given up on trying to stop me.

Q: Your patience had paid off?

Monique: We moved to Haiti in '86. We ended up buying a house in Carrefour, a suburban section of the southern part of the metropolitan area. It was a slap in the face of the Haitian bourgeoisie. How could a rich surgeon from the States buy a house in Carrefour? Poor people are supposed to live in Carrefour. The residence was near the voodoo temple.

Q: So you actually moved to Haiti to stay?

Monique: Well, after Duvalier fled the country in 1986, there was a movement afoot for members of the Diaspora to return home. So we went to Haiti. The children were about to graduate and they did not want to go to Haiti. I could not believe it. The members of the New Age church had predicted in one of their seances that I would move to Haiti. There I was, after so many years, living again in Haiti. Although I did not really believe them, I started to save some money.

My husband had lost a significant amount of money. He had gone from a net worth of over a million dollars to almost nothing. He basically had to start over. I got a job in Haiti. I worked as a coordinator for adult education in the countryside. I felt privileged to have had this experience. It was like a gift.

Q: But there was a lot of political instability in the country?

Monique: Oh yes, there was. Seven men armed with automatic weapons came and shot up my house one night. We all thought that we were going to be killed. We screamed our hearts out. They finally left. I later broke my leg trying to fix up the house. A few weeks later, they shot up my car, and my husband was car-jacked. He had a fracture of the arm. The teacher I used to work with was assassinated. It was a very traumatic experience.

Our house was on top of the mountain, overlooking a small cemetery. I started to renovate the cemetery, planting trees all over. I started to make a lot of friends. Children started to come around to learn how to read and write. I was very busy. They warned us that we had to leave the country. I said, "No way!"

I had my mattress on the floor my aunt lent me, my suitcase, and the icebox. I would stay awake at night and sleep by day. One night, they came into the house and stole all my belongings. I had no phone, no electricity. I couldn't call anybody. I found my keys on the floor, my purse inside out, whatever money I had was gone, and my passport was gone. I was naked on the bed because it was hot. I took off all of my clothes. I could have been harmed. Somebody, my guardian angel, was looking over me that night. I came out unscathed. Whoever came in saw me naked and didn't touch me. I started crying. I just cried and cried and cried.

While I was going through this ordeal, I felt ostracized by everyone. First, they did not like the fact that I had chosen to live in Carrefour, away from the upper class. They ostracized me because I was working for popular education. They ostracized me because of the way I treated my maids. They ostracized me because I made the choice to return to my voodoo heritage and visited the temple. I was isolated, but I would not trade my experience for the world. Okay, I say, no, I do a lot of self-talk with myself. So I will tell, talk to myself, and say okay, why do I do this, why, how can you change this?

Q: You are really a strong woman aren't you?

Monique: So I talked to myself twice and I went to sleep and I didn't leave the house until I became comfortable again, going back in the garden, going back to my work, and doing all this.

Q: How did you readjust to life here after those experiences?

Monique: You know, it was very hard. In a way, when we moved to Ft. Pierce, I remember feeling very confused and scared. I didn't know if I was in Haiti or if I was here. I remember my son coming from school. I was taking a nap at the apartment where we live. The place was very small. We had no furniture. We had a mattress on the floor. We lived like this for almost a year. When my son turned the key in the lock, I went into a panic attack. I rushed to the door, trying to hold it back. Only then, I realized where I was. I was no longer in Haiti. At night, if I hear shooting, I would wake up thinking that I was in Haiti. Those were very difficult times from an emotional standpoint.

Q: You were experiencing symptoms of Post-traumatic Stress.

Monique: Post-traumatic, yeah. This was tough. My husband was irritable, moody, and was difficult to get along with. He was angry at the world. I encouraged him to return to his old familiar environment and resume his practice. He did go back without any problems.

Q: How did those experiences that you went through affect your way of treating patients?

Monique: You know, I feel like when I see my patient, that there is always hope. Who am I to say this is hopeless case? Whatever happens to somebody, I know that somehow, the person can survive. So I will give a chance to people. My experience gave me a better appreciation for human suffering. I learned to show tolerance and empathy towards people. I was never going to take anything for granted anymore. I harbor no angry feelings towards anyone. Whatever happened was part of life. Life has ups and downs. And I think that everybody's life, and I think mine, has those, too. And I have to survive. I realize that forgiveness is a gift that I must make to myself.

Q: You don't want to give anybody power over you by keeping grudges against them?

Monique: So I said I can understand where you were coming from, where they were coming from, or what their experience is and I know my husband had a lot of bad experiences. He had a lot of baggage, he had hang-ups, so I was able to understand that and not take it personally. After spending the night crying, I would wake up and I would say, "Oh, oh, that's a beautiful day out there, it is over. Get a life, Monique!" The tears were gone.

And I was able to help people less fortunate than I was. When I was in the countryside and I saw children hungry, women powerless, women, and I see illness, I see all kinds of things and I say, "God, how lucky I am." And that really gave me strength.

Q: There you are, you have survived your demons about your own religious identity, you have survived a major, life-threatening event, you have survived assassination attempts, you have survived financial fall, and there you are. Where does it end?

Monique: I survived my son's physical illness and mental illness. Which this thing was really the biggest thing in my life. All the suffering I had, everything I went through, I would say that was the worst. When Paul, Jr., turned about 14, something changed. He became very depressed, very withdrawn. Then he refused therapy. He was extremely angry and when he got ejected from school, he was so violent that one day, he threw a glass at the side of his father's head. He was arrested and the court would not accept his plea of insanity. He was incarcerated and I had to get him out of jail. Everything, assassination, Haiti, everything was really pale in comparison. It was pure hell. Now I look at him and say, "This is so wonderful." I had to take a restraining order against him at one point, after he threatened to kill me. He blamed me for not being around and letting him lose control. The court finally ordered a psychiatric evaluation. A Jewish psychiatrist who knew nothing about the Haitian culture saw him. They asked all sorts of silly questions and were planning to send my son to the pig farm in North Carolina. I was fed up. I told my husband, Paul, "If your friend, the Jewish psychiatrist, does not stop talking about putting my son away, I do not know what I might do." The first time I went there the psychiatrist asked me, "Well, are you doing any voodoo on your kid?" He was asking questions like this: Do you think maybe it's a good idea if we take him away from you, send him somewhere, where he stays away from the family because of your religion? And I said, "Uh uh." They moved down to Florida and I had my family keep him for me until he was 18.

Q: What is he doing now?

Monique: He has been living with a girlfriend for the past two years. He has a full-time job and is very sweet now. His girlfriend came to, they had dinner with me on Sunday, and when they had dinner and I was looking at him in amazement. I could not believe it was the same person who had put me through a real nightmare. And to me it's my greatest accomplishment. My in-laws were against me, my husband was confused, everybody, so that was the only time in my life I really felt that I was completely alone. But I said, you know, I would just go to bed and cry and cry and cry and I would wake up in the morning and say, you know what, God, I know I'm going to see that. I'm going to see the end of this story. I know it. It took years. It took about seven years. He graduated from the Art Institute of Fort Lauderdale in Business.

Q: What a wonderful story! Thank you very much.

CONCLUSION

It seems like a very long time ago since we took our journey into the beginning of times. The world, as we established, has not always been patriarchal. During the Sumerian era, women dominated. Mother Goddess prevailed, granting her subjects with the gift of fecundity, love, and abundant life. There were as many goddesses as human needs. Then Father God entered, the organizing principle of a new world order, a new philosophy and new monotheistic religion with its three branches, Judaism, Muslim, and Christianity. The world has not been the same then. Fanaticism would prevail. To ensure the perpetuity of the newly created system, the leaders would not hesitate to either go to war or subjugate other humans. People who stood in the way were exterminated. Civilizations were destroyed. In the name of God and civilization, far away lands were discovered and appropriated without any respect for human life. Women were considered inferior and Blacks were considered sub-human or not human at all. A whole philosophy was developed to justify the two great evils of the world, racism culminating in slavery and sexism.

Negroes were first to offer some resistance to this hideous system of exploitation. At the turn of the eighteenth century, the Negroes from the plantation of St. Domingue were restless. They were the first to use guerrilla tactics to combat their much bigger enemy. General Leclerc army was defeated. Their exploit was to be played down. The last thing the slave owners of South Carolina wanted was for the Negroes to start having ideas and mount a similar armed movement. The slaves would escape from the plantations in defiance of established rules, facing certain death if caught. Maroonage was alive and well in some of the Caribbean islands, especially in Jamaica. In the U. S. it took the form of the Underground Railroad movement, featuring the courage of Harriet Tubman.

Later on, women would develop an organized and lasting response that spanned centuries. Negroes fought for freedom. Often it seemed that the destiny and the struggle of the two groups were one in linked. Alliances were made. White women saw the fight against slavery as their fight, too, not hesitating to push Black women aside when it was perceived to be advantageous to do so.   The women's rights movement witnessed several historical waves.

The defeat of Communist and Marxist ideology was supposed to give way to a global market where people are no longer defined by their social or economic class, but by their association to groups whose even the true essence is ill defined and controversial. In the communist era, when one referred to a member of the proletariat, everyone knew who was being referred to. In the post-modernist era, the situation is blurred and confusing. Many will question the very essence of entities like African-Americans, women, gays, and lesbians. Political correctness has become the terminology *du jour*. These different groups are feeling more and more alienated. They are living in era of so-called opulence to which they do not feel they belong. To women and Blacks, who have not benefited from the capitalist economic explosion and the rise of America from rags to riches, post-modernism has all the characteristics of disaster. The conservative agenda, along with the Christian coalition, have found a powerful ally in the media eagerness to re-construct reality. This is often done by omission of important elements of the events or by superficial analysis by strategically chosen expert. The psychosocial reality of women and Blacks can easily be ignored or simply discarded. Discourse about the exploitation of women, Black history of slavery, racism, and the destruction of family life can be discounted as irrelevant. Attempts at promoting gender studies and race relations debates are pooh-poohed by the same media. It seems that the whole era has been struck by what Linda Nicholson calls "historical amnesia." Vibrant and promising minority leaders that could become the standard bearers for the struggle of the minorities have been made into icons that are adored by people across all ethnic groups and genders.

In the post-modernist era, feminism seems to have become a dirty word. Ask any outspoken and educated woman if she is a feminist and you are likely to see some hesitation, and if you do get an answer, it might be an evasive one. The feminist movement has been victim of a well-orchestrated backlash. So has discourse about revolution, fight for justice, and equality. Such words are often talked about in a very derogatory way. Almost three-quarters of a century of cold war has chipped away at the attractiveness of Marxism as a liberating ideology. Oppressed groups no longer have a unifying and motivating philosophy to guide them through their struggle. The lack of success of some women and Blacks has given way to despair and apathy. Some have even resorted to indiscriminate violence to resolve their conflicts. They have turned this violence against their families and against themselves by using drugs. Capitalism's shiny cities over the hill has no room for them, therefore they are not feeling particularly sorry when civil unrest defaces them, destroys them, or burns them down. Repeated riots in recent times prove this.

Post-modernism is in danger of turning feminism into a completely passive movement that is totally disconnected from politics and social agitation. It might live up to its description as "hyper-intellectualized" and theoretical discourse with no "real" constituency. Or it might become the refuge for all the radical, third wave feminists who have lost track of the original goals of the movement and have reduced it to the affirmation of femininity through outlandish hair coloring and provocative dress code. This movement may suit White feminists just fine. It could be that second wave feminists feel that they have fought a good fight, they have gained celebrity status, and are ready to enter the Women's Hall of Fame. Maybe the second wave feminists are satisfied that their goals of equality and equal pay have been or are about to be achieved. However for the millions of Black women who are unemployed and are still grappling with such basic issues as day care, single parenthood, poverty, access to health care, domestic violence and drug-infested neighborhood, the double burden of racism and sexism still heavily weighs on their shoulders. For them, the feminist goals are far from being achieved.

The traditional brand of feminism and its elite have been accused of losing touch with the real issues that women are confronting today. Maybe it is time that minorities are accepted at the debate table as equal partners. It might mean relinquishing control and yielding to the desire of Black women to set their own priorities and create their own agenda. Can anyone blame Black women who have been at the receiving end of both racism and sexism for wanting to shape their own destiny? What can be a better statement of empowerment for a

Black woman than to know that her voice is being heard not because she was endowed with singing talents, but because she, too, can identify and denounce the ills of our society? Womanism is that new liberating movement which calls for a revived feminist consciousness that is more attuned to the needs of Black women and other minorities.

Will the adepts of that movement be able to resist the lure of post-modernism and its media blitz? Will they be able to resist the proliferation of talk shows where your most intimate bedroom fantasies, bar encounter mishaps, and sexual deceits can become national television material, while more substantive events are reconstructed and sanitized into tidbits fit for consumption on the evening news menu?

Can the adepts of the movement resist the trap of assimilation without acknowledgment of their individuality and special attributes in the name of superficial multiculturalism and national unity?

Are the proponents of a classless, color-blind society ready to make room at the table for Black men, Black women, and other minority groups and treat everyone as equal partners with equal voices?

Will the feminist strategists finally acknowledge that standing on the battlefield in opposition to the disappearing and endangered Black men would not be in the best interest of Black women and would amount to putting the last nail in the Black race's coffin?

Today's reality is that the journey that started out by the denunciation and the confrontation of a crudely and bitterly oppressive world, where no one was ashamed to show the ugly face of racism and exploitation of women, seems to have come back to the starting point. This time, the manifestations of racism are more sophisticated and much subtler. The proponents of racism can hide behind the mantle of new language, double talk, political correctness, and the "T" word (tokenism). None of these otherwise decent, family loving, and God fearing people will ever admit that they are racist.

Until this situation changes, Black women must prepare themselves. They must heed Bell Hooks' call for self-recovery in "Sisters of the Yam." Before she can do that, she must come to grip with who she is. Bell Hooks' call to Black women to continue to de-colonize their minds and to resist the devaluation of Black women is often misunderstood, even by Black men who see Black women's self-affirmation as threatening.

Furthermore, Black women must fully understand their role as links between God and the universe, as interconnected agents that create a web whose destiny is to re-institute harmony between mankind and the ecology. To truly experience nature as an ally, one must first realize that nature has been misused and abused. For abused and exploited people, nature is where the healing will start. Their closeness to nature has given Native Americans their courage and their strength of character. Such a movement is begging for new leaders, a new ideology that will carry the struggle forward. I believe that ecofeminism will provide that cementing and unifying force. Charlene Spretnak says it very clearly, "It is our refusal to banish feelings of interelatedness and caring from the theory and practice of ecofeminism that will save our efforts from calcifying into well-intentioned reformism, lacking the vitality and wholeness that our lives contain. We need to find our way out of the technocratic alienation and nihilism surrounding us by cultivating and honoring our direct connections with nature."[66]

Black women's return to nature will have to start with the recapture of their ancestral African soul that is rooted in traditions of caring, closeness, and respect for Mother Earth, the source of life. Such a soul is far remote from the violence and the dilapidated neighborhood and the chaos that has become the labels attached to Black families in America. The just societies of ancient and traditional Africa, as demonstrated by Oba T'Shaka, Ph.D., were able to develop human beings, men and women, who lived according to the just principles of harmony, truth, balance,

---

[66] See Spretnak, C. Reference No. 73

justice, and right order.   (Return To The African Mother Principle of Male –Female equality, Vol. 1) Black women can take inspiration from Isis, the great mother goddess of the Egyptians. She is the goddess with ten thousands of names, one for each of her worshipers' needs. She is both spirit and flesh. She is the incarnation of the harmony that must exist between human and nature.   Isis was the goddess who put the dismembered body of her husband, Osiris, back together and blew life back into him. The analogy with the situation of Black men in America is quite striking. Black men in America are not in their rightful place as leaders of their families. Instead, they are entombed in the entrails of the prison system. They are lost in the abyss of drug addiction.   They are represented in disproportionate numbers in the major epidemics like AIDS, hypertension, and other diseases. Black men are still invisible in the Corporate Boardroom of America. Black men are not in college. Will the Black woman rise and become the Isis that will save Blacks from extinction? When one member of society benefits, the whole society benefits. Otherwise, Black men will continue to be entombed in the entrails of the prison system and the abyss of drug addiction until they are completely extinct. Black women are the last hope for the survival of the race.

Black women need to move away from the stage of passive acceptance of degradation and inequality, as established by

Downing and Roush in their five-stage developmental model, to the final stage of active commitment to the creation of a non-sexist world. (Downing, N.E., & Roush, K.L., 1985) From passive acceptance to active commitment, a model of feminist identity development for women. (The Counseling Psychologist, 13, 695-709)

REFERENCES

1. Aristotle. <u>Philosophy of Aristotle: Aristotle's Works and Method</u>. Monarch Notes, 01-01-1963.

2. <u>Ancient Civilizations</u>.   Young Students Learning Library. Newfield Publications. 01-01-1996.

3. Anderson, S. E. <u>The Black Holocaust for Beginners</u>. Writers and Readers Publishing Inc. New York 1995.

4. Blaustein, Albert P. & Zangrando, Robert L<u>. Civil Rights and African Americans</u>. Northwestern University Press 1991.

5. Bourke, Vernon J., <u>The Pocket Aquinas</u>. Washington Square Press 1960.

6. Budge, E.A. <u>Wallis: Osiris & The Egyptian Resurrection</u>. Dover Publications 1973.

7. Cherry, Andrew L. Jr. <u>The Socializing Instincts, Individual, Family and Social Bonds</u>. Praeger 1994.

8. Chesler, Phyllis, Ph.D., "A Wolf in Feminist Clothing," Vol. III, On The Issues, 03-01-1994, pp 8+.

9. Bailey, Cathryn, "Making Waves and Drawing Lines: The Politics of Defining the Vicissitudes of Feminism," Vol. 12, Hypatia, 06-22-1997, pp 17(12).

10.   Bawer, Bruce, "Notes on Stonewall: Is The Gay Rights Movement Living In The Past?," Vol. 210, The New Republic, 06-13-1994, pp 24(5).

11. Borysenko, Joan Ph.D. <u>A Woman's Book of Life: The Biology, Physiology, and Spirituality of the Feminine Life Cycle</u>. Riverhead Books 1996.

12. Brock, Rita Nakashima. "Casting Stones: The Theology of Prostitution," Vol. 6, On The Issues, 6-01-1997, pp 21-25.

13. Brown, Lyn Mikel & Gilligan, Carol. <u>Meeting at the Crossroads: Women's Psychology and Girls' Development</u>. Ballantine Books, New York, 1992.

14. Cosentino, Donald J. <u>Sacred Arts of Haitian Vodou</u>. UCLA Fowler Museum of Cultural History. South Sea International Press Ltd. 1995.

15. De Beauvoir, Simone. <u>The Second Sex</u>. Vintage Books, New York 1989.

16. Draper, John William M.D., LL.D., <u>History of the Intellectual Development of Europe: Chapter XIII, History of the World</u>, 01-01-1992.

17. Deutscher, Penelope. "The Only Diabolical Thing About Women..." Luce Irigaray on Divinity, Hypatia, 9-22-1994, pp 88(24).

18. Estes, Clarrissa Pinkola, Ph.D. <u>Women Who Run With The Wolves: Myths and Stories of the Wild Woman Archetype</u>, Ballantine Books. January 1997.

19. Felder, Deborah G. <u>The 100 Most Influential Women of All Time. A Ranking Past and Present</u>. Citadel Press Book, 1996.

20. Flaubert, Gustave. <u>Madame Bovary</u>. Bantam Classic 1989.

21. Fleming, Thomas C. "The African Mother Principle," The Sun Reporter, 04-27-1995.

22. Foot Moore, George. <u>History of Religions: History of the World</u>, 01-01-1992.

23. Foucault, Michel. <u>The History of Sexuality, An Introduction, Vol</u>. Vintage Books Edition, March 1990.

24. Gachago, Miriam. "Gender Analysis in Socio-Economic Activities." <u>Women Magazine</u> 01-1997, pp12-5.

25. Gale F. Raymond. <u>Who are you? The Psychology of Being Yourself</u>. Prentice-Hall 1974.

26. Gilligan, Carol. <u>In A Different Voice, Psychological Theory and Women's Development</u>, Harvard University Press 1982, 1993.

27. Gower, Rebecca; Salm, Steven; Falola, Toyin. "Swahili Women Since The Nineteenth Century: Theory and Empirical Considerations On Gender Identity And Construction, (Re-conceptualizing African Women: Toward the Year 2000)," Vol. 43, Africa Today, 07-18-1996, pp 251(18).

28. Gladstone, Brooke. "Gender and Advertising," Talk of the Nation (NPR) 8-11-1997, Washington, DC.

29. Goldsby, Richard A. "Why The Shortage of Black Professors?" Journal of Blacks In Higher Education, The, 09-30-1993, pp PG.

30. Gray, John Ph.D. Men are from Mars, Women are from Venus, HarperCollins Publishers 1992.

31. Hale, Jacob, "Are Lesbians Women?" Vol. 11, Hypatia, 03-01-1996, pp 94...

32. Hale, Thomas A. "Griottes: Female Voices From West Africa, Vol. 25." Research in African Literature, 09-22-1994, pp 71(21).

33. Healy, Melissa. "Welfare Cases Drop 20% In U.S., Study Finds..." Los Angeles Times, 05-10-1997., pp A-1.

34. Herrnstein, Richard J., Murray Charles. The Bell Curve: Intelligence and Class Structure in American Life. Free Press Publications. January 1996.

35. Horney, Karen, M.D. New Ways In Psychoanalysis. W. W. Norton & Company. New York 1966.

36. Hooks, Bell. Killing Rage, Ending Racism. Henry Holt & Company, 1995.

37. Hooks Bell. Sisters Of The Yam: Black Women And Self-Recovery. South End Press 1993.

38. Iredale Paul, "Up to 50 Million Females Missing In India," Reuters, 11-19-1995.

39. Jacklin, Carol Nagy, "Female and Male: Issues of Gender." American Psychologist, Vol. 44, No. 2, Feb 1989

40. Jacobson, M.D., Alan and Parmelee, M.D., Dean X., <u>Psychoanalysis: Critical Exploration in Contemporary Theory and Practice</u>, pp 209-210, Brunner/Mazel, 1982.

41. Jae-In Kim, "A Study On Gender Roles In The Elementary And Secondary School Textbooks." Women's Studies Forum, 1 Jan 1993.

42. James, George G. M. Stolen Legacy, <u>Greek Philosophy Is Stolen Egyptian Philosophy</u>. Africa World Press, New Jersey 1992.

43. Kane, Emily & al. "Family Status and Criticism of Gender Inequality At Home and At Work..." <u>Social Forces</u>, 06-01-1994, pp 1079(24)

44. Kaplan, Paula J, Ph.D. <u>The Myth of Women's Masochism</u>. Dutton, New York, 1985.

45. Keen, Ernst.   <u>Psychology And The New Consciousness</u>. Brooks/Cole 1972.

46. Knapp, Bettina, "The Archetypal Woman Fulfilled: Isis, Harmony of Flesh/Spirit/Logos..." Vol. 50, <u>Symposium</u>, 03-01-1996, pp 28(12).

47. Kyriakidou, Dina. "Aristotle, Ancient Lyceum Believed Unearthed in Athens," Reuters. 01-14-1997.

48. Lerner Gerda, <u>The Creation of Feminist Consciousness from Middle Ages to Eighteen-Seventy</u>. Oxford University Press, New York, 1983.

49. Lerner, Gerda. <u>The Creation of Patriarchy</u>. Oxford University Press. New York 1986.

50. Leuchtag, Alice, "The Culture of Pornography," Vol. 55, <u>The Humanist</u>, 05-15-1995, pp 4...

51. Lieberman, Carole M.D & <u>Lisa Collier, Bad Boys, Why We Love Them...</u> Dutton, Penguin Books, USA 1997.

52. Maher Adrian, "'90s Swingers Give Monogamy the Kiss-off," Trends Home Edition, Los Angeles Times, 02-12-1998, pp E-1.

53. Mahoney, Michael J., <u>Human Change Processes, The Scientific Foundations of Psychotherapy</u>. Basic Books 1991.

54. Manzo, Anna Rosales, "The Afro-Asiatic-Euro Connection: Discovering The Ancestral Soul," <u>Reunion</u>, 12-01-1994.

55. Masson Jeffrey Moussaief. <u>The Assault On Truth, Freud's Suppression Of The Seduction Theory</u>. Collins Publishers, Toronto 1984.

56. McAllester Matthew, "Love's Database/Are Online Connections-- Where The Brain, Not The Body, Does The Seducing-- Changing Romance?" <u>Newsday</u>, 02-12-1998.

57. McDonald Marjorie, <u>Not By The Color Of Their Skin: The Impact Of Racial Differences On The Child's Development</u>. International University Press 1973.

58. "MidLife Women's Network: Can we talk? Couples Communication," Vol.4, <u>Midlife Woman</u>, 01-01-1995, pp 1-4.

59. Milburn, Trudy, "Bridging Cultural Gaps," Vol. 86, <u>Management Review</u>, 01-01-1997.

60. Modleski, Tania. <u>Feminism Without Women: Culture And Criticism In A Postfeminist Age</u>. Isis, 1992.

61. Moyers, Bill. <u>Genesis, A Living Conversation</u>. Double Day, New York 1996.

62. Muller, J.P. & Richardson, W.J. <u>Ouvrir Les Ecrits De Jacques Lacan</u>. Editions Eres 1987.

63. New Living Translation. <u>Holy Bible</u>. Tyndale House Publishers. 1996.

64. Ng, Sik Hung & al. "Feminist Identities And Preferred Strategies For Advancing Women's Self-Concept." <u>The Journal of Social Psychology</u>, 10-01-1995 pp 56...

65. Ogede, Ode S, "Counters To Male Domination: Images Of Pain In Igede Women's Songs (Women as Oral Artists)." <u>Research in African Literatures</u>, 09-22-1994, pp. 105(16).

66. Orr, Catherine M. "Charting the Currents of the Third Wave." Vol.12, <u>Hypatia</u>, 06-22-1997, pp 29 (17).

67. Osmowo, Maxine. "Girls Speak Out: Commercial Sex Workers (Prostitution)," <u>Contemporary Women's Issues Collection</u>, 1-01-1995, pp. 6...

68. Otto, Friedrich, "New Age Harmonies, A Strange Mix Of Spirituality And Superstition Is Sweeping Across The Country," <u>TIME</u>, 12-07-1987, pp 62.

69. Peseschkian, Nossrat. <u>In Search of Meaning, A Psychotherapy of Small Steps</u>. Springer-Verlag, Berlin Heidelberg 1985.

70. Prabhupada, A.C. Bhaktivedanta Swami. <u>Bhagavad-Gita As It Is</u>, Bhaktivedanta Book Trust, Vaduz, Lichtenstein

71. Pratap Anita, "New Delhi, Cover Stories: Killed by Greed And Oppression In India, The Ancient Custom Of Dowry..." <u>Time International</u>, 09-11-1995, pp 46+.

72. Pringle, Heather. <u>New Women Of The Ice Age</u>. Discover, New York, April 1998).

73. Purcell, Edward. "The First Europeans, Native Americans, And The Forced Immigration Of Black Africans," Vol. I, <u>Immigration: Social Issues in American History</u>. Oryx Press, 01-16-1995.

74. Rodwell J.M. <u>The Koran</u>. Everyman 1996.

75. Roberts, J.M. <u>A Short History of the World</u>. Oxford University Press. New York, 1993.

76. Rosser, Sue V. <u>Biology and Feminism, A Dynamic Interaction</u>. Twayne Publishers, 1992.

77. Rossi, Alice C. <u>The Feminist Papers, From Adams to De Beauvoir</u>, Northeastern University Press, 1988.

78. Roth H. Mark. <u>Zaire, The Slave Trade, Countries of the World</u>. Bureau Development, Inc. 1991.

79. Rousseau, Jean-Jacques. <u>Emile</u>. Everyman 1996.

80. Rowbotham, Sheila.   <u>Hidden From History, 300 Years Of Women's Oppression And The Fight Against It</u>. Pluto Press.

81. Ruether, Rosemary Radford, "Ecofeminsm: Symbolic And Social Connections Of The Oppression Of Women And The Domination Of Nature." <u>Lila-Asia Pacific Women's Studies Journal</u>, 01-04-1994, pp. 63-72.

82. Sandler, Joseph & al. <u>The Techniques Of Child Psychoanalysis, Discussions With Anna Freud</u>. Harvard University Press 1980.

83. Sandroff, Ronni. "State of the Couple Report," Vol. IV, <u>On The Issues</u>, 06-01-1995, pp 20+.

84. Saint Augustine. <u>Works of Saint Augustine: The Confessions</u>. Monarch Notes, 01-01-1963.

85. Slater Robert Bruce, "The Growing Gender Gap In Black Higher Education," <u>Journal of Blacks in Higher Education</u>, The, 03-31-1994, pp PG.

86. Spretnak, Charlene. <u>Ecofeminism: Our roots And Flowering In Reweaving The World</u>. Diamond and Orenstein, 1990.

87. Stabile, Carole A. "Postmodernism, Feminism, And Marx: Notes From The Abyss." Vol. 47, Monthly Review, 7-17-1995, pp 89.

88. Sundstrom, Karla, "Healing Through Responsible Agency Within Feminist Spirituality," Vol. 17, <u>Bulletin of Simone De Beauvoir Institute</u>, 0-01-1997, pp 153-159.

89. Thompson, Patricia J., "Dismantling The Master's House: A Hestian/Hermean Deconstruction Of Classic Texts," Vol. 9, <u>Hypatia</u> 9-22-94.pp 38.

90. Van Howe, Annette, "Remembering The Women Of History." <u>The Humanist</u>, September 19, 1996.

91. Verner, Brenda J. "Why Feminism Has Failed To Lure Black Women: Africana Womanism," Chicago Weekend, 03-12 & 19-1995.

92. "Violence Against Women Fact Sheet," <u>Contemporary Women's Issues Collection</u>, 01-01-1995, pp 1-14.

93. Watson, Raymond K., & al.   "Effects Of Interpersonal Communication Process Variables On Outcomes In An International Conflict Negotiation Simulation," Vol. 136, The Journal of Social Psychology, 08-01-1996, pp. 483(9).

94. Welsing, Dr. Frances Cress, The Isis Papers, The Keys to the Colors. Third World Press. Chicago 1991.

95. Witham Larry. "Movement Focuses On Healing Gays." The Washington Times, 02-06-1995, pp.25.

96. Whitman, David, Friedman Dorian, Tharp Mike, Griffin Katie. "Welfare, The Myth Of Reform," U.S. News and World Report, 01-16-1995, pp 30-39.

97. Wolfe, Alan. "The Gender Question: Women And Men In The Mirror Of Feminist Theory," The New Republic, 6 Jun 1994.

98. Wollstonecraft, Mary. A Vindication Of The Rights of Woman. Penguin Books. London, England. 1992.

99. World History. The World Almanac and Book of Facts 1997, 11-15-1996.

100.   Wright, Peggy A.   "Bringing Women's Voices To Transpersonal Theory..." Vol. 17, ReVision, 01-01-1995, pp 3.

101. Wright, Robert, "Feminists Meet Mr. Darwin: The Evolutionary Psychology Of The Female Mind." The New Republic, 28 Nov 1994.